11-95

the **SOUND ON SOUND** book of

# desktop
# digital studio

Printed in the United Kingdom by MPG Books, Bodmin

Published by: Sanctuary Publishing Limited, Sanctuary House, 45-53 Sinclair Road, London W14 0NS, United Kingdom

www.sanctuarypublishing.com

Cover design: mouse image © Nick Veasey/Untitled

Sound On Sound web site: www.sospubs.co.uk

While the publishers have made every reasonable effort to trace the copyright owners for any or all of the photographs in this book, there may be some omissions of credits, for which we apologise.

ISBN: 1-86074-324-2

the **SOUND ON SOUND** book of

# desktop
# digital studio

p a u l   w h i t e

Also available by Paul White from Sanctuary Publishing

*Creative Recording I – Effects & Processors*
*Creative Recording II – Microphones, Acoustics, Soundproofing & Monitoring*
*Home Recording Made Easy*
*MIDI For The Technophobe*
*Live Sound For The Recording Musician*
*Recording & Production Techniques*
*Music Technology – A Survivor's Guide*


The BASIC series

*basic DIGITAL RECORDING*
*basic EFFECTS & PROCESSORS*
*basic HOME STUDIO DESIGN*
*basic LIVE SOUND*
*basic MASTERING*
*basic MICROPHONES*
*basic MIDI*
*basic MIXERS*
*basic MIXING TECHNIQUES*
*basic MULTITRACKING*

# contents

## CHAPTER 8

# introduction

*The Digital Desktop Studio* is written for anyone who wants to record and create music with a computer rather than with traditional studio hardware. A decade ago computer music meant MIDI sequencing and perhaps a little audio editing, but now it's possible to set up a complete multitrack studio within a Macintosh or PC computer, complete with software-driven effects and synthesisers. This makes for a compact and powerful solution, but there are also complexities associated with the setting up and operation of such a system. The beginner may feel overwhelmed by the information presented in software manuals, but *The Digital Desktop Studio* helps the newcomer focus in on what's necessary to get the job done.

*The Digital Desktop Studio* is not a substitute for a software manual but is rather a book designed to provide a thorough overview of the process of using computers for MIDI sequencing, audio recording and audio editing, as well as for sound synthesis and effects processing. In some respects, it's like a "master" manual, designed to help you make sense of your various hardware and software manuals. It doesn't matter whether you use a Mac or a PC, or what software you use for that matter; this book deals with concepts common to all platforms.

Various types of desktop system are explored, including those that rely on a little external hardware as well as the ones that don't, and the benefits and compromises of each type are clearly explained. There's also a simple but practical introduction to MIDI and sequencing, as well as a whole chapter explaining those elusive terms that crop up so often when working with computer audio, such as sample rate, bit depth, S/PDIF, AES/EBU, ASIO, VST and so on. There's also a comprehensive glossary included at the back of the book. Jargon is avoided wherever possible, but it's used where it's essential, and it's explained simply and clearly.

Desktop studios provide a wonderful opportunity to make music and have fun at the same time, and I'd like to help you make the most of that opportunity.

## chapter 1

# desktop studios

The project studio paradigm has changed dramatically over the past decade or so. Where once the mixer and multitrack tape recorder took centre stage, these days the home studio is more likely to be based around a computer, combined with a little external hardware. Today's computers are built to meet the needs of multimedia (tackling both sound and picture) as well as processing text and spreadsheets, and because they are mass produced in huge numbers they are relatively inexpensive, considering the enormous computational power they place at our disposal. In short, computers provide us with the means to set up music studios hugely more powerful than anything that has gone before and are available at a fraction of the cost of the traditional tape-based recording set-up. The catch, if there is one, is that computer-based systems can be complicated to set up. Sophistication brings power, but it also bring complexity.

One reason why things are often more complicated than we'd like is because the music market represents only a tiny fraction of the overall computer market. The manufacturers of computer audio products, such as soundcards and music software, often have to work very hard to get around operational limitations that would not exist if computers were designed solely as musical tools. Because of the ways in which pieces of computer hardware and software interact, and because of the number of permutations available, putting together a computer-based music studio is no casual matter. Furthermore, technology is opening up new possibilities every few months, so musicians with a background in traditional recording hardware may not even know the extent of what today's computer-based desktop studio has to offer. The aim of this introduction, therefore, is to examine the role of computers in music making, specifically to find out what traditional recording and sound creation tasks they can undertake. Once the possibilities have been explored, I'll take a look at some practical arrangements and try to match them with different recording requirements. The remaining chapters will then examine these functions in detail.

# computers and music

If you're used to working with a tape machine and a mixer, you may be uncertain of what the practical benefits of a computer audio system are, although most musicians will be aware that computers can be used as MIDI (Musical Instrument Digital Interface) sequencers. The first computer to really make an impression in this area was the Atari ST, not least because the manufacturers had the foresight to include MIDI In and Out ports as part of its basic specification. It was on the Atari that we saw MIDI sequencers develop beyond being just interesting toys to become serious tools for music production.

The beauty of MIDI is that musical performances are stored relatively efficiently as note data (as opposed to audio material, which takes upwards of 5Mb of memory per track per minute depending on the data format). This MIDI data is then used to control – or, in effect, to play – external hardware synthesisers in real time. Today a large number of soundcard-based and software synthesisers also exist, however, and these will be investigated later.

Because MIDI files are vastly smaller than audio files, the data transfer rate of MIDI is such that even a modest computer can handle it without being over-taxed. Anyone not yet *au fait* with MIDI will find a working overview in chapter two, although for more details the reader should delve into *MIDI For The Technophobe* or *BASIC MIDI*, which are also available through Sanctuary Publishing. It's interesting to note that the Atari ST, which ran with a clock frequency of only 1MHz, is still capable of MIDI timing of a rock-solid accuracy that equals or exceeds that of modern 500MHz computers, thanks to its simpler, more direct operating system.

# adding audio

When audio recording via computers became possible, it soon became clear that the faithful old Atari couldn't keep up with the increased workload, which signalled the start of music software development for the Apple Macintosh platform and, later, the PC. Other types of computer may also be used for musical applications, but these are now so rarely supported by software designers that, to all intents and purposes, Macs and PCs are the only viable computers for the serious musician.

The first audio programs were stand-alone applications designed to record and edit stereo audio files. Incoming audio was digitised, either via an external converter box or a computer expansion card, and was then recorded onto a hard drive. In the early days, the sizes of hard drives were measured in tens of megabytes rather than gigabytes, and so storage space was both limited and very expensive. As the prices of hard drives fell and computers grew faster, multitrack recording software also became available. However, it was only when MIDI sequencing and audio recording were integrated into the same piece of software that the desktop studio as we know it today was born. Of course, stereo editors are still important pieces of software in music production, especially as the equipment required to create audio CDs is now relatively inexpensive. As a rule, these will run on the same system as a MIDI-plus-audio sequencer, so the only additional expense will be the editing software itself and the CD burner.

A modern sequencer can provide dozens of tracks of MIDI recording and a dozen or more audio tracks, the precise number of tracks being determined by the available computing power, the speed of the hard drive and the interface. A speedy drive running with a SCSI interface can handle upwards of 32 simultaneous tracks of audio playback, whereas an internal EIDE drive may only cope with around twelve to 20 tracks. If these terms don't mean much to you at the moment, chapter three explains the most important computer audio terms and concepts.

# the user interface

All modern sequencers use a graphic interface so that blocks of sound or MIDI information can be copied, divided or moved around. For example, you may want to duplicate a successful chorus section, edit down a rambling solo or remove a link section that isn't working out as well you'd hoped. Audio and MIDI recordings are visible within the same window, which is clearly a great advantage over having the audio on a separate recorder, as the integrated approach actually allows you to see that your sections of audio – song choruses, for example – are where they should be relative to the MIDI data. Figure 1.1 shows both audio and MIDI tracks placed on the the main Arrange page of a modern sequencer.

To transfer MIDI into or out of a computer (other than the Atari ST, which has a built-in MIDI interface), you'll need either to install a separate MIDI interface or to use one of the MIDI synthesisers that has a direct "to host" computer connection. If you're using a soundcard synth or a virtual software synth, no MIDI interface is required as the MIDI information never has to leave the computer.

PC users will find a MIDI interface included as a part of most general-purpose soundcards, especially those developed for games or multimedia use, while Mac users will need to buy an external hardware MIDI interface unit. Larger MIDI systems (ie those comprising two or

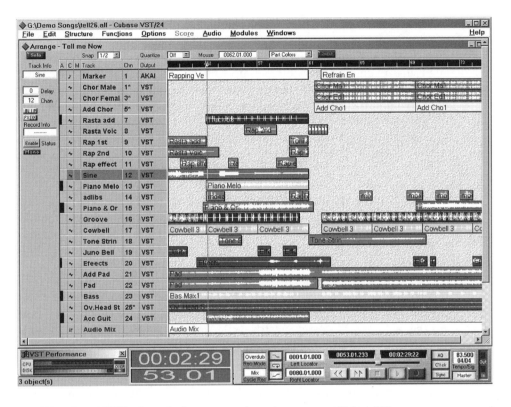

Figure 1.1: Audio and MIDI tracks on the Arrange page of a modern sequencer (Cubase VST)

more multitimbral hardware MIDI instruments) may require a multiport MIDI interface to overcome the maximum channel capacity of MIDI – one MIDI port can accomodate a maximum of 16 different musical parts. Multiport MIDI interfaces are most often supplied as a separate hardware box rather than as part of a soundcard.

# the audio interface

Some kind of audio interface is required for audio to be transferred into or out of a computer. All but the lowest level modern desktop Macintosh computers (from Power PCs onwards) have a built-in stereo in/stereo out interface, but although this might get you up and running you'll probably want something better for serious use. PC owners will find stereo audio ins and outs on the same games soundcard as their MIDI port, but again something better may be advisable for serious work. Similarly, if you want to use an external mixer to combine your audio tracks, you'll need to buy an audio interface with multiple outputs.

These extra outputs may be either digital or analogue, depending on your choice of soundcard or interface. This may seem confusing at the moment, but chapter five outlines the various types of practical set-ups. In the main, your system set-up will be dictated by your working methods and by your budget. For example, most musicians working alone can manage with a stereo-in audio interface as they tend to record only one or two tracks at a time, but where there's a need to record multiple performers at once on different tracks then an audio interface with multiple inputs will be needed.

# audio mixing

With software sequencers being able to handle multiple tracks of audio material, they clearly need to be able to handle the mixing of those tracks because few soundcards have as many physical audio outputs as the sequencer has audio playback tracks.

Mixing is generally accomplished by using the processing power of the host computer, although other solutions are available that use DSP (Digital Signal Processing) cards to do some of the work. To keep things simple, I'll start by looking at native systems (ie the ones that rely entirely on the host computer for everything).

The mixing capability of a sequencer is limited by its available computing power, but these days virtually all software provides the ability to mix tracks and to automate level changes, in much the same way that a hardware automated mixer can record fader movements. EQ also takes up a certain amount of processing power, so the usual methodology is to call up EQ on just those channels that need it rather than offer full EQ facilities on every channel. In this way, audio tracks can be mixed down to two outputs (or more if available), which may then be routed to a stereo recorder. This simplest of set-ups presupposes that either software- or soundcard-based instruments are used for all MIDI tracks. If you're using external hardware synths, an external hardware mixer will invariably be needed to be combine your computer audio data with the sounds from your MIDI synthesisers. All of the common options are investigated in chapter five.

# plug-ins

In "real" studios, mixers tend to be used in conjunction with effects such as delay and reverb, and while some audio interfaces with multiple ins and outs (used with the appropriate software) allow you to configure some of their connectors as sends and returns for use with external effects boxes, modern computers are powerful enough to allow you to use a reasonable number of native real-time plug-in effects at the same time as playing back audio and MIDI. (The term *native* simply means that the host computer provides the power to create the various effects.) There are various plug-in platforms that are available, and the one you use will depend on what sequencer software you're using. There are also proprietary plug-in systems which are allied to specific types of hardware, such as Digidesign's ProTools (which uses Digidesign-compatible TDM plug-ins) and the PC-based system Soundscape.

# VST

The most common native plug-in format, VST (Virtual Studio System), was pioneered by Steinberg, the manufacturers of Cubase, and the technology was then shared between various other companies to produce the nearest thing we currently have to a standard plug-in format. VST plug-ins are available in both Mac and PC versions, and are normally found in a pull-down menu accessible from within the mixer page of the host sequencer. VST plug-ins are available to handle all of the usual studio effects and processes, such as compression, limiting and gating, as well as reverb, echo, chorus and flanging. However, they go a lot further; there are also plug-ins for vocoding, pitch correction, creative distortion, spectral enhancement, noise removal, click suppression and other functions too numerous to list.

The VST standard has now evolved into VST II, and in this version plug-in parameters can be controlled via MIDI information. This has enabled plug-in designers to create effects that can be automated under MIDI control.

All plug-ins will take up some of a processor's power, so there will always be a limit to how many you can run at once. However, as with a conventional mixer, effects like reverb and echo can be used in the effects send and return loop of the virtual mixer so that a single plug-in can be applied to as many channels of audio as required without taking up any more processor capacity. Processors such as compressors or equalisers still have to be used on a per-channel or per-group basis, though, and so are patched in via virtual channels or group insert points, again much in the same manner as on a hardware console. More information on the subject of using and understanding mixers can be found in *BASIC Mixers*, also from Sanctuary Publishing.

# virtual instruments

Just when it seemed that the VST revolution had given us everything we could possibly dream of inside our computers, virtual synthesisers started to make an impression. Computer-based synths have been around for many years, but they tended to be clumsy and they hogged processor power. Now there are rather more refined software synths available, some of which are designed as stand-alone applications and some of which come as VST instrument plug-ins. Because the VST standard has been enhanced since its inception, allowing plug-ins to both generate and respond to MIDI messages, MIDI-controlled VST instruments can be designed that will work with any VST-compatible sequencer. Stand-alone (non-VST) software synths can still be used from within many of the more popular sequencer packages, but only if additional drivers are included that will allow them to receive MIDI instructions from the sequencer and to route audio data into the sequencer's mixer.

VST synths have the advantage of being readily compatible with any sequencer that supports the latest VST instrument plug-ins, and they're also easy to configure. VST instrument plug-ins appear on exactly the same type of pull-down menu as any other VST plug-in, although the exact way in which these are presented varies according to the manufacturer of the sequencer. Again, it's possible to automate the current generation of VST plug-ins via MIDI, which means that there's already a way to send MIDI to these devices without having to install special drivers. Instead of the sequencer track data being sent to a MIDI port or a soundcard driver, it's simply routed directly to the appropriate plug-in.

A significant advantage of using a virtual synth is that it's possible to have a control interface covered with virtual (on-screen) knobs, just like the real thing, and the automation capabilities of VST mean that adjustments can be made in real time and recorded as part of a song. The down-side to this is that, the more synth notes are played at once, the more computing power is required, which will eventually result in a compromise in the number of audio tracks and processing plug-ins that can be used at the same time. This is why it's never really possible to determine exactly how many tracks a system is capable of playing back at once; it all depends on what else the computer has to do at the same time.

Samplers are also available in software-only forms, some of which will read commercial sample CD-ROM formats. As you might expect, these will hog some of a computer resources, but even so the concept is an attractive one, especially if it isn't necessary to play back a huge number of voices at the same time. They also tend to use the computer's own RAM as sample memory, although the hardware-sampling capability built into some of the cheaper multimedia soundcards uses separate on-board memory.

# mastering and editing

As well as allowing the user to perform multitrack recording and MIDI sequencing, the computer can also help in compiling a selection of best mixes into an album. The usual approach is to use a stereo-editing software package that can be used to tidy up the beginnings and ends of mixes. The relative levels should be adjusted between tracks, EQ applied where necessary, and of course the lengths of the gaps between tracks should also be set. Other processes may also be applied, such as compression or limiting, which will help to refine the material until it sounds as good as possible. The finished album can then be recorded to any destination, from a cassette deck to a DAT machine or a MiniDisc recorder, or it may be stored as an MP3 file ready for distribution on the internet. Alternatively, a number of audio CDs may be burned.

# more cool stuff

The musical use of computers isn't limited to multitrack recording, MIDI sequencing and mastering, although these are the more common applications. Computers can also help in composing music. At one end of the scale there are programs such as Band In A Box, which produces a complete MIDI arrangement based on your choice of chords and musical style, while at the other extreme there are programs like KOAN Pro that create music (via MIDI) by using an algorithmic method based on a set of mathematical rules and random selections. Or for something really off the wall there is software like Metasynth, which enables the user to turn drawings or even photographs into sound, with various filtering algorithms to make the results more or less musical in the conventional sense. The principle at work here is that each pixel of the photograph is used to control the level, pitch and pan position of a separate oscillator. The results, which are not always musical in the traditional sense, may then be saved as audio files.

The great thing about programs like Band In A Box and KOAN Pro is that the resulting MIDI data can be loaded into a favourite MIDI sequencer package and then changed around until something desirable is achieved. There's also a fair amount of shareware available – either on the internet or on the cover discs of computer magazines – which can be pressed into creative use, although it's important to scan these programs for viruses before copying them onto a computer. One PC program I tried from a company called Syntrillium simulates wind chimes, and comes complete with a choice of scales, sounds and weather conditions!

Most serious MIDI sequencers will also allow the user to produce a pretty decent printed score generated from MIDI compositions. Although some musical knowledge is necessary to wring the best out of score-writing software, even a novice with a few good musical ideas should be able to print out a score for their latest epic that's clear enough for a visiting musician to understand. As long as the piece is played along to the sequencer's click track, whatever is played on the keyboard will appear on the score. It's that simple.

Other, less obvious functions include the removing of hiss and clicks from previously-recorded material, or even from vinyl records. The latter facility is popular among musicians wishing to transfer their vinyl collections to CD while leaving the hiss and crackles behind.

# practicalities

On the face of it, a suitable computer fitted with MIDI and audio interfaces, and running suitable software, can perform the same functions as a conventional recording studio. Although this isn't too far from the truth, there are some other things that will be needed before a studio is truly complete. The most obvious is a monitoring system (a combinations of an amplifier and speakers) that will enable you to hear what's happening, and you may also choose to invest in a stereo recorder such as a DAT machine, a MiniDisc recorder or a CD burner. Monitoring arrangements and studio set-up considerations are discussed in more detail towards the end of this book.

To record "real" sounds rather than relying entirely on MIDI sound sources, you'll need a reasonably good studio microphone or two. Very few audio interfaces come with good-quality mic amps that are built in, so in most cases a separate microphone pre-amplifier will be needed, which should be plugged into the line input of your soundcard or audio interface.

# hardware assistance

The outcome of this technological escalation is that, given a computer and the right software, it's possible to do some amazing things without using any external hardware except for a monitoring system, a MIDI keyboard and a mic pre-amp. However, even with a fast computer you may still end up in a situation where you want to do more things at the same time than the computer is capable of handling. In this case, it's possible either to use specialised DSP-based computer expansion cards to take over some of the more labour-intensive functions or to add external hardware. For example, I mentioned earlier that you might prefer to use hardware synths rather than (or in addition to) virtual synths, and the same applies to samplers, drum machines and some effects.

With soundcards, there are high-end DSP-based systems available, such as ProTools and Soundscape, which handle all of the hard-disk recording, mixing and plug-in activity via their own DSPs, or there are also more affordable solutions on the market such as the Yamaha SW1000XG and Lexicon's Core II, which combine hardware mixing, audio I/O (In/Out) and digital effects on a single card. Here, however, it's important to watch out for how well these will integrate into the existing system. For example, can the hardware be accessed via the existing sequencer package, or does it come with its own support software that will restrict its use in some way? In fairness, most MIDI-controllable hardware can be controlled from a control map set up in the native sequencer package, but this isn't always particularly seamless. The ideal system is one in which the hardware is supported directly by the sequencer software, as is the case with ProTools hardware used from within Logic Audio or Cubase VST.

# the upgrade spiral

The world of computer music is anything but static, so it makes sense to buy the most powerful computer that your finances will allow. Even so, you should still be prepared to upgrade to a newer and faster model in a year or two in order to maintain a state-of-the-art system. Some money may be lost in the process, but probably much less than would be lost because of the depreciation on a comparable hardware-based studio system that has no upgrade path. Of course, if the new system does all that's desired of it now, why change it at all?

One reason for the existence of the upgrade spiral is that music software undergoes frequent revisions as more features are added. Naturally these features are very attractive, but more features means that more computing power is needed to run them. Another reason is that more software is becoming available that will run at the same time as a main sequencer package. (I'm thinking now of software-based plug-ins, such as audio-processing effects and software-based instruments like synthesisers, samplers and drum machines.) It's true that it's not vital to subscribe to all of these modern wonders – it's possible to buy a system that only does what's necessary and then stick with it – but the temptation to keep up with technological development is almost overwhelming.

Alternatively, if upgrading to the latest machine proves to be prohibitively expensive, you may prefer to content yourself with being a year or two behind the state of the art and instead upgrade by buying bargain-priced, second-hand computers as they become available. My own system is more than two years behind the current technology available, but it's still more than powerful enough for my own requirements.

# the rest of the studio

The fact that computers and recording software are such good value for money can lead the user into believing that he or she can make do with equally cheap components in the rest of the studio, but this simply isn't true. Premium items such as capacitor mics and mic pre-amps are now much more affordable than they used to be, but they still seem expensive when compared with the cost of computers, considering that they only do one job and computers are capable of doing so much. There is a school of thought that says that most of the money available to the user should go into the computer, but this is not the way to plan a good studio. I would advise to budget for a good microphone, decent cables and, if possible, a mic pre-amp/voice channel. It's possible to still use an old dynamic microphone previously used for gigs, but in most instances a capacitor mic will provide noticeably better results on vocals and acoustic instruments. A good hardware reverb is also a real benefit, if it can be patched it into the system.

The same applies to monitor speakers. If they aren't accurate, it's impossible to know what a recording really sounds like. Good-quality monitor loudspeakers should be used, placed on rigid stands and set up properly, as described in chapter eight. It's not necessary to monitor loudly, but there has to be enough volume to overcome the physical noise made by the fans and drives of the computer. If possible, computers should be placed in a ventilated cupboard, which will reduce the noise, but be careful not to block off ventilation. Lining the cupboard with an inch-thick layer of furniture foam (fireproof, of course) will help to damp out the noise.

# your task...

This book can never be a substitute for the manuals that come with a computer, software and external hardware. It's aim is to illustrate the kinds of things that a computer can do and the various configurations that you might consider depending on your working methods. It also offers some advice on recording and mixing, although the other books in this series should also be consulted if you need more in-depth guidance in these areas. Hopefully, after reading this book, rather than being overwhelmed by the barrage of information flung at you by manuals you'll be in a better position to know how to use them and obtain the answers that you need.

Before it's possible to begin to make music on a computer, it's necessary first to learn something about the machine. This includes being aware of all of the basic functions, such as creating, loading and saving files, using the mouse and so on, but it's also useful to be aware of how to diagnose faults and recover from crashes. Having friends who use the same type of computer can help immensely, even in they don't use it for music, and if you can gain enough experience to re-install a damaged operating system then you're well on your way.

You're much less likely to run into problems if you buy your system preconfigured and tested, but you should also be aware that playing games, loading programs from magazine cover disks or accessing the internet can cause problems with music software, not to mention lay your computer open to the risk of picking up computer viruses. If you must use the same computer for both jobs, I'd recommend that you ask your supplier to install a second hard drive with a separate operating system that you can use exclusively for music. In this way, the computer will behave like two completely different machines, depending on the drive from which you boot up. Those with limited computer experience should ask the computer supplier to set this up for them and to show them how to choose the start-up drive.

A further useful safeguard is to make a back-up copy of the drive to CD-ROM, along with its freshly-installed operating system and music software, as soon as it's set up. You may even be able to persuade the supplier to do this for you. In the event of a fatal crash, this back-up can be copied back onto the hard drive (after it has first been erased and reformatted), which will restore the system back to its original condition. Of course, this will result in the total loss of any data that has been recorded to the drive since the system's original installation, which is why it's so important to make regular back-ups of important files. Reformatting the drive may also erase the invisible files that some companies use in conjunction with key disk copy protection, so it's important to uninstall any such software prior to reformatting the drive.

## chapter 2

# introducing MIDI

For users who have already had some experience with MIDI, it may not be necessary to read all of this chapter; but it should help to bring those coming from a more traditional recording background up to speed without burdening them with unnecessary complexities.

First of all, what does MIDI stand for? Answer: Musical Instrument Digital Interface. However, before starting to explain how MIDI works and how to use it, it might be more useful to ask what kind of things it can do. It should be noted that MIDI isn't only applicable to keyboard players, but because the keyboard is the best-suited instrument on which to generate MIDI information the majority of MIDI music is made using keyboards. There are practical alternatives for musicians who prefer to pluck, bow, blow or hit things, but I'll be referring to keyboards during this explanation.

## the MIDI virtual orchestra

The combination of MIDI and a suitable sequencer (which is a large part of the thrust of this book) will enable the user to record all of the different musical parts of a score from the keyboard one at a time, and then hear them playing together in perfect synchronisation, each part played back with a chosen synth sound. The sounds can be changed even after recording has been completed, and the tempo of the finished recording can also be changed. It's also possible to experiment with musical arrangements by copying verses and choruses to new locations within a song.

The reason why MIDI allows the user to perform all of these amazing functions is that it isn't a system for transmitting sound at all; rather, it's actually a system for transmitting instructions to devices that produce sounds. Take the analogy of a traditional musician, for whom the musical score provides the instructions and the player's instrument provides the sounds. MIDI works in much the same way, except in the context of MIDI the score is electronic and the sounds that are heard are produced by banks of synthesisers.

# introducing the MIDI sequencer

At its simplest, MIDI means that a keyboard player can play several electronic instruments from a single keyboard rather than having to dash around the stage whenever a change of instrument is required. However, shortly after the introduction of MIDI came the MIDI sequencer, a special type of multitrack recorder that is capable of recording not sound but MIDI information.

Whatever the type of MIDI system used, a MIDI keyboard (or other suitable MIDI instrument) with MIDI In, Out and Thru sockets on the back panel will be essential. The keyboard should also have *velocity sensitivity* (and virtually all serious keyboards do), which means that the instrument will respond like a real instrument in that, the harder the keys are hit, the louder the notes will be. If the keyboard doesn't have velocity sensitivity, all of the notes will sound at the same level, like an organ. The master keyboard may be "dumb" (ie with no built-in sounds), or it may be a conventional keyboard synthesiser with built-in sounds.

# the MIDI link

Linking MIDI instruments is accomplished by means of standard MIDI cables, which are available from most music shops. As with computers, MIDI data is stored in a digital form, which may be though of as a kind of ultra-fast Morse code for machines. The method of MIDI connection is quite straightforward, as we shall see shortly, but what is more important at this early stage is to appreciate precisely what musically-useful information can be passed from one MIDI instrument or device to another. This following description covers the most important and basic aspects of MIDI, but in the interests of keeping this introduction quick and simple it is by no means comprehensive.

# the anatomy of a note

When a key is depressed on a MIDI keyboard, a signal known as a Note On message is sent from the MIDI Out socket, along with a note number identifying the key. When the key is released, a Note Off message is sent. This is how the receiving MIDI instrument knows which note to play, when to play it and when to stop playing it. Up to 128 different notes can be handled by MIDI, where each key on the keyboard has its own note number. The loudness of the note depends on how hard the key is hit, which is really the same thing as saying how fast the key is pushed down. This speed, or *velocity*, is read by circuitry within the keyboard and used to control the volume of the sound being played.

The pitch of the note is determined by the location of the key which is pressed, although it's quite possible to transpose MIDI data before it reaches its destination. However, in order to keep things simple, let's assume that, unless otherwise stated, pressing a key results in the corresponding musical note being played.

# MIDI note data

As the information determining Pitch, Note On, Note Off and Velocity exists in the form of electronic signals, it's possible to send those signals along cables to control a second MIDI instrument some distance away from the controlling keyboard. This works as follows: a small computer inside the keyboard monitors the physical motion of the keys and converts these actions to MIDI messages, which appear at the MIDI Out socket of the keyboard. If the MIDI Out of the keyboard currently playing (which is called the *master* keyboard) is plugged into the MIDI In socket of a second MIDI instrument (which is called the *slave*) then the slave is able to play the notes as performed on the master keyboard. This simple MIDI connection is shown in Figure 2.1.

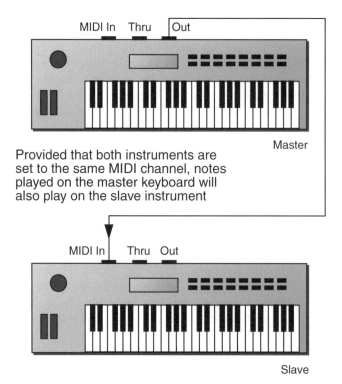

Figure 2.1: Midi master/slave set-up

# what do those MIDI sockets do?

MIDI Out sends information from a controlling MIDI device (the master) to other MIDI devices that it is controlling (slaves).

MIDI In receives MIDI information, which is then passed on to the MIDI thru socket unchanged. However, if any of the incoming information is "addressed" to the instrument in question, it will act on that MIDI data exactly as if it were being controlled directly from a keyboard.

MIDI Thru sends a copy of the MIDI In signal to multiple destinations, thus allowing several MIDI instruments to be linked together.

# the synthesiser module

The ability to link a second instrument via MIDI means that the sounds of both instruments can be played by using just one keyboard. This may be convenient, but it's hardly likely to revolutionise music as we know it! However, a little further thought will reveal that the second instrument doesn't actually need a keyboard at all because all of the playing is done on the master keyboard.

This leads nicely onto the subject of MIDI modules, which are simply the sound-generating and MIDI-interfacing electronics of a keyboard instrument packaged in a rather more compact and generally less expensive box. There's also no reason why multiple modules shouldn't be controlled from a single master keyboard, but in order to appreciate the full implications of this it's important to understand the concept of MIDI channels. These are the means by which certain messages are "addressed" so that they are recognised by certain instruments and ignored by others.

# MIDI channels

In a typical master/slave MIDI system, the way in which the instruments are linked together like a daisy chain means that all of the slaves will receive the same MIDI information. The MIDI channel system was devised in order to allow the master instrument to communicate with just one specific slave without all of the others trying to play along with it. The basic idea is that MIDI note messages are tagged with an invisible address label which carries their MIDI channel number. The messages are therefore only acted upon when they are received by a MIDI instrument or device set to the same MIDI channel number. All other MIDI devices will politely ignore the message.

There are 16 MIDI channels, which are, logically enough, numbered one to 16, the idea being that MIDI information sent on channel one will only be acted upon by slave instruments also set to receive on channel one. For example, if the master keyboard were set to MIDI channel one, and then three different MIDI instruments set to receive on channels one, two and three were connected, only the instrument set to channel one would respond. The other modules would still receive the information, but the MIDI data would tell them that the information wasn't not on their channel, so they would ignore it.

By switching channels on the master keyboard, up to 16 different MIDI instruments set to 16 different channels can be addressed individually, even though they are all wired into the same system. The concept of MIDI channels will become vitally important when we move onto the subject of MIDI sequencers.

# Omni mode warning!

If a MIDI instrument is inadvertently set to Omni mode (an option usually found in the MIDI Set-up menu), the system won't behave as expected. Most MIDI instruments can be set to receive on any of the 16 MIDI channels, but if Omni mode is used then this will allow a MIDI instrument to respond to all incoming data, regardless of its channel. In other words, everything that comes along the MIDI cable is played, which is roughly analogous to one member of an orchestra trying to play all parts of a score at the same time. For regular, 16-channel operation, instruments should be set to Poly mode. There will be more about modes later.

# more about modules

So far I've described modules as being MIDI synthesisers in boxes without keyboards, and this definition is true enough, as far as it goes. However, a great many modern modules actually contain several independent sound-generating sections, each of which can be addressed on a different MIDI channel.

These sound-generating sections are often known as *parts*, because in a typical system each section can be made to play a separate musical part. For example, a 16-part multitimbral module can play back up to 16 different musical sounds at the same time, each part controlled via a different MIDI channel. For most purposes, a multi-part module can be visualised as being analogous to several synthesisers sharing the same box. The same is also true of most computer soundcards that have MIDI synth sections.

# multitimbrality

Modules capable of playing two or more different parts with different sounds are said to be multitimbral, although the individual synthesiser sections they contain are rarely entirely independent of each other. For example, they will all share the same set of front-panel controls, and some parameters may affect all of the voices globally. What's more, on low-cost modules (and also budget soundcards) the outputs from the various parts are usually mixed to stereo, and they then emerge from a single stereo pair of sockets. Modules also usually include effects sections, which have to be shared between the parts in some way. However, it's invariably the case that independent control may be exerted over the choice of available sounds (or *patches*, as they call them in synthspeak) that are selected, the relative levels of the different voices, the left/right pan positions and the amount of effects (such as reverberation) added to each part.

Drum machines are a special type of MIDI module, and are equipped with their own built-in sequencers which allow them to store and replay rhythm patterns and complex arrangements based on permutations of those patterns. The main difference between a standard synth patch and the way in which a drum machine organises its sounds is that a synthesiser tends to interpret incoming MIDI note data as different pitches of the same basic sound, whereas a drum machine produces a different drum, cymbal or percussion sound for each MIDI note. Most multitimbral synthesiser modules and computer soundcards usually have one part dedicated to drum sounds, so it's no longer essential to buy a separate drum machine, although it may prove desirable to make use of the preset rhythm patterns that drum machines invariably provide.

# MIDI thru chains

The master instrument in a simple MIDI chain sends information from its MIDI Out socket, which must be connected to the MIDI In socket of the first slave. The MIDI Thru of the first slave is then connected to the MIDI In of the second slave and its Thru connected to the MIDI In of the next one and so on. The result is a daisy chain, and while this can be infinitely long in theory, this turns out to be untrue in practice. What actually happens is that the MIDI signal deteriorates slightly as is passes through each instrument, and after it has gone through three of four instruments it starts to become unreliable, and soon notes start to become stuck or refuse to play at all.

One solution is to use a MIDI Thru box, which takes the output from the master keyboard and then splits it into several Thru connections, which

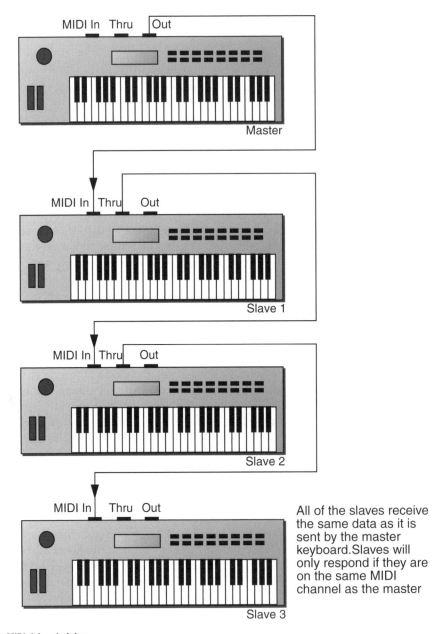

All of the slaves receive the same data as it is sent by the master keyboard. Slaves will only respond if they are on the same MIDI channel as the master

**Figure 2.2: MIDI daisy chaining**

feed the individual modules directly. Figure 2.2 shows the standard method of daisy chaining, while Figure 2.3 shows the same system wired using a MIDI Thru box. A MIDI Thru box is a relatively simple and inexpensive device which splits a single MIDI signal several ways. Thru

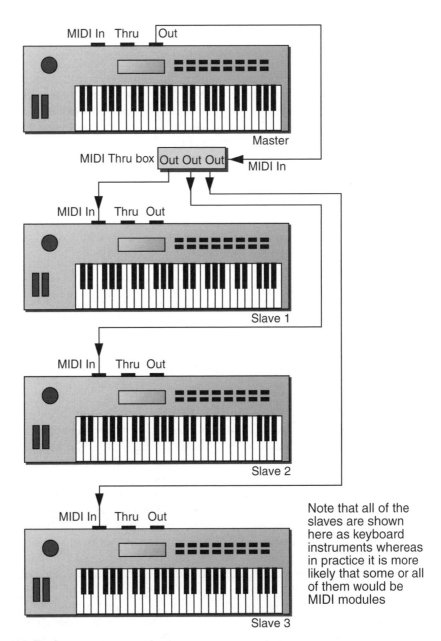

MIDI In  Thru  Out

Master

MIDI Thru box Out Out Out  MIDI In

MIDI In  Thru  Out

Slave 1

MIDI In  Thru  Out

Slave 2

MIDI In  Thru  Out

Note that all of the slaves are shown here as keyboard instruments whereas in practice it is more likely that some or all of them would be MIDI modules

Slave 3

**Figure 2.3: MIDI Thru box**

boxes may also be used in combination with daisy chaining; if an instrument is fed from a Thru box, its Thru socket may be linked to another module to form a short daisy chain. The only proviso here is that these individual chains are no more than two or three devices long.

# MIDI programs

Modern synthesisers are mainly programmable, which means that they have the ability to remember many different sounds, each identified by a patch or program number. New instruments inevitably come with some preset factory patches (which can't be changed), along with space for users to store their own patches. MIDI can allow direct access to up to 128 patches, sometimes numbered from 0 to 127 and sometimes from 1 to 128. (Even standards don't always turn out to be all that standard!) The buttons that are used to select the patches on the master keyboard also enable patch information to be transmitted via MIDI to the slave synthesiser modules. This enables the user not only to play the modules remotely but also to select the sound or patch to which they are set.

Instruments containing more than 128 patches must have these organised into two or more banks, each containing a maximum of 128 patches. This is because MIDI Program Change messages can only access 128 patches directly. MIDI Bank Change commands are used to switch from one bank to another.

# MIDI controllers

In order to help the keyboard player to imitate the expression of a real instrument, a typical MIDI synthesiser or master keyboard has two or more performance wheels mounted to the left of the keyboard. These are used to control pitch bend and depth of vibrato. Like the keys, these wheels generate MIDI information that can be used to control a slave module. Further control may be provided by means of foot switch or pedal inputs, which allow a conventional volume pedal to be used as a means of varying MIDI control functions, such as level or filter frequency. Because pedals and wheels can be set to any position, rather than simply be either on or off, they are known as *continuous controllers*. Other MIDI controllers are available to perform functions that can be either on or off.

Continuous controllers actually work in a series of small steps, with values from 0 to 127 (or 1 to 128). The different devices which allow a musical instrument to be controlled in this way include performance wheels, joysticks, levers, pedals, foot switches, breath controllers and ribbon controllers, among others. It's not necessary to worry about MIDI channels or other technicalities when using controllers because the data automatically goes to the same destination (ie the same MIDI channel) as the notes that are being played on the keyboard.

# pitch-bend scaling

By changing parameters in the MIDI Set-up menu, MIDI instruments can often be "scaled" so that, for example, the maximum travel of the pitch-bend wheel might cause a pitch shift of as little as one semitone or as much as a whole octave. It's important to ensure that any instruments likely to play at the same time are set with the same scaling values, especially for events such as pitch bend, or when a note is bent on the master keyboard the sound on that instrument might go up by a third and the sound from the slave by a fourth! For general use, most people set up a pitch-bend range of two semitones, so that, from the centre position of the wheel, a range of a whole tone either higher or lower is available. Most pitch-bend wheels are spring loaded so that they automatically return to their central position when released.

Note that, although the pitch-bend wheel is involved in the controlling of expressiveness, it doesn't fall within the category of MIDI controllers group but rather exists in a group of its own.

# more controllers

On an instrument that is designed to work with the MIDI controller governing master volume, turning up the master volume slider on the master keyboard will send the appropriate control information (controller number seven, for point of reference) over the MIDI channel and the receiving synth will respond to it. A multitimbral module receiving a message concerning master volume control will vary the volume of whichever part is being addressed according to the MIDI channel of the controller keyboard.

Another common MIDI controller is the sustain pedal, which prevents the note envelopes from entering their Release phase until the pedal is released. This function operates rather like the sustain pedal on a piano. A full listing of controller numbers and their functions is included for reference, as you may find some interesting uses for them when you start to do some serious sequencing.

# controller listing

| | | | |
|---|---|---|---|
| 0 | Bank select | 5 | Portamento time |
| 1 | Modulation wheel | 6 | Data entry |
| 2 | Breath controller | 7 | Main volume |
| 3 | Undefined | 8 | Balance |
| 4 | Foot controller | 9 | Undefined |

| | | | | |
|---|---|---|---|---|
| 10 | Pan | 80-83 | General purpose 5-8 |
| 11 | Expression | 84 | Portamento control |
| 12 | Effect control 1 | 85-90 | Undefined |
| 13 | Effect control 2 | 91 | Effects depth (effect 1) |
| 14 | Undefined | 92 | Tremolo depth (effect 2) |
| 15 | Undefined | 93 | Chorus depth (effect 3) |
| 16-19 | General purpose 1-4 | 94 | Celeste depth (effect 4) |
| 20-31 | Undefined | 95 | Phaser depth (effect 5) |
| 32-63 | LSB for control changes 0-31 | 96 | Data increment |
| | (where greater resolution is | 97 | Data decrement |
| | required) | 98 | Non-registered parameter |
| 64 | Damper/sustain pedal | | number LSB |
| 65 | Portamento | 99 | Non-registered parameter |
| 66 | *Sostenuto* | | Number MSB |
| 67 | Soft pedal | 100 | Registered parameter number |
| 68 | *Legato* footswitch | | LSB |
| 69 | Hold 2 | 101 | Registered parameter number |
| 70 | Sound variation/exciter | | MSB |
| 71 | Harmonic content/compressor | 102-19 | Undefined |
| 72 | Release time/distortion | 120 | All sound off |
| 73 | Attack Time/Equaliser | 121 | Reset all controllers |
| 74 | Brightness/expander gate | 122 | Local control |
| 75 | Undefined/reverb | 123 | All notes off |
| 76 | Undefined/delay | 124 | Omni mode off |
| 77 | Undefined/pitch transpose | 125 | Omni mode on |
| 78 | Undefined/flange or chorus | 126 | Mono mode on |
| 79 | Undefined/special effect | 127 | Poly mode on |

Not all controllers deal with performance control. In addition to the last four controller numbers, which change MIDI modes, there are also Bank Change messages, an All Notes Off message (used to cut off all notes that may still be playing), Local On/Off and a Reset All Controllers message, which ensures that all controller values are reset to their default values.

The initials MSB and LSB stand for Most Significant Bit and Least Significant Bit, which is roughly computerspeak for coarse and fine adjustments. Both MSBs and LSBs have a possible numerical range of 0 to 127. Variable controllers have values of between 0 and 127, while switched controller are usually set at 0 for off and 127 for on. Most modern instruments will also accept any value of 64 and above as on and any below 64 as off. Pitch bend, however, can provide control in two directions, so its default position is midway between the two extremes, at 64. The sequencer will take care of most of the obscure MIDI dialogue to and from your keyboard and modules for you, but when it comes to editing MIDI sequence data it's helpful to know what the more common controllers and their values mean.

# MIDI modes

Instruments are generally set to Poly mode for conventional operation, although some older instruments default to Omni mode every time they are switched on. Because the vast majority of work is done in Poly mode, most users rarely give MIDI modes a second thought. For reference, though, there are actually four different MIDI modes, which are defined as follows:

- Mode one: Omni On/Poly. The instrument will play polyphonically (ie more than one note simultaneously), but MIDI channel data is ignored. Whatever is sent to it, on whatever channel, will be played by it. Some older instruments still default to Omni On mode when powered up, so they must be switched back to Omni Off before being used.

- Mode two: Omni On/Mono. The monophonic equivalent of mode one. This is hardly ever used.

- Mode three: Omni Off/Poly. The "normal" MIDI mode, especially for sequencing or multitimbral operation. In mode three, the instrument responds only to messages on its own MIDI channel and plays polyphonically.

- Mode four: Omni Off/Mono. The monophonic equivalent of mode three. Mode four is used mainly by MIDI guitar players who need to have each string working on a separate MIDI channel in order to be able to bend notes or apply vibrato on independent strings. Because each string of a guitar is in mono (ie it can only play one note at a time), it makes sense to use the receiving synth in Mono mode to mimic the way in which a real guitar is played.

# non-registered parameter numbers

Because not all synthesisers use the same type of synthesis, it would be impossible to provide a standard range of controllers that were able to access every parameter that had an influence over the sound being produced. Some parameters are common to all instruments, and these are known as registered parameters, but in order to allow manufacturers to provide access to all of the relevant parameters present on different instruments the non-registered parameter (NRPN) system was added to the MIDI specification.

The registered parameters are pitch bend sensitivity, fine tuning, coarse tuning, change tuning program and change tuning bank. The vast majority of controls are non-registered, but for precisely this reason it's usually necessary to have some form of customised hardware interface or editing software with which to access them. Because they are non-defined, the user has no means of knowing what they are unless they are detailed in the MIDI specifications at the back of the instrument manual. NRPNs are mainly used to provide access for software writers who are designing editing programs, although the more sophisticated MIDI user may also be tempted to make use of them.

# aftertouch

Another source of information concerning the control of musical performance is channel aftertouch, which is produced by some keyboards when the keys are depressed hard. A pressure sensor under the keyboard sends out a lot of MIDI data corresponding to how hard you push down on a key after playing a note, so if you're not using aftertouch on your master keyboard it should be turned off in order to cut down on unnecessary MIDI traffic. Also, when working with a computer sequencer, unnecessary controller data takes up a lot of memory.

Aftertouch can be assigned to trigger various functions, such as brightness, loudness, depth of vibrato and so on. It's a useful way of adding expressiveness to a performance, but it should be kept in mind that channel aftertouch affects all of the notes that are playing at any one time, not just the one that's being depressed.

A few instruments feature polyphonic aftertouch, which means that, when a key is depressed, the controller data which is sent applies only to that note and not to all of the notes that are currently playing. Polyphonic aftertouch can generate a vast amount of MIDI data, and so therefore must be used sparingly. Very few instruments support this facility.

Another less-common feature is release velocity. All touch-velocity instruments generate MIDI note velocity, depending on how quickly the keys are depressed, but on an instrument with release velocity there is also information generated to indicate how quickly they are released.

# sound banks

Where a synthesiser module contains two or more banks of sounds, a MIDI Bank Change message (also a form of controller message, involving controller numbers 0 and 32) is then used to access the different banks. Not all instruments use standard Bank Change messages, but the relevant controller values are supplied in the handbooks of MIDI instruments as part of MIDI implementation tables.

# assignable controls

Instruments often allow the user to designate which physical control device relates to a specific MIDI controller, so the modulation wheel on a synth could be redirected to control something quite different, such as the amount of reverb applied or the brightness of the sound.

How much you want to get involved with the various controllers is up to you. At first you'll probably be happy to use the pitch bend and modulation wheels and the sustain pedal, but as you become more familiar with MIDI you may be attracted to the possibilities of using a sequencer to automate your performance by using it to control levels, create automated panning, change effects, change patches and so on. The encouraging thing about MIDI is that you can start off very simply, making music right from the beginning, and then you can try out more ambitious things as you grow more comfortable with the concept.

# channel voice messages

Most of the MIDI messages discussed so far are only accepted by the receiving device if they are on the same channel as the sending device. This type of message is called a MIDI Channel message for that reason. MIDI Note On and Note Off messages are also Channel Messages, as are all other types of performance data relating to velocity, pitch bend, controller data, program changes and so on. There are other MIDI messages that are not channel specific.

# MIDI clock

Unlike channel-specific messages, MIDI messages related to synchronisation and sequencer control have no channel address, so are received by all of the instruments in the MIDI system. Perhaps the most important of all of these system messages is MIDI clock.

MIDI clock is a tempo-related timing code comprising 96 electronic ticks for each four-beat-long bar of music. These ticks are inaudible, but they are recognised by any drum machine or sequencer set to External MIDI Sync mode, enabling the slave machine to stay in sync with the master. MIDI clock may be used to synchronise a drum machine with a sequencer. In this case, the slave machine must be set to External MIDI Sync, which means that it will follow the tempo generated by the master device exactly.

# start, stop and continue

The slave device also needs to know when to start and stop, so MIDI also includes Start, Stop and Continue messages. On their own, these are only of any use if a master starts to play from the very beginning of a song, because otherwise the slave won't know the position from which it's supposed to start. To get around this, the MIDI Song Position Pointer message was also added to the MIDI specification.

# song position pointers

MIDI Song Position Pointers, or SPPs, are quite invisible to the user. On starting the sequence, a message is sent to the receiving device, which informs it of the position from which to start. As a result, the slave device can lock up almost instantaneously with the master, even if a song is started halfway through.

# MIDI machine control

There is also a MIDI protocol for controlling compatible tape machines and hard-disk recorders, which is known as MIDI Machine Control (MMC). This allows remote access to the main transport controls and sometimes to the record status buttons of a multitrack recorder, which can be useful, particularly if the multitrack recorder is on the opposite side of the room to the sequencer.

# limitations of MIDI

MIDI might seem to be instantaneous, but by computer standards it's quite slow. What's more, it moves data in single file; it is a serial system. When a chord is played, all of the Note On messages are sent sequentially. However, because MIDI is still pretty quick compared to the resolution of human hearing, the notes appear to sound at the same time. Even so, if 64 notes were played at once, for example, the delay between the first and the last might be audible.

In reality, the speed of MIDI is seldom a limitation when dealing only with notes, but if you're trying to replay a multipart MIDI sequence that also contains lots of controller information then you could end up with the MIDI equivalent of a traffic jam, resulting in timing errors. In practice, it's wise to use controllers only when necessary and to switch off the master keyboard's aftertouch whenever it's not needed. The better sequencers give priority to MIDI note timing when traffic gets heavy so that timing problems are less likely to be audible.

# active sensing

MIDI also includes something called active sensing (although this isn't always implemented), which checks that a connection exists between devices. In effect, the receiving device looks for regular confirmation that the MIDI connection is intact, and in order to do this a regular stream of Active Sensing messages is sent by the transmitting device. If the receiving device doesn't get back an "all's well" message within the allowed time, it shuts off all notes that are playing. If it didn't do this and the MIDI cable was accidentally unplugged between a Note On being sent and a Note Off being sent, the receiving instrument would continue to play indefinitely. This is sometimes known as a stuck MIDI note.

# MIDI song select

Because MIDI sequencers can hold more than one song in their memories, MIDI also includes a Song Select message. As you might expect, tunes can requested by number in the range of 0 to 127. Think of it as a MIDI jukebox that accepts requests via MIDI Song Select numbers! This facility is most often used with hardware sequencers in situations where musicians may rely on them to provide live backing tracks.

# tune request

If a Tune Request command is sent, all of the MIDI instruments in the system that have a tuning routine will give themselves a quick maintenance check and retune themselves to their own internal reference.

# system-exclusive messages

System-Exclusive (Sysex for short) messages are part of the MIDI System Message portfolio, but, whereas the rest of MIDI is pretty precisely defined, Sysex is provided so that manufacturers can build instruments with different facilities but which still conform to the MIDI specification. Rather than using the MIDI channel system for locating their targets, Sysex messages contain an ID code that is unique to the type of instrument for which they are intended. Where two or more identical instruments are being used in the same system, it's often possible to assign an additional ID number of between one and 16 to each one so that no two have exactly the same ID. If they did, they'd all respond to the same Sysex data.

In the main, Sysex allows those people who write sound-editing software to gain access to all of the sound-generating parameters that might need adjusting. The programming parameters of analogue and digital synths tend to be quite different, so manufacturers have to be allowed to specify exclusive codes to access their specific set of parameters, just as they provide NRPNs to access certain unique parameters using MIDI controllers.

Because Sysex messages are only recognised by the type of instrument for which they are designed, there's no risk of your drum machine trying to interpret a message intended for one of your synths and getting its brains scrambled.

# patch dumping

Usually, only advanced users of MIDI have more than a passing association with MIDI Sysex data, but anyone can use it at a basic level for copying patches or banks of patches from a synth into a MIDI storage device such as a sequencer or MIDI data filter. Here's how it works.

Most modern MIDI instruments have a Sysex dump facility tucked away in their MIDI configuration pages somewhere. All you have to do is connect the MIDI Out of the instrument to the sequencer's MIDI input, start recording on the sequencer and then start the dump procedure. The Sysex data will be recorded in exactly the same way as MIDI notes are recorded. However, the Edit list will look like it's full of completely meaningless data.

Sysex dump data usually takes several seconds to record, after which it can be played back into the instrument at any time to restore the patches that have been saved. It's advisable not to quantise the Sysex dump after recording it because then it may not play back properly.

# compatibility

Most new MIDI instruments support most MIDI features, but few are actually compulsory. About the only thing that can be taken for granted is that a MIDI synth will send and receive MIDI note data, although virtually all devices will accept MIDI Program Change messages and velocity information. If a MIDI message is received by an instrument incapable of responding to that message then the message is ignored.

The back pages of the relevant equipment manual should include a table displaying which MIDI facilities are supported, on which an "O" will show that the facility is present and a "X" will show that it isn't supported. This is known as the MIDI Implementation Table, and it can be very informative.

# MIDI merge

If there is a need to split the same MIDI signal to two or more destinations, it's possible either to fit the Thru connectors to the various MIDI instruments or to use a MIDI Thru box. However, merging two streams of MIDI data isn't quite so simple. MIDI data is quite complicated, and so, if two MIDI cables were joined with a Y-lead, the result would be a jumble of meaningless data. Instead, a special device known as a MIDI merge box is required. Figure 2.4 demonstrates how a MIDI merge box might be used to combine the MIDI outputs from a keyboard and from a dedicated sound-editing device, enabling both to be fed into a sequencer at the same time.

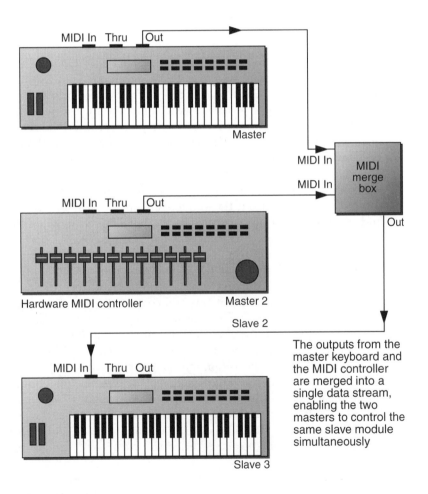

**Figure 2.4: Basic MIDI merging**

Merge facilities are necessary when a sequencer must be controlled by a master keyboard and still receive MIDI sync signals at the same time, or in order to play two keyboards into a sequencer at the same time. A merge facility is necessary at any time that a MIDI device needs to be controlled from two places at the same time. Although stand-alone MIDI merge boxes are available, most of the more sophisticated multiport MIDI interfaces include two or more mergeable inputs.

# MIDI sync

In a self-contained desktop studio environment, sync may not be an issue, but you'll need to know something about the way MIDI handles sync if you need to lock your sequencer to another sequencer, a tape recorder or a video machine.

# tape sync

The simplest MIDI sync system is FSK (Frequency Shift Keying), which records a series of electronic tones onto a spare track of the tape machine that will later provide a sync reference for the sequencer. This system provides a set of invisible timing pulses, rather like the sprocket holes in a roll of cine film. The sync tones are related to tempo, so more sync pulses are recorded per second as the the tempo increases.

A small hardware box known as a MIDI/tape sync box is needed to turn the MIDI sync data from the sequencer into recordable bursts of tone and vice versa, although many drum machines have this facility built into them. To synchronise a sequencer to tape using FSK, it's first necessary to program the entire drum part – complete with any tempo changes – and then play back the piece while recording the sync code output from the MIDI/tape sync box onto one track of a tape recorder. Some tape machines have dedicated sync ins and outs, while on others you have to use the audio ins and outs. On analogue tape machines, make sure that the noise reduction is bypassed, as this can prevent time code from being reproduced accurately. You should be aware that sync code is normally recorded onto the highest-numbered tape track (which will obviously be track four on a four-track machine), and if the machine has a special provision for handling sync codes this will invariably be found on the highest-numbered track. While recording the sync code, the sequencer MIDI Out feeds the MIDI In of the MIDI/tape sync box, and the audio out of the MIDI/tape sync box is recorded to tape.

To run the sequencer in sync with the tape machine, the tape output from the sync track that has just been recorded must be plugged into the sync in socket on the MIDI/tape sync box and the tape must be started from the beginning. The sequencer should be set to External MIDI Sync, whereupon it will automatically start to play when it receives the sync code from the tape machine, and it should stay in time with the tape until the tape machine is stopped.

Basic FSK synchronisation is simple, but the problem is that, whenever the tape is stopped, it must be wound right back to the beginning again in order to establish the sync, which can be very frustrating. Furthermore, unless the sequencer has more than one input with a MIDI a merge facility, it's impossible to record new parts onto the sequencer while locked to tape because the sequencer's MIDI In is occupied by the MIDI Out from the FSK sync box. Of course, a separate MIDI merge box can still be used to combine the MIDI output of the master keyboard with the MIDI out of the FSK sync box.

However, there is a refinement of the original FSK sync code, called Smart FSK, which makes life easier. With this system it's no longer necessary always to play the tape from the start in order to obtain synchronicity. This refined system is designed to work with MIDI SPPs (Song Position Pointers) so that the tape machine can be started anywhere in the song and the sequencer will always find the right place. Most modern MIDI equipment can generate and read SPPs, and the whole process works without any further intervention from the user.

# SMPTE

SMPTE is often used with video, or it is used to synchronise music with other forms of professional systems. It was originally designed to synchronise the soundtracks of films, so that the music ran alongside the action taking place on the screen, but it is now supported by many MIDI interfaces. Unlike Smart FSK, SMPTE is based on real time, and is measured in hours, minutes and seconds, with further subdivisions to accommodate individual frames of TV and film material. Because it is independent of tempo, a whole tape can be recorded, or *striped*, with code before any recording or programming takes place. SMPTE is available in a number of frame formats to accommodate both TV and film, the most common of which are 24, 25 and 30 frames per second. Conversion from real time to a MIDI tempo setting is carried out by the sequencer software, and most sequencers provide SMPTE support in a way that is very clear to the user. The starting tempo of a piece of music and the location are also stored within the tempo map, along with the amount and the time location of any subsequent tempo changes in the song. Tempo map data is invariably stored as part of the song file on the sequencer.

For those interested in such things, SMPTE stands for the Society Of Motion Pictures And Television Engineers, although to cover both US and European TV formats the term SMPTE/EBU is now used. American TV operates at 30 frames per second (fps) and film at 24fps, while European TV has a frame rate of 25fps. Apart from the more common 24, 25 and 30fps formats, the standard also includes *drop frame*, which is used for converting some specialist video formats. The system is so named because whole frames of picture are periodically discarded in order to eliminate cumulative timing errors which would otherwise cause noticeable sync problems. Drop frame is not generally used in audio-only applications.

It is normal to set the SMPTE format to the local TV standard, which in Europe means 25fps. Because individual frames of picture are too coarse a measurement for audio data, additional resolution is gained by dividing individual frames up into smaller units of time. (MTC can be treated in exactly the same way, even though there are slight technical differences in the data format.)

# MTC

By far the most common sync system used in modern sequencers is MTC (MIDI Time Code). MTC is a MIDI-specific variation on the traditional SMPTE protocol, and it offers the same choice of frame rates. Because MTC information is carried directly via MIDI, the hardware necessary to sync with it can be simpler. Some digital recording systems even output MTC directly, which means that no other hardware is needed. In those instances when MTC is not directly supported by a digital recorder, third-party interface boxes are often available. (The Alesis ADAT BRC remote controller outputs MTC, for example.)

Another dedicated sync code goes by the name of DTL (Direct Time Lock), and this is used exclusively by Mark Of The Unicorn's sequencing package Performer. Hardware support for this format is limited and is less popular in the UK than in its native USA.

# General MIDI

Most soundcards and many synthesisers include a bank of what are known as General MIDI, or GM, sounds. These comprise a bank of 128 standard preset sounds that ensure nominal compatibility between instruments made by different manufacturers. General MIDI was a relatively late addition to the MIDI specification, but it's extremely useful because it means that commercial MIDI files can be produced and you can be pretty sure of what types of sounds are going to be used to play back your composition. The GM sound set is tightly defined concerning the sounds that are included and the patch locations in which they reside. The set includes a number of standard pop and classical sounds as well as synth sounds and sound effects, and they are all located at the same patch numbers, regardless of the instrument or its manufacturer.

General MIDI is relevant only to those instruments bearing the GM logo. Furthermore, a GM machine may also be able to function as a non-GM machine, in which case it will have a dedicated GM mode or a separate bank of GM sounds for those occasion on which General MIDI operation is required.

GM also includes drum sounds, and specifies the keys on which the various drum sounds are mapped. A bass drum will always be a bass drum, even if it doesn't sound exactly the same on every machine.

Furthermore, GM specifies the minimum performance capability of the machine, in terms of multitimbrality and polyphony. Essentially, the aim is to allow a MIDI sequence that has been recorded over one GM module to be played back on any other GM module without the need to remap patches, move drum note allocations or worry about running out of parts or polyphony. This doesn't mean that all GM synths have to sound exactly the same, but it does mean that, for example, a piano preset voice on one machine must be in the same patch location as a similar-sounding piano preset voice on any other GM machine. For this reason, it's useful to have at least one GM-compatible instrument in your collection so that you can play commercial GM-format MIDI files or sequences made by any musicians with whom you may collaborate.

## polyphony and multitimbrality

GM instruments allow the user to play back 16 parts on 16 MIDI channels, with a total polyphony of at least 24 notes. If more notes than the instrument can handle are played, note robbing takes place and previously-played notes start to drop out. The whole idea of specifying a minimum level of polyphony is to ensure that you don't run out of polyphony when you're trying to play a MIDI song file that conforms to the GM format.

## Roland's enhanced GS format

Much of the present format of General MIDI owes its existence to Roland's own protocols, and so it's hardly surprising that Roland have gone one step further and devised an enhanced version of General MIDI which they call GS. Machines compatible with GS offer several alternative banks of GM types sounds, which gives the user more choice while still remaining within the GM remit. With GS, the basic GM set occupies one bank (Bank 0), with up to seven banks of variations All of the variation tones of a piano will still sound like pianos, although they will all be subtly different. Further banks are provided for sounds known as sub-capital tones, which are less obviously related to the main GM capital tones. A Bank Change command allows the user to switch between the banks.

Yamaha have also introduced their own expanded General MIDI format, which they call XG. Like Roland's GS mode, this builds on the basic General MIDI sound set and includes several banks of alternative sounds. Most Yamaha XG instruments also support Roland's GS format.

# basic definitions of General MIDI

- A GM instrument must support all 16 MIDI channels simultaneously, in order to provide 16-part multitimbrality.

- Percussion parts must be on MIDI channel ten, and must include a minimum set of 47 standard sound types, including the most common drum and latin percussion sounds. These must all be mapped in accordance with the GM standard.

- GM instruments must be capable of 24-note polyphony, and notes must be allocated dynamically. The specification allows eight notes to be reserved for percussion, which leaves 16 for all of the other instruments.

- All 128 preset sounds are defined by their type and patch location. Although there is some variation in sound between modules, the contents of each patch location is quite rigidly defined, right down to the dog barks, helicopters and gunshots featured in the special effects section.

- All GM instruments must respond to the same set of MIDI Controllers, and the default ranges set for these controller must be standard. The MIDI controller implementation includes the ability to change the master tuning and the range of the pitch-bend wheel via MIDI, Reset All Controllers (which resets all MIDI controllers to their default values) and All Notes Off (which silences any notes currently playing). All GM machines must also respond to pitch bend, velocity and aftertouch.

# General MIDI voice table

Note: some manufacturers number their patches from 0 to 127 rather than from 1 to 128.

| Program Number | Instrument | Program Number | Instrument |
|---|---|---|---|
| 1 | Acoustic grand piano | 37 | Slap bass 1 |
| 2 | Bright acoustic piano | 38 | Slap bass 2 |
| 3 | Electric grand piano | 39 | Synth bass 1 |
| 4 | Honky-tonk piano | 40 | Synth bass 2 |
| 5 | Electric piano 1 | 41 | Violin |
| 6 | Electric piano 2 | 42 | Viola |
| 7 | Harpsichord | 43 | Cello |
| 8 | Clavichord | 44 | Contrabass |
| 9 | Celesta | 45 | Tremolo strings |
| 10 | Glockenspiel | 46 | Pizzicato strings |
| 11 | Music box | 47 | Orchestral harp |
| 12 | Vibraphone | 48 | Timpani |
| 13 | Marimba | 49 | String ensemble 1 |
| 14 | Xylophone | 50 | String ensemble 2 |
| 15 | Tubular bells | 51 | Synth strings 1 |
| 16 | Dulcimer | 52 | Synth strings 2 |
| 17 | Drawbar organ | 53 | Choir aahs |
| 18 | Percussive organ | 54 | Voice oohs |
| 19 | Rock organ | 55 | Synth voice |
| 20 | Church organ | 56 | Orchestra hit |
| 21 | Reed organ | 57 | Trumpet |
| 22 | Accordion | 58 | Trombone |
| 23 | Harmonica | 59 | Tuba |
| 24 | Tango accordion | 60 | Muted trumpet |
| 25 | Acoustic guitar (nylon) | 61 | French horn |
| 26 | Acoustic guitar (steel) | 62 | Brass section |
| 27 | Electric guitar (jazz) | 63 | Synth brass 1 |
| 28 | Electric guitar (clean) | 64 | Synth brass 2 |
| 29 | Electric guitar (muted) | 65 | Soprano sax |
| 30 | Overdriven guitar | 66 | Alto sax |
| 31 | Distortion guitar | 67 | Tenor sax |
| 32 | Guitar harmonics | 68 | Baritone sax |
| 33 | Acoustic bass | 69 | Oboe |
| 34 | Electric bass (Finger) | 70 | English horn |
| 35 | Electric bass (Pick) | 71 | Bassoon |
| 36 | Fretless bass | 72 | Clarinet |

| Program Number | Instrument | Program Number | Instrument |
|---|---|---|---|
| 73 | Piccolo | 101 | FX 5 (brightness) |
| 74 | Flute | 102 | FX 6 (goblins) |
| 75 | Recorder | 103 | FX 7 (echoes) |
| 76 | Pan flute | 104 | FX 8 (sci-fi) |
| 77 | Blown bottle | 105 | Sitar |
| 78 | Shakuhachi | 106 | Banjo |
| 79 | Whistle | 107 | Shamisen |
| 80 | Ocarina | 108 | Koto |
| 81 | Lead 1 (square) | 109 | Kalimba |
| 82 | Lead 2 (sawtooth) | 110 | Bagpipe |
| 83 | Lead 3 (calliope) | 111 | Fiddle |
| 84 | Lead 4 (chiff) | 112 | Shanai |
| 85 | Lead 5 (charang) | 113 | Tinkle bell |
| 86 | Lead 6 (voice) | 114 | Agogo |
| 87 | Lead 7 (fifths) | 115 | Steel drums |
| 88 | Lead 8 (bass and lead) | 116 | Woodblock |
| 89 | Pad 1 (new age) | 117 | Taiko drum |
| 90 | Pad 2 (warm) | 118 | Melodic tom |
| 91 | Pad 3 (polysynth) | 119 | Synth drum |
| 92 | Pad 4 (choir) | 120 | Reverse cymbal |
| 93 | Pad 5 (bowed) | 121 | Guitar fret noise |
| 94 | Pad 6 (metallic) | 122 | Breath noise |
| 95 | Pad 7 (halo) | 123 | Seashore |
| 96 | Pad 8 (sweep) | 124 | Bird tweet |
| 97 | FX 1 (rain) | 125 | Telephone ring |
| 98 | FX 2 (soundtrack) | 126 | Helicopter |
| 99 | FX 3 (crystal) | 127 | Applause |
| 100 | FX 4 (atmosphere) | 128 | Gunshot |

# General MIDI drum map

| Note Number | Drum Sound | Note Number | Drum Sound |
|---|---|---|---|
| 35 | Acoustic bass drum | 43 | High floor tom |
| 36 | Bass drum 1 | 44 | Pedal hi-hat |
| 37 | Side stick | 45 | Low tom |
| 38 | Acoustic snare | 46 | Open hi-hat |
| 39 | Hand clap | 47 | Low mid tom |
| 40 | Electric snare | 48 | High mid tom |
| 41 | Low floor tom | 49 | Crash cymbal |
| 42 | Closed hi-hat | 50 | High tom |

| Note Number | Drum Sound | Note Number | Drum Sound |
|---|---|---|---|
| 51 | Ride cymbal 1 | 67 | High agogo |
| 52 | Chinese cymbal | 68 | Low agogo |
| 53 | Ride bell | 69 | Cabasa |
| 54 | Tambourine | 70 | Maracas |
| 55 | Splash cymbal | 71 | Short whistle |
| 56 | Cowbell | 72 | Long whistle |
| 57 | Crash cymbal 2 | 73 | Short guiro |
| 58 | Vibraslap | 74 | Long guiro |
| 59 | Ride cymbal 2 | 75 | Claves |
| 60 | High bongo | 76 | High woodblock |
| 61 | Low bongo | 77 | Low woodblock |
| 62 | Mute hi conga | 78 | Mute cuica |
| 63 | Open hi conga | 79 | Open cuica |
| 64 | Low conga | 80 | Mute triangle |
| 65 | High timbale | 81 | Open triangle |
| 66 | Low timbale | | |

# MIDI sequencers

All of the original MIDI sequencers handled only MIDI. There was no audio capability until some years later, when fast computers and hard drives became affordable. Even now, it makes sense to look at the MIDI capabilities of a sequencer as being separate to its audio potential.

A modern MIDI sequencer might more accurately be called a multitrack MIDI recorder. In the context of recording, the term *track* refers to a means of recording a musical part in such a way that it may be edited, erased or re-recorded independently of the other parts. For those familiar with the concept of multitrack tape, MIDI sequencing draws a close analogy with that way of working, although the tracks contain MIDI data rather than sound.

A typical MIDI sequencer will provide 16 tracks as a bare minimum, and often many more. The reason why we should need more than 16 sequencer tracks when there are only 16 MIDI channels will become evident shortly.

# musical layers

Using a MIDI sequencer, numerous separate musical parts can be recorded at different times, either by playing the parts one at a time on a MIDI keyboard, by entering note and timing data manually, or by a combination of live playing and editing. The individual parts may be monophonic or they may comprise chords, while a difficult part may be split over two or more tracks that are set to the same MIDI channel and then recorded in several takes. Once they have been recorded, these parts may then be played back via any MIDI-compatible synthesiser or collection of synthesisers.

Unless you have a sequencer with a built-in synthesiser, you'll need a synthesiser, a synthesiser module or a soundcard in order to play back compositions. The number of different musical parts that can be played back at once is limited by the number and type of synthesisers available. Fortunately, most modern synthesisers and PC soundcards are capable of playing back up to 16 different sounds at once, each controlled by a different MIDI channel.

# composing with MIDI

As with much traditional composition, MIDI composing usually starts at the keyboard. Instead of writing down a score, however, the composer will record sections of music into the sequencer against an electronic metronome set to the desired tempo. The composition can be played back at any stage over a suitable synthesiser. Those composers who can't play well enough to play the parts in real time can enter notes directly into the sequencer in much the same way as a composer would write notes onto manuscript paper.

# the benefits of MIDI

Perhaps the best reason for using a MIDI sequencer is that it's not necessary to hire an orchestra or a band of session musicians; even a relatively inexpensive multitimbral synthesiser will provide all of the required sounds, even though few people would argue that a MIDI orchestra sounds as good as the real thing. Also, just like in the written score, if you're not happy with something you've done you don't have to start again from scratch; you can simply erase any unwanted notes and "write" in new ones. It doesn't really matter whether the finished piece is played by a bank of synths or by an orchestra that's been hired to reproduce the composer's original work as faithfully as possible. Both are valid methods of making music.

# sequencer set-up

In a typical set-up, a master MIDI controller – usually (but not invariably) a keyboard – is connected to a sequencer via a MIDI cable, and when the sequencer is set to Record any notes played on the keyboard are recorded as MIDI data into whichever sequencer track has been selected for recording. In a simple system, there might be 16 MIDI tracks set up so that each is on a different MIDI channel, and if the MIDI output of the sequencer is fed to a 16-part multitimbral module then all 16 tracks can be played back at once. If only an eight-part multitimbral module is available then only eight different sounds can be played back at once, in the same way as an eight-piece ensemble can only play a maximum of eight different lines of music at the same time. Figure 2.5 overleaf shows a basic sequencing system.

If you have a keyboard that includes a synth (as shown in the diagram), simply select Local Off and connect it up like any other synth module. Local Off isolates the synth's keyboard from its sound-generating circuitry so that, in effect, it behaves as if it were a separate dumb keyboard and MIDI synth module. This is necessary to prevent the formation of a MIDI loop. (See the 'Checklist' section at the end of this chapter for more troubleshooting details.)

# click track

Although a sequencer could be treated as being little more than a multitrack recorder for MIDI information, its real power lies in the way in which it allows recorded data to be modified and edited. When a recording is made, the sequencer is normally set to the tempo of the desired recording and a metronome click is generated so that the performance can be synchronised with the internal tempo of the sequencer. In this way, the MIDI data is arranged in musically meaningful bars, which ultimately makes editing the timing of notes or copying and moving sections of the MIDI recording much easier and more accurate.

If you don't want to be tied to tempo at all, you can simply turn off the metronome click and play as you would when recording onto a conventional a tape recorder. The practical disadvantage of working in this way is that you can't then use the internal beat and bar structure to plan your edits, and you won't be able to use the quantise function because the timing of your performance will be quite independent of the sequencer's internal clock.

For music that incorporates a succession of tempo changes, it's generally possible to enter a new tempo at the location of any bar or beat. The more sophisticated sequencers are even equipped with a graphic tempo-editing mode, by which it may be possible to draw curves to create smooth tempo increases or decreases.

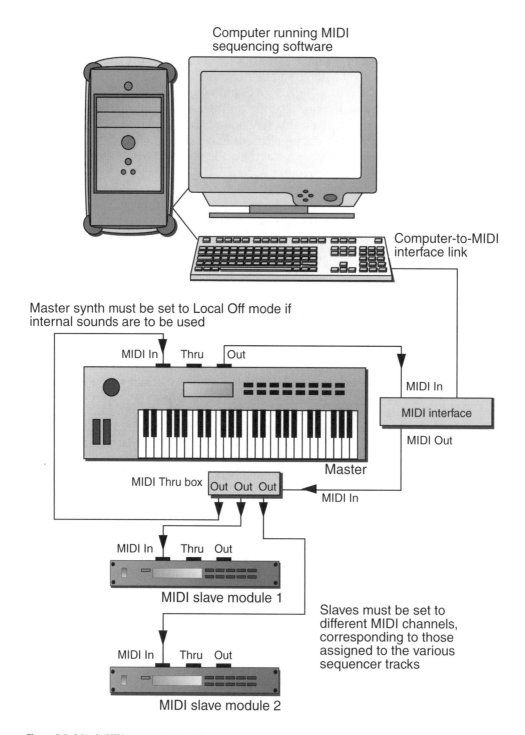

Figure 2.5: A basic MIDI sequencer system

# quantisation

The ability to quantise MIDI data after it has been recorded is a useful feature for those composers who aren't possessed of a perfect sense of timing. Essentially, when something is quantised the timings of the notes are changed, and each note is pushed to the nearest exact subdivision of a bar. For example, if you're working in 4/4 time and you select 16 as your quantise value, every note will move to the nearest point on an invisible grid that divides the bar into 16 equal chunks.

The quantise function will only produce meaningful results if the original recording was made in time with the metronome click of the sequencer. Furthermore, if your timing is really bad, you may find that, on quantising, some notes snap to quantisation positions a step away from their originally intended positions. Over-quantising a performance can also strip away the feel of the music, so it's important to use this function with care.

The more recent computer-based packages allow the user to unquantise data as well as quantise it. You should be warned, however, that some less advanced software sequencers perform what is known as destructive quantise, so if you think that it might be possible that you'll need to go back to the original version it's vitally important to keep a copy of the original track.

# percentage quantise

More sophisticated sequencers offer a percentage quantise function that allows the notes you've played to be shifted towards the exact quantise division by a percentage. For example, if a 50% quantise value is set then the note will move to a position halfway between where the note was actually played and the position of the nearest quantise division. This is great for tightening up playing without losing the feel of a piece.

Yet another quantise-related function is *swing*, which can gradually turn the quantise grid of a 4/4 rhythm into a 2/4 rhythm.

# tracks and channels

A sequencer track is simply somewhere to record one layer of a composition. The MIDI information contained in that track can then be configured to be played on any MIDI channel or any combination of MIDI channels. (Figure 2.6 shows the Arrange page of a popular computer-based sequencing package, and describes the layout of the

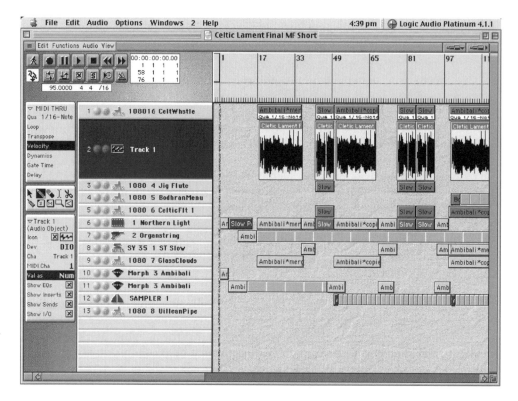

**Figure 2.6: The Arrange page of a sequencer package**

tracks and the way in which recorded sequences are represented.) It's also possible to have an arrangement where several different tracks are all recording MIDI data set to the same channel. For example, if you're recording a complicated drum part, you might want to put the bass and snare drum on one track, the cymbals and hi-hats on another and any tom fills on yet another. Not only does this make it easier to play the parts, but it also makes them less confusing to edit if you want to make any changes.

# rechannelling

Modern sequencers convert incoming MIDI data to the channel appropriate for the track on which you're recording regardless of the channel to which the master keyboard is set. This process is known as rechannelling. Once you've completed recording one track, all that you need to do then is to select the next track and start playing. You don't have to keep changing the MIDI channels on the master keyboard.

# cut, copy and paste

Like a word processor, a MIDI sequencer allows the user to move things around as well as to delete or replace wrong characters (in this case musical notes). If you want to use the same phrase or chorus more than once, it can be copied and duplicates can be pasted into new locations, which will mean that you won't have to play the same material time and time again. Copying is usually done graphically, by dragging highlighted sections of the track and dragging them to the desired position with the mouse. Long sections can be broken up into smaller sections using on-screen tools such as the scissors.

Unless you deliberately filter out certain types of MIDI data (and some sequencers have the facility to do this), you'll find that your sequencer captures everything sent by the master keyboard, including messages governing Note On/Off, Velocity, Pitch, Modulation, Aftertouch and other controller information, along with MIDI Program Change and Bank Change messages. That means that, if programs on the master keyboard are changed halfway through the recording of a song, that particular Program Change message will be recorded and will cause your synth to change patches every time the song is played back. If you find something weird happening, look in the Event Edit list and find out what's in there that isn't note data.

A sequencer track must also be told what synthesiser sound it is expected to control, and so in addition to entering the MIDI channel (which informs it of which instrument or part of a multitimbral instrument it is controlling) it's also necessary to enter the program number of the patch that you want to hear. If the synthesiser supports MIDI Bank Change messages, you also need to tell it in which sound bank the sound is located.

A MIDI Program Change recorded during the count-in period of a track will ensure that the synth that is being used for that track switches to the correct patch before playing commences.

# playback

When a MIDI sequence is played back, the sequencer transmits the MIDI information to the receiving synth in exactly the same order as it was originally played, and with the same timing. However, it's possible to change the tempo after the material has been recorded without affecting the pitch (unlike on a tape recorder, where you're dealing with sound rather than MIDI data).

# sequence editing

In the editing pages of a typical sequencer, it's possible to change the value, start time, length and velocity of any of the notes that have been played. It's also possible to build up compositions by entering the notes manually, by placing new notes onto the quantise grid in non-real-time, in much the same way as you would write notes on manuscript paper. On packages that have a scoring facility, it's also possible to enter notes directly onto the score.

# destructive and non-destructive editing

Although quantising is irreversible on some budget sequencers and sequencing packages, all professional systems will allow the user to unquantise something at a later time if required. In fact, many reversible procedures are made possible because the original recorded data isn't actually changed at all – changes are heard only because the data is processed in real time, as the sequence plays back. Such features are said to be non-destructive, because the original performance data is left intact. Even so, you should still save your work to disk regularly so that, if something goes wrong, you'll be able to return to the previously-saved version and pick up your work from there.

A number of other related, non-destructive editing options are often made available, including the ability to transpose music (either as it's played or after it's been recorded), the ability to make the music either louder or softer by adjusting the overall velocity, and the ability to use the same piece of data at different points within the same song. On some systems it's even possible to compress the dynamic range of MIDI data, which can help to even out the differences between the louder and softer notes, and this is roughly analogous to the way in which a hardware compressor affects audio signals. It may also be possible to delay or advance tracks in relation to each other in order to change the feel of a piece of music.

Of course, some edits are permanent, such as moving a note to a new time or pitch, or erasing or adding a note. These are known as destructive edits. Fortunately, there's usually an undo function that will allow you to reverse the last edit you did, destructive or not.

# MIDI drums

It's just as possible to sequence the sounds from a drum machine as it is for any other type of MIDI sound module. However, the drum machine's

External MIDI Sync will have to be switched off first or the drum machine's internal patterns will start to play every time the sequencer is turned on.

Because it's difficult to play a complete drum part in one go on a keyboard, it's common practice to spread the drum part over several sequencer tracks. This will make it easier to edit drum tracks later.

# the MIDI interface

Other than the ageing Atari ST, computers don't usually have MIDI sockets, and this means that you'll need to buy an external MIDI interface or a PC soundcard with a built-in MIDI interface, or you'll have to use a synth module that comes with a built-in MIDI interface.

MIDI Interfaces for older Apple Macintosh machines plug into the modem or printer port on the back of the computer, while the newer G3 iMacs and later use the USB (Universal Serial Buss) interface. PC users will need either an interface card fixed inside their computer or an external interface that can be plugged in. Most PC soundcards include a MIDI interface facility, although it may also be necessary to buy a special adaptor cable in order to make use of it. As a rule modern PCs include USB interfaces. Usually, if the manufacturer of your sequencing software also produces a MIDI interface then you should use it, as you'll find that there will then be less likelihood of running into a problem with its compatibility with your system.

# multiport MIDI interfaces

A basic MIDI interface provides a single MIDI output socket, which means that you're restricted to a maximum of 16 MIDI channels. However, you may wish to use two or more multitimbral synthesisers in order to create a composition with more than 16 parts, or, as is more often the case, you may have several multitimbral synthesiser modules and want to change from one to the other without having to reconnect MIDI leads. In order to do this you should use a MIDI interface with multiple output ports (physically separate MIDI outs that can each source 16 MIDI channels of MIDI data). This will provide you with, in effect, several different sets of 16 MIDI channels, which can all be used at the same time.

Within the sequencer, the ports may be designated by number or letter, so that you have 16 channels on port A, another 16 on port B, a further 16 on port C and so on. If a different 16-part multitimbral synth module

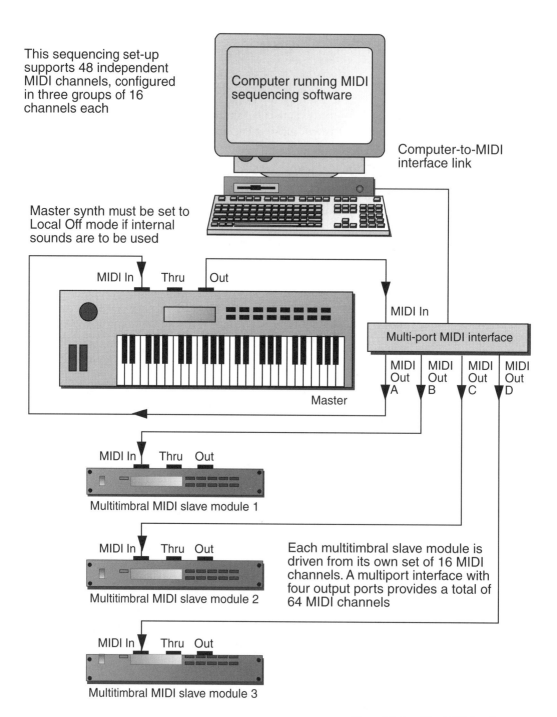

This sequencing set-up supports 48 independent MIDI channels, configured in three groups of 16 channels each

Computer running MIDI sequencing software

Computer-to-MIDI interface link

Master synth must be set to Local Off mode if internal sounds are to be used

MIDI In    Thru    Out

MIDI In

Multi-port MIDI interface

MIDI Out A    MIDI Out B    MIDI Out C    MIDI Out D

Master

MIDI In    Thru    Out

Multitimbral MIDI slave module 1

MIDI In    Thru    Out

Multitimbral MIDI slave module 2

Each multitimbral slave module is driven from its own set of 16 MIDI channels. A multiport interface with four output ports provides a total of 64 MIDI channels

MIDI In    Thru    Out

Multitimbral MIDI slave module 3

Figure 2.7: A multiport MIDI interface

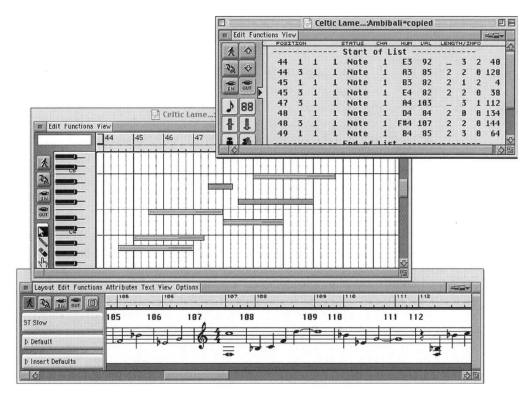

Figure 2.8: Common sequencer edit pages

is connected to each port of a four-port interface, there will be 64 different sound sources available, each of which can be addressed individually by specifying a MIDI channel along with a port designation (A, B, C or D). Figure 2.7 shows how a multiport system might be configured. It's important to realise that a multi-port interface must be supported by the sequencing software.

# sequencer user interfaces

The manufacturers of most leading software sequencing packages have adopted the style of interface pioneered by Steinberg in their Cubase software, which is based around the analogy of multitrack tape. In Cubase the sequencer tracks are depicted as individual, vertically-stacked strips, with musical bars running from left to right. Once a section of a track has been recorded, it shows up as a strip running from the start location to the end location. This sequence may then be dragged to a new position in the same track, or it may even be moved to a completely different track so that it plays back with a different sound.

Sequence blocks may also be copied, split into shorter sections or deleted as required.

This Arrange page handles basic recording and arranging. There are also other pages which address various aspects of editing, scoring, audio recording and audio mixing. The Edit pages usually allow the user to examine (and change) recorded data as a list of MIDI events, displayed graphically as a grid display resembling the roll of a player piano or, in the case of "score" versions, as a conventional musical score. Most sequencers also have the facilities to graphically edit controller information. Figure 2.8 shows some of the Edit pages on a popular software sequencer.

If your choice of sequencer includes score-writing facilities, you'll be able to print out sheet music for your compositions on a suitable printer. Some musical literacy is still useful, however, as the computer doesn't always interpret what is played in the same way that a trained score writer would.

Because sequencer screens can hold a lot of detail, and because it's sometimes useful to be able to view more than one page at a time, it's a good idea to buy the biggest monitor that you can afford. In any event, you shouldn't consider buying anything smaller than 17 inches. It's even better to have a computer that can support multiple monitors.

# MIDI file format

MIDI sequence data is usually stored in a file format that is specific to the software manufacturer, although some of the more popular sequencing packages allow the user to transfer song data from one computer platform to another and, in some case, even from one manufacturer's software sequencer to another's.

On those occasions where there is no easy way to translate song files between sequencers, it's still possible to save work as a standard MIDI file and transfer it that way, although only up to a maximum of 16 tracks at a time. Most computers will read DOS-formatted floppy disks, so if you're transferring MIDI files from a Mac to a PC you should first format a disk in DOS format on the Mac and then save your song as a standard MIDI file. Use the MIDI File Import Facility (usually found in the File menu) to open the song in another sequencer. If you're using a computer with no floppy drive, you can transfer files as e-mail attachments if you have a modem attached to your computer. When e-mailing files to Mac users, it's vital to use a suitable file compression utility first so that the file type is preserved.

# key features of sequencers

Every sequencer is different, but all should be capable of the following core MIDI functions:

- Real-time recording, by which a MIDI performance can be played in real-time from keyboard and recorded in much the same way as by a tape recorder.

- Step-time recording, by which notes are keyed in one note at a time. The positions and lengths of the notes is determined by the user, after which they can be played back at any tempo. With a piano-roll type of editing screen, it's also possible to draw notes directly onto the quantise grid and then use the mouse pointer to stretch them to their desired lengths. A package with scoring facilities will allow the user to place conventional musical symbols onto a stave.

- Synchronisation facilities. Although a MIDI/audio sequencer can form the basis of a complete recording studio, it's still sometimes useful to be able to run a drum machine, tape recorder or hard-disk recorder at the same time. In order to make the tempo of a sequencer synchronise to that of another MIDI device or tape machine (equipped with a suitable sync interface), it must be equipped with sync facilities, and these are sometimes omitted on very cheap sequencing software. There are several sync options, but the most commonly-used types are MIDI clock and MTC (MIDI Time Code). More sophisticated interfaces may also support SMPTE time code. With Alesis ADAT machines, an interface with an ADAT nine-pin sync socket is required in order to obtain sample-accurate synchronisation.

- Multiport interface support. In a complex MIDI system, one set of 16 MIDI channels may not be enough. A multiport MIDI interface that is compatible with the sequencing software will provide several separate MIDI outputs, each with its own set of 16 MIDI channels. This should not be confused with a simple multi-output interface, across which multiple output sockets carry duplicates of the same MIDI data. This is really just a combination of a single-port interface and a MIDI thru box.

- File Import. MIDI sequencers usually save song data in a proprietary format, which other sequencers may not be able to read. The most common method of MIDI file transfer is to use the standard MIDI file (SMF) format. You should note that, if your sequencer includes the ability to handle audio, your audio tracks will not be transferred as part of a standard MIDI file.

SMFs were devised in order to allow complete interchangeability between MIDI song files, and it also makes it possible for third-party companies to provide commercial sequencer files that can be read by any machine. However, SMFs can only handle the basic 16 MIDI channels; they can't cope with multiport data.

- Editing. A typical sequencer will include a number of editing tools to enable you to change your composition after it has been recorded. These range from the ability to change individual notes to the ability to change entire arrangements and swap instruments. The main editing operations are listed below:

  (i)    Quantisation. This is the ability to automatically move notes to the nearest accurate subdivision of a bar (16ths of a bar, for example). The user can set the number of quantise subdivisions in a bar prior to quantising. Percentage quantise and swing functions are also very useful.

  (ii)   Transposition. With this function, notes can be transposed by any amount without altering their lengths, while entire compositions or sections of compositions can easily be shifted to a different key.

  (iii)  Copy, cut and paste. These functions allow any section of music to be copied to different tracks or locations in the song. This is useful for duplicating repeated sections, such as choruses, or for doubling up a line of music on two tracks by copying a part, then assigning the copy to a different instrument sound to the original. The cut function allows unwanted material to be removed.

  (iv)   Mute. This allows the user to mute individual tracks, and can be useful if you've just played three solos but you're not sure which one was the best.

  (v)    Solo. This function mutes all of the other tracks so that you can hear the solo'd track in isolation.

  (vi)   Cycle. This allows the user to continually loop around a specific section of music while recording or editing. This mode is also useful for rehearsing parts prior to recording

  (vii)  Undo. This allows the user to reverse or undo the last edit or recording operation.

# MIDI wiring

The setting up of a basic MIDI sequencing system starts at the keyboard. It's here that the MIDI information that is to be recorded originates. The master keyboard is connected via its MIDI Out to the MIDI In of the MIDI interface. As mentioned earlier, if your keyboard includes a synth section (if it makes sounds, in other words) then it should be switched to Local Off and a MIDI cable should be patched from the sequencer's MIDI Out to the keyboard's MIDI In. If there are other MIDI modules in the system, these can be daisy-chained in any order by feeding the MIDI Thru of one piece of gear into the MIDI In of the next. Alternatively, a thru box may be used.

If you have master keyboard that doesn't have a Local Off facility, consult the manual accompanying your sequencer to determine if you can disable the MIDI Thru on the track being recorded. Most sequencers provide for this eventuality.

Up to three modules can normally be chained in a Thru-to-In chain without problems, but longer chains may suffer from stuck or missed notes due to the MIDI signal becoming corrupted. In this case a multiple-output MIDI Thru box should be attached to the output of the sequencer, and each module (or short chains of two or three modules) should be fed from separate outputs on the thru box.

# MIDI timing

If you try to send to much MIDI data at once – for instance, if you have all 16 channels trying to play a large musical chord at exactly the same time – you may cause a MIDI traffic jam, in which case the notes will be spread out slightly. This is most noticeable when there are several sounds with fast attack that are quantised to the same beat. Using lots of other MIDI control data can also slow things up, but the better sequencing software packages give priority to note timing, which helps to reduce the problem.

If you encounter this type of timing problem, there are several things that can be done to improve things. Try putting the most time-sensitive parts (such as drums) onto the first few tracks and the less critical parts (such as slow-attack strings) onto the later tracks, because the first track is usually dealt with first in terms of timing priority.

Timing problems may be exaggerated by older keyboards or instruments that take longer than they should to send out or respond to information. Some early MIDI keyboards took around 10ms to send a MIDI message after a key had been depressed, and a slow module or synthesiser could take the same time to respond to an incoming MIDI note message. Modern instruments are generally better, but some models are still noticeably faster than others. If you're aware that you have a slow instrument, try entering a small negative delay offset to the relevant track so that it plays back just before the other tracks. Not only will this tighten up the timing of that track but it will also help to make sure that there aren't too many MIDI events occurring at the same time.

It's also possible to apply a little negative track delay to those tracks carrying slow-attack sounds, such as strings or brass, so that the notes fire a fraction of a second earlier than the rest of the quantised material.

# checklist

If you've connected up your system as described but no sound comes out, here are a few things to check:

- Ensure that everything is switched on and that your synth modules are set to Multi or Sequencer mode (assuming that you want to use them multitimbrally). Also, make sure that your synths are set to the same MIDI channels as those on which you're sending data.

- If you're working on a sequence that includes controller data, make sure that you haven't just turned down all of your modules using controller seven, as you might do to perform a fade. If you've done this, they'll stay turned down until you send them new controller seven values to turn them back up again!

- Check your MIDI cable connections, and don't rule out the possibility of a faulty MIDI lead. Some modules have a combined MIDI Out/Thru socket, and if so you should ensure that MIDI Thru is enabled. (Check the handbook for that particular piece of equipment.) To help narrow down the problem, most sequencers have some form of visible indicator that tells you when they're receiving MIDI data, and many modules are equipped with an LED or some other indicator that blinks when data is being received.

- If two or more instruments are trying to play the same part, the chances are that you've either got more than one module set to the same MIDI channel or that something's been left set to Omni. If your master keyboard plays its own sounds whenever you try to record on any track or channel, check that the synth is really set to Local Off. On some instruments, Local Off reverts to Local On every time the power is switched on.

- If the playing of a single note results in a continuous burst of sound, stuck notes, or apparently limited polyphony, the chances are that you have a MIDI loop. In a MIDI loop, MIDI data generated by the master keyboard passes through the sequencer and somehow gets back to the input of the master keyboard, where it starts its round trip all over again, rather like acoustic feedback. This usually happens when a keyboard synth is used as a master keyboard and Local Off hasn't been selected. You should also check your MIDI cabling. If you have no Local Off facility, disable the sequencer MIDI Thru on the track to which you're recording.

## chapter 3

# the technical stuff

It would be nice to be able to tell you that making music on a computer is as simple as turning it on, hitting Record and recording it, but before you can get to that stage there are things that you'll need to know. While you can certainly drive a car without knowing anything about mechanics, the same isn't true of computers. You don't have to know everything, but you won't get far without some basic knowledge of what the hardware and software is up to. Buying a ready-configured system flattens the learning curve considerably, and unless you're a computer expert I strongly recommend that you follow this route. Even so, you'll still need a certain amount of background information so that you can make sense of what's going on. This chapter explains some of the more common concepts and standards that you'll encounter along the way, but don't feel you have to read it all in one go. Treat it as a source of reference if that suits you better.

## digital basics

All digital audio equipment designed to accept analogue signals – such as the outputs from microphones – must convert the analogue input into a digital format before it can process it or record it. In the case of sound, the analogue signal voltage varies in proportion to changes in air pressure. A rapidly vibrating string, for example, will create equally rapid fluctuations in air pressure which a microphone can convert to variations in voltage.

Digital systems use binary numbers to measure amounts, and in the case of the signal from a microphone the digital data measures the changing analogue voltage by using a succession of ones and zeros. These digits are represented in the circuit by the presence or absence of a nominally-fixed voltage. In essence, converting an analogue signal into digital information involves measuring the analogue voltage at regular intervals and then turning these measurements into a series of binary numbers

Sound needs to be sampled and measured several tens of thousands of times per second if the end result is going to be of CD quality. If you have enough instantaneous measurements per second, the original sound can be accurately recreated up to the highest frequency limit of human hearing.

# sampling theory

This process of measuring and digitising minute sections of the input signal is known as sampling, and Figure 3.1 shows what happens when a signal is sampled. Each sample is a discrete measurement taken at one point in time, and the more often these measurements are made, the more accurately the curves of the original analogue signal are followed.

Sampling theory states that you must take a sample at a minimum of twice the frequency of the highest frequency that you are likely to encounter if the output is to be reconstructed accurately. If the sampling frequency is less than twice the highest frequency, additional frequencies will be introduced based on the sum and difference between the sampling frequency and the audio frequency. These frequencies won't have been present in the original signal and so will sound musically unpleasant.

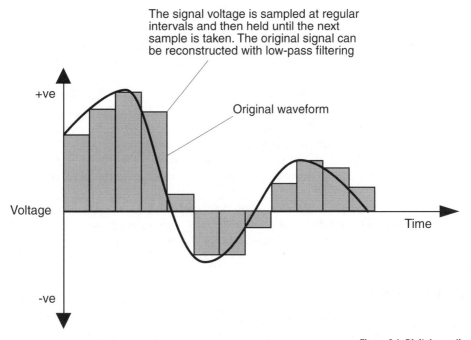

The signal voltage is sampled at regular intervals and then held until the next sample is taken. The original signal can be reconstructed with low-pass filtering

Original waveform

+ve

Voltage

Time

-ve

**Figure 3.1: Digital sampling**

The creation of unwanted frequencies by sampling at a rate that is too low is known as aliasing, and to prevent this it is necessary to filter out any frequencies in the original signal that are above half the sampling frequency. Because no filters are perfect, the sampling rate must be a little higher than twice the maximum audio frequency, which is why for an audio bandwidth of 20kHz a minimum sampling frequency of 44.1kHz is used. If you're thinking that 44.1kHz is an odd kind of number (why not 45kHz or 50kHz?) then you're right; but, as is so often the case, the reasons are historic.

The other major factor affecting audio quality is the accuracy with which individual samples are measured. Basically, the more digital bits that are used to represent each sample, the more accurate the measurement. CDs and DAT tapes use 16-bit sampling, although many digital multitrack recorders and signal processors now use 20- or 24-bit conversion.

Digital sampling proceeds in steps – there are no halves or thirds of a bit – and the number of steps depends on the resolution of the analogue-to-digital converter used. Eight bits will provide only two to the power of eight steps, which works out as 256. That means that your loudest signal could have 256 steps but that your quieter sounds will have considerably fewer. This allows for a rather poor level of resolution, and causes what's known as quantisation distortion, an effect that gets more noticeable at lower signal levels.

Quantisation distortion actually sounds like noise. The main difference is that it disappears in the absence of a signal, unlike most other sources of noise. Nowadays, eight-bit sound is rarely used, other than in some undemanding computer applications. Using more bits allows for a vast improvement in resolution, and most current digital processors use 16-, 20- or 24-bit resolution converters. Each bit in a linear sampling system equates to 6dB (decibels) of dynamic range, so an eight-bit system can only provide a dynamic range of 48dB at best – about as noisy as a cheap cassette recorder. 16-bit resolution gives a maximum dynamic range of 96dB, while 20- and 24-bit systems can still give practical dynamic ranges in excess of 120dB.

So far, then, we know that an audio signal can be represented by a series of numbers, but these numbers also have to be recorded and replayed with exactly the same timing relationship if the result is to be accurate. This is where sample rates come in.

# sample rates

Simply stated, the sample rate is the number of times per second that an audio waveform is "measured" during the analogue-to-digital conversion process. This sampling must be done at precise intervals, and is generally controlled by a very accurate crystal clock. As long as the same sample rate is used for both analogue-to-digital and digital-to-analogue conversion, the replayed audio will be of the same length and pitch as the original.

Although the minimum sample rate for serious audio work is 44.1kHz, less critical work is sometimes done at 32kHz (which reduces the audio bandwidth to under 15kHz), while broadcasters prefer to work with a rate of 48kHz. Most DAT machines and soundcards support sample rates of both 44.1 and 48kHz, but it's important to note that everything in a system must be set to run at the same sample rate or your final audio recording won't play back at the same speed as that at which it was recorded. If you're planning on making CDs then you should always work at 44.1kHz, whereas if you're producing material for broadcast purposes then it's best to stick to 48kHz.

Recent system have been introduced that run at double the current standard sampling rates, so now rates of 88.2kHz and 96kHz can be added to the list. These produce a slightly better sound quality in theory, but in practice few people can detect a difference. My own view is that 96kHz sample rates only provide a sonic advantage if the most esoteric equipment is used to make recordings of acoustic instruments in a very sophisticated studio.

# the high sample rate argument

The regular sampling rate of 44.1kHz provides an audio bandwidth of 20kHz, which exceeds the hearing range of most humans. However, there is a school of thought that believes that recording with a much wider audio bandwidth will produce a better and more accurate sound. The sample rate of 96kHz doubles the *audio* bandwidth to 40kHz, and although these frequencies are actually inaudible there are plausible arguments to explain why these recordings should sound better.

One theory is that the very harsh filters used to block out everything above 20kHz in a 44.1kHz system impart their own sonic signature to the sound. This was certainly true of early digital converters, and although the new ones are much better there may still be some audible artefacts generated by the filtering.

Another theory is that, in real life, frequencies above the range of human hearing emanating from different instruments interact to form audible frequencies, which are then recorded. However, if the instruments are separately miked using a 20kHz system, these high frequencies are removed before the sounds are combined, and so some of the sonic character is lost.

It's up to you whether you use a 24-bit/96kHz or 16-bit/44.1kHz system, but bear in mind that the number of tracks that you'll be able to run at any one time, and the amount of processing that you'll be able to apply, will be reduced as you work with more bits and/or higher sample rates

# why more bits, anyway?

Current CDs use a 16-bit/44.1kHz format, so why should it ever be necessary to record using more than 16 bits? The answer is that, whenever a digital signal is processed by a change in its level or the addition of EQ, it loses a little of its resolution. Furthermore, a 16-bit signal only has maximum resolution when recorded at its maximum level. Quieter sounds are recorded using fewer than 16 bits, and the resolution is correspondingly lower. By recording and processing using more bits that necessary for the final delivery medium (probably CD), you can preserve the maximum resolution possible right through to the end of the project. If, on the other hand, you record everything at 16-bit resolution, your final mix might have a resolution that's only equivalent to 13 or 14 bits. Again, this is of little concern when dealing with pop music, which generally has a very limited dynamic range, but with acoustic music extremely quiet passages may end up being more noisy and more distorted than they need to be.

# dither

A recording made and mixed with a resolution of 24 bits can be reduced to one of 16 bits using a process know as *dithering*, which preserves much more of the original dynamic range of the signal than simply truncating or discarding the least-significant eight bits. Essentially, a tiny amount of pseudo-random noise is added to the signal in order to dither very low-level digital information, but in order to prevent this noise from compromising the apparent signal-to-noise ratio of the recording it can be mathematically configured so that it appears high in the audio spectrum (usually above 15kHz, where the human ear is least sensitive). This refinement is known as *noise-shaped dithering*.

Without getting too technical, dithering allows the music to remain audible as it fades down into the noise floor, just as it does with analogue tape. Without dither, the signal will grow progressively more distorted at lower levels and will then cease abruptly as the least-significant bit is lost. Most stereo-editing software packages include the facility to dither 24-bit or 20-bit audio down to 16 bits, and it should be noted that dithering should always be the last process applied to the signal if it is to be effective.

Although a 24-bit/96kHz sample rate may seem to be unnecessarily esoteric at the moment, it pays to be aware of it because 24-bit/96kHz audio may become the standard hi-fi format once DVD has become widely adopted. In any event, most serious audio equipment is now compatible with 24-bit/96kHz sample rates whether that resolution is necessary or not, and as storage capacities rise and processors become more powerful there will be less concern about conserving resources by working at 16-bit/44.1kHz resolution. Already, RAM (Random Access Memory) and computer hard drives are orders of magnitude cheaper than they were a few years ago, so data storage is no longer the major cost concern it once was. However, we're still pushing computers pretty hard when it comes to processing, and as high-resolution 24-bit/96kHz audio takes around three times as much processor power per minute than CD quality 16-bit/44.1kHz rates, you can expect a dramatic drop in the number of tracks, plug-ins and virtual instruments you can have at your disposal if you choose to use it.

# digital connections

Unlike analogue systems, in which every signal needs to be sent down a separate cable, digital systems allow two or more signals to be sent along the same cable while they still remain completely separate. The physics behind this apparent magic is not important at this stage, but the terms *clocking* and *sync* need to be explained.

The best way to understand what's going on is to look at an example. Lets say that you have a computer studio set-up with a digital input and you want to transfer some music from a DAT (Digital Audio Tape) recorder into your computer in the digital domain. The first step is to connect the digital output from your DAT machine phono connector (probably an S/PDIF) to the digital input of your computer interface or soundcard. S/PDIF is a standard connection protocol developed by Sony and Philips and is designed to be used with consumer digital equipment. It may be provided on some equipment as an optical port, as an alternative to – or in addition to – the phono co-axial connector. Commercial-format adaptors are available for converting co-axial S/PDIF to optical, and vice versa. Now comes the clocking part.

When the DAT machine plays, a highly-accurate crystal clock controls the rate at which the samples of data are played back, ensuring that the material is the same length and at the same pitch as the original. In order that these little slices of data can be transferred into a computer, the soundcard's sampling clock has to be running at exactly the same rate as that of the DAT machine. If the DAT machine and the computer soundcard are allowed to run independently, their clocks will always run at slightly different speeds, even if they're both set to the same frequency. The result would be clicks and crackles in the audio as the two clocks drifted in and out of sync with each other.

Although digital co-axial S/PDIF connections use the same type of phono connectors as those used by audio cables, it's important to use a proper digital cable if problems are to be avoided. Conventional audio phono cables often appear to work fine, but the problem is that they don't provide accurate signal transmission. The result is an increase in error rate. You may not hear anything obviously wrong, however, because the error-correction system employed by the receiving piece of equipment will mask minor errors, but if the error rate becomes too high these errors may result in clicks or other audible glitches.

The reason why cheap audio cables don't work properly is that digital audio data takes up a much greater bandwidth than analogue audio. At the high frequencies involved, impedance mismatches reflect back some of the signal back along the cable, and these "echoes" compromise the signal-to-noise ratio of the system to such an extent that, at some point, zeros may be misread as ones or vice versa. 70-ohm digital cable is required to do the job properly. This will minimise reflections and maintain the signal's integrity.

Some S/PDIF connections use an optical connector, via which the data is transmitted over fibre-optic cables rather than as electrical signals. The Alesis ADAT optical format uses the same type of connector, so it's important not to get the two types mixed up. Both systems use the same types of transmitting and receiving devices, but their data formats are very different. No damage will be done if you try to connect an ADAT interface to an S/PDIF or vice versa, but no signal transmission will take place either.

Optical cables also differ in quality just as much as coaxial cables. There are two areas where optical signals can be degraded: the termination and the fibre-optic cable itself. The optical quality of the cable (or lightpipe, as it's sometimes called) determines the maximum distance over which the signal can travel before errors start to become a problem. The terminations affect how efficiently light enters or leaves the cable, so there will be more loss if the signal has to pass through a lot of terminations. If you need cable lengths of more than a couple of metres, it's worth investing in high-quality optical cables rather than continuing to use the budget ones that come with most pieces of digital audio equipment.

# clock sync

Fortunately, the digital data carried along an S/PDIF cable also carries the clock signal from the first machine, and this is used to synchronise the clock in the receiving device. However, the receiving device usually has to be placed into Digital Sync mode for this to happen. (Figure 3.2 shows a DAT machine feeding to the input of a soundcard.) DAT machines without a word clock input facility default to Digital Sync mode automatically if they are switched to digital input. This auto switching system is sensible, as there are no normal circumstances in which you'd want to accept a digital input while the receiving DAT machine was running from its own internal clock (Internal Sync mode). Nevertheless, on some computer audio systems Digital Sync mode must be selected manually. The rule is that the source

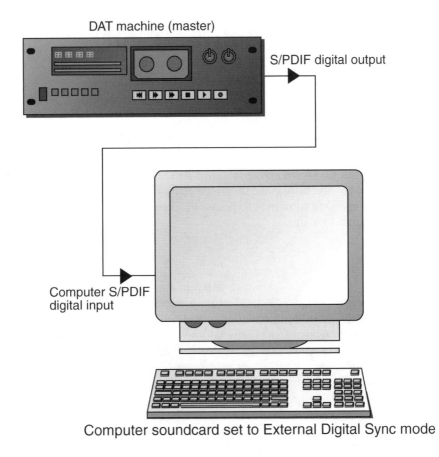

DAT machine (master)

S/PDIF digital output

Computer S/PDIF
digital input

Computer soundcard set to External Digital Sync mode

**Figure 3.2: Digital connection (soundcard feeds DAT machine)**

device runs from its own clock (Internal Sync mode) and the receiving device is set to Digital Sync mode. Multiple devices can be cascaded in this way, but stringing more than four digital devices together in a chain may cause problems due to the progressive corruption of the clock signal.

More serious equipment uses the so-called AES/EBU digital interface, which can usually be identified by the fact that it uses XLR connectors rather than phono leads. In any event, the sockets are normally marked clearly on the rear panels of the equipment. Both S/PDIF and AES/EBU carry a stereo signal with a clock, but they operate at different voltage levels and so are not strictly speaking compatible (even though you can sometimes get away with using an adaptor lead between the two). AES/EBU is balanced, has a nominal five-volt level and can use conventional mic cables over short distances, while S/PDIF is an unbalanced 75-ohm system operating at around 0.5 volts requiring digital 75-ohm co-axial cable for it to work properly. You may get away with using audio phono leads over very short distances, but this isn't recommended because, although everything may seem to work fine, you might find that you end up with occasional unexplained clicks in the audio stream. Longer AES/EBU cable should use digital-grade balanced cables.

The main advantage of S/PDIF is that DAT IDs and CD track IDs are carried as part of the data format, while with AES/EBU these are stripped out. The optical version of S/PDIF (sometimes known as *Toslink*) is also useful in those situations where the screen connector of a co-axial cable might cause ground loop problems. On the other hand, AES/EBU ignores the SCMS (Serial Copycode Management System) copy protection system which is used in some DAT machines to prevent cloned tapes from being re-copied in the digital domain.

# word clock

The majority of professional systems have a word clock facility, which simply means that the sample clock is fed via separate sockets rather than relying on the clock embedded in the digital audio signal. In complex set-ups, this can be more accurate and less prone to clock corruption or jittering timings. Word clock usually travels via unbalanced cables terminated with bayonet-fitting BNC connectors, and as with other digital interconnects it will normally be clearly labelled on the rear panel of the equipment. Like any other digital clocking system, there can only be one master; all of the other pieces of gear act as slaves and lock to the master clock.

In a professional studio, the word clock may come from a separate, high-accuracy clock generator with multiple outputs that synchronises everything in the studio, but in a project studio system it's more likely to originate from the digital console (if there is one) or from a digital tape machine synchroniser. It's also quite common for systems to include a mixture of equipment, where some is locked to a master word clock while other devices (usually without a word clock input) are synchronised via S/PDIF or AES/EBU. You should be aware that many semi-pro pieces of studio gear have rather poor master clocks which can introduce jitter into the rest of the system, resulting in a degradation of both the audio quality and the signal-to-noise ratio. (The problem of jitter is explained in the section covering 'Digital Audio Quality' below.)

Using word clock has a number of advantages, not least being that it avoids long daisy chains of equipment. Chains of this type can introduce clock instability, as each piece of equipment will try to lock to the one before it. In extreme cases, this can result in either glitches or a total loss of sync. The other advantage is that a high-quality, low-jitter master clock can be used to control everything, which should result in better audio performance.

## sample-rate converters

In situations where you want to work at one sample rate but some or all of the source material is at another, sample-rate conversion will be necessary. This may be accomplished either with an external hardware box, which will take in a digital signal at one sample rate and output it at another in real time, or it can be done with a software program. For example, if you have recordings made on a DAT machine at 48kHz and you wish to master a CD (which requires audio sampled at 44.1kHz), you'll need to convert the sample rate of the audio before the CD can be compiled. If not, the CD will seem to play OK but the audio will be slowed down and the pitch will have dropped by a factor of $^{44.1}/_{48}$ (around 10%).

## digital audio quality

If digital audio is just a matter of storing and retrieving numbers, how is it that some systems sound better than others? While it's true that digital audio data is simply a stream of numbers, they must be the right values and delivered at exactly the right time if the original audio signal is to be adequately represented. The weakest link in the chain is probably the analogue-to-digital (A/D) converter, the job of which is to sample the incoming audio signal and convert it into a stream of numbers. The part of the circuit that actually performs the measuring is actually a very highly-refined digital voltmeter, and if this instrument doesn't measure the signal accurately then the numbers will be wrong and the result will be distortion.

The measurements also have to be made at precisely regular intervals (the sample rate), but poor analogue-to-digital design, bad circuit-board layout, shoddy clock design and other factors can result in jitter. Jitter occurs when the sampling period varies slightly, rather than being constant, and a consequence of this is that the audio waveform is sampled just before or just after the correct time, resulting in the wrong value being stored.

Finally, the sampling theorem according to Nyquist states that, for the accurate reconstruction of a signal, the sampling rate must be equal to or greater than the highest frequency component of the signal being sampled. The human ear is capable of hearing only up to 20kHz or so, but that doesn't mean that sounds stop at 20kHz. The harmonics produced by plucked metal strings and struck bells and cymbals can go much higher than that, so these must be removed before sampling takes place. Various filtering strategies are used to achieve this, all of which involve the construction of a very steep low-pass filter. No filter is perfect, however, and the steeper the response, the more the filter tends to ring or resonate at the cut-off point. This ringing can impart a harsh quality to the sound, a fault much in evidence in first-generation CD players of the early Eighties. Modern converters are much better in this respect, thanks to technologies such as oversampling, single-bit converters and improved filter design. These differences explain why some "CD-quality" soundcards sound rather better than others.

# software plug-ins

In conventional studios, mixing consoles are used in conjunction with outboard effects boxes such as delay and reverb units, although some digital consoles also feature built-in effects. However, using an audio interface with a computer can severely restrict the flexibility with which you can patch in hardware effects. While some audio interfaces with multiple ins and outs allow the user to configure some of their connectors as sends and returns for use with external effects processors, the lack of audio channels and the routing limitations imposed by the host sequencing software may make this impractical. If you're using a stereo in/stereo out soundcard then clearly any form of external effects patching is likely to be limited to processing the whole mix.

Fortunately, modern computers are powerful enough to run a reasonable number of native virtual plug-in effects at the same time as they play back audio and MIDI. In other words, instead of the effects existing as hardware boxes you buy them as pieces of software that "plug into" your main audio program. There are various formats of plug-ins to choose between depending on the sequencer which you're using, and there are also different systems allied to specific types of hardware, such as Digidesign's ProTools system, which uses Digidesign-compatible TDM plug-ins.

# common types of plug-ins

Digidesign were the first company to take the plug-in concept seriously, developing Sound Designer II for the Macintosh. The development of SDII plug-ins was opened up to third-party developers, and they were designed mainly to handle things like EQ, compression, limiting and other mastering functions. Despite its continued use in many professional applications, SDII is no longer supported by Digidesign, and so no new plug-ins are being written in this format.

Today, Digidesign produce AudioSuite off-line plug-ins for use with ProTools 4 and upwards, as well as the TDM (Time-Division Multiplexing) real-time range, which run exclusively on ProTools hardware. Other software manufacturers (such as eMagic) also support AudioSuite plug-ins, as well as the increasingly common VST format, and sequencers that can support ProTools hardware can generally access TDM plug-ins, although not at the same time as VST plug-ins. This latter restriction is due to the fact that the ProTools hardware requires the Digidesign DAE (Digital Audio Engine) to run TDM plug-ins, which run on a Digi DSP card rather than on the computer's processor, and this arrangement doesn't allow native VST plug-ins to be run at the same time. Nevertheless, some software allows some tracks to use VST, and others TDM, by running both sets of drivers.

On the PC side, Microsoft created Direct X as a part of the multimedia aspect of Windows, and Direct X handles both DirectSound soundcard drivers and DirectShow plug-ins (often still referred to as DirectX). The majority of Windows music software supports this plug-in architecture.

Another plug-in format with a multimedia background is Adobe Premier, which was originally designed to complement the PC and Mac video-editing package of the same name. Premier is an off-line format plug-in (ie audio files are processed in non-real time), like Audio Suite, and is supported by a number of popular sequencing and editing programs, including eMagic's Logic Audio and Bias Peak.

Of course, not everyone wants to support a standard plug-in format – MOTU (Mark Of The Unicorn) developed their own format, MAS, for use with the Mac version of their Digital Performer sequencing software. Versions of several popular plug-ins have been created to run in this format, but to my knowledge no other platforms support MAS plug-ins. Although MOTU's Digital Performer can't use VST plug-ins directly, TCWorks' Spark program includes a "shell" section that allows a matrix of up to 20 VST plug-ins to be used as a single plug-in inside software compatible with both Digital Performer and VST.

Steinberg's PC-only editing software, Wavelab, also started life in a proprietary plug-in format that could work in real time on faster machines and off-line on slower machines. Current versions of Wavelab also run with VST plug-ins and DirectShow plug-ins, which means that there is little incentive for anyone to develop further plug-ins in the Wavelab-only format.

Digidesign's low-cost 001 system (running a simplified version of ProTools software) uses a proprietary plug-in format which is essentially a real-time version of AudioSuite (RTAS), and many of the popular mainstream plug-ins are being released in this format, while VST (Virtual Studio Technology) is supported on both the Mac and the PC. The latest incarnation of this can both generate and be controlled by MIDI, which allows for the automation of plug-ins as well as making it possible to use VST instruments such as virtual synths and samplers.

# VST plug-ins

The VST plug-in format was created by Steinberg in order to enable software-generated effects to be added to the audio tracks within the mixing environment of a MIDI/audio sequencer. By making the VST protocol openly available to anyone who wanted to use it, Steinberg have brought the user as close to a plug-in standard as he's likely to get, although not all music software provides VST support. Various third-party companies produce VST-compatible plug-ins for both PC and Macintosh computers, although some specific plug-ins are available for only one or the other of these two platforms.

The software of the two major European players, Steinberg (Cubase VST) and eMagic (Logic Audio), allow the user to be able to run run VST plug-ins, as do many stereo editing packages, and because VST development information is freely available to anyone who wants to use it a number of shareware and freeware plug-ins have been created by enthusiasts to augment the already impressive list of commercial offerings.

VST plug-ins are placed within a VST folder on the hard drive of the

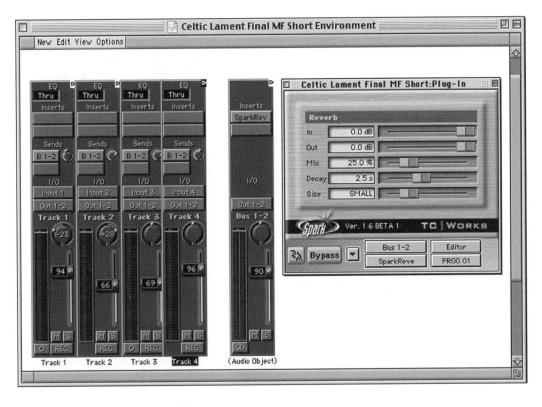

**Figure 3.3: VST effects in Logic Audio**

computer, where they can be accessed by any audio program that is VST compatible. In other words, you can use the same VST plug-ins in your MIDI/audio sequencer as you can in your stereo editor, although the first time you try to run a VST plug-in from a newly-installed piece of audio software you may be asked to locate the VST folder. Programs often come bundled with their own set of VST plug-ins, so if you find that you've ended up with more than one VST folder it's probably best to move all of your VST plug-ins to a single folder and then direct the software to use this folder the next time it asks for the location of your VST plug-ins.

Plug-ins are generally called up from a drop-down menu accessible from the insert points of the mixer page of the host sequencer, although some software may use an "Add Plug-in" dialogue. The exact system will vary from sequencer to sequencer, but as a rule plug-ins may be placed in channel insert points, where single channels are to be treated, or they may be placed in an aux/send return loop, where multiple channels require processing with the same effect. This system functions very much like the aux send/return on a regular console, allowing varying amounts of the same effect to be set up on each channel. Figure 3.3 shows how both insert and aux send/return VST effects are set up within Logic Audio.

VST plug-ins provide equivalents to pretty much all of the regular studio effects, such as compression, limiting, gating, reverb, echo, chorus, flanging and so on, but VST reverb plug-ins that sound as good as a reasonable outboard reverb processor demand a lot of computing power. For this reason you may wish to use an external reverb processor, if your mixing arrangements make this possible. If everything is being mixed internally and you don't have a soundcard with on-board effects chips, you'll either have to rely on plug-in effects or you'll have to record your tracks via hardware effects boxes. Clearly the latter method will prevent you from making any subsequent adjustments to the effect parameters or level, and if the effect is stereo you'll have to record onto a pair of tracks in order to keep the effect in stereo.

In addition to the more usual studio effects, there are also VST plug-ins available for vocoding, pitch correction, creative distortion, spectral enhancement, noise removal, click suppression, hum removal and numerous other functions. The number of VST effects on the market is growing all the time, so it pays to check out music internet sites and music magazines for the latest updates and additions.

When they were first introduced, it was only possible to set up VST plug-ins via on-screen controls, and user settings could be saved for later use, but there was no way to automatically adjust the plug-in parameters during the course of a piece of music. Clearly, automation has introduced a lot of creative potential, and so Steinberg came up with the VST II standard, where plug-in parameters can be controlled with MIDI information in much the same way as hardware effects boxes can be controlled via MIDI.

All plug-ins will take up some of your processor's power, so there'll always be a limit to how many you'll be able to run at once. Therefore, effects like reverb are best used in the effects send and return loop of the virtual mixer, if this facility is available. In this way, a single plug-in can be applied to as many channels of audio as required. As with hardware outboard equipment, processors such as compressors or equalisers, which treat the entire signal rather than adding an effect to the dry (un-effected) signal, still have to be used on a per-channel or per-group basis via channel or group insert points.

# time and pitch manipulation

There are lots of tricks that you can do using the audio manipulation facilities provided by your sequencer, and many of these will extend beyond what you might expect from a simple multi-effects unit. For example, there are very powerful filters available that can process any sounds to make them appear synthetic, and there are devices that will distort sound in interesting ways. Built-in facilities vary from one software package to another, but pitch changing and time stretching are supported by most packages. These are invaluable tools for massaging audio sample loops, but you may also find others which will allow you to maximise levels, de-noise a signal and so on. Some of the more processor-intensive processes work off-line (in other words, they aren't real-time plug-ins), so you can use them even on a slower machine; you'll just have to wait around a while for the results.

Pitch-to-MIDI conversion is also fairly common, and allows a monophonic recording of an instrument to be analysed in order that a MIDI track may be produced which mirrors the note and pitch-bend information of the original track. This is useful when you need to have a MIDI instrument playing along in unison with a real instrument that you've just recorded. Some software even offers the quantisation of audio tracks, enabling the timing of things such as drum parts and guitar riffs to be tightened up. In my experience, this can work well, as long as you don't process a section that's too long, and as long as the original audio isn't too complex. As with so many things, you'll need to experiment in order to determine what will work and what won't.

# virtual instruments

After VST effects hit the market, VST instruments followed, and some of these are pretty spectacular, often being based on digital models of popular vintage instruments. Computer-based synths have been around for many years, but there was previously no standardisation of operation and generally no way of using them within other software packages unless support was specifically built in by the designers of the host program. The introduction of VST instruments changed all of that.

Stand-alone (non-VST) software synths can often be used from within the more popular sequencer packages only if drivers are included that allow the synths to receive MIDI instructions from the sequencer and to route audio into the sequencer's mixer. VST instruments, on the other hand, have the advantage of being readily compatible with any sequencer that supports VST musical instruments, and as a rule they're as easy to configure as VST effects. The exact details differ from one sequencer to another, but usually a VST instrument will function much like a mixer audio channel, and can usually be routed to any possible destination within the mixer. Furthermore, it may also be possible to insert regular VST effects after the instrument in order to provide more sonic capability.

The plus side of using virtual synths is that you can have a control interface covered with virtual knobs, just like the real thing, and the automation capability of VST means that you can make adjustments in real time that are recorded as part of a song. When the emulation is of a pre-MIDI instrument, which had no facilities to save and recall patches, this is clearly a big advantage. Moreover, monophonic instruments such as the MiniMoog can be emulated in multivoice format in order to provide polyphony.

However, there's also a negative side to virtual instruments, and the most obvious problem is the drain on processing resources. As a rule, the more notes that are played at once, the more computing power is required. Computing power is allocated to replaying audio tracks, creating effects and creating VST instruments, and so overdoing things in any one of these areas will eventually compromise the others. This is just one reason why it's never possible to predict exactly many tracks a system is capable of playing back at once; it all depends on the virtual effects and instruments that are running at the same time.

# other VST instruments

So far, I've only mentioned VST synths, some of which are digital models of existing analogue instruments, some are emulations of other digital hardware synths and some are newly-designed instruments in their own right. However, it's also possible to create VST drum machines and samplers, and some of the software samplers currently available can read commercial sample CD-ROM formats, the most common being the Akai S1000 and S3000.

# software samplers

Like virtual synths, these take up a significant proportion of a computer's resources, but the concept is an attractive one. Whereas hardware samplers have their own RAM, software samplers tend to utilise the host computer's RAM, and so it makes sense to install as much RAM as possible if you're intending to make serious use of a software sampler.

Software samplers have a distinct advantage over hardware models

**Figure 3.4: eMagic EXS24 software sampler**

insofar as they have a much clearer graphic interface, and instead of arcane multitimbral modes you simply open a separate sampler in each track where you need sample playback. Because the computer's own RAM is used for sample playback, the available sample memory can be much higher than that of a conventional hardware instrument. Most software samplers will also import commercial sample CD-ROMs in Akai S1000/3000 format, and possibly Roland and E-mu format as well.

Having a software sampler that can run within the VST plug-in environment also means that the sampler output can be further processed using standard VST effects, such as delay, chorus or reverb. Different plug-ins can be used for each track, up to the limit of your computer's processing capacity.

There are several software samplers available, but there are some advantages in buying one that's specifically designed to run within the sequencer program you normally use. Not least of these is that this gives you the ability to access the sampler directly, without leaving the sequencer program, and in some cases the sequencer's audio recording and editing facilities may be used to create and edit new samples.

eMagic's EXS24 sampler is designed specifically for users of that company's Logic Audio program, and handles file imports (Akai only at the time of writing) by converting samples to its own format and then storing them on the computer's hard drive. As hard drive space is now very cheap, this is a very practical way of working, and one thing you'll notice right away is that samples stored on the computer's hard drive load up in seconds, whereas on a hardware sampler they may take a couple of minutes. Samples are selected for loading on a pull-down menu, rather like selecting synth patches.

Whereas conventional audio tracks rely on disk access, samplers work directly from RAM, so there's no drain on disk access capacity other than when actually loading or saving samples. Furthermore, because the sampler doesn't have to create sounds in real time, the processing load tends to be lower than it is with a software synthesiser. However, there is some processor loading, as samples still have to be repatched, filtered, modulated, enveloped and so on.

# ReWire

Not all audio software is designed to slot together as neatly as VST, so Steinberg and a software company called Propellerhead Software co-operated to develop a piece of software called ReWire, which allows audio to be routed between different programs in real time. ReWire is available for both Macs and PCs, and can be thought of as a multichannel software audio cable – in fact, rather like a length of multicore. This virtual multicore can accommodate up to 64 channels of audio at any one time at pretty much any standard bit resolution and sample rate. A further benefit is that audio data transferred via ReWire can be delivered with sample-accurate synchronisation. Indeed, different applications can be locked to the sampling rate. Also, common transport control commands such as Play and Stop may also be sent via ReWire. One of the first applications of ReWire was to allow Propellerhead Software's Rebirth virtual analogue drum synth to run alongside Steinberg's Cubase VST software. This system works by making it possible to patch the output from a virtual synth directly into the mixer section of Cubase, where it can be further processed with VST effects. Furthermore, ReWire isn't limited to Cubase users; there are also some other leading manufacturers of sequencers who support it.

# software drivers

Hardware is linked to sequencing software by an invisible piece of computer code known as a *driver*, so in order for a system to work it must have a driver that is compatible with both the host sequencer software and with the hardware interface. If your host software and your audio hardware both support ASIO or ASIO II then it's reasonably safe to assume that the two will work together, assuming that the driver works properly. (I say reasonably safe because the internet sites for hardware manufacturers frequently feature updated driver software that either improves performance or fixes bugs.)

# ASIO

ASIO stands for Audio Stream Input Output Technology, and was first designed as part of the Cubase VST software. Its latest incarnation, ASIO II, is another Steinberg innovation that establishes a standard protocol for audio drivers that bypass the slower parts of the host computer's operating system and can be shared across platforms and between other manufacturers who support the protocol. To date, both Opcode and eMagic support ASIO and ASIO II, although eMagic tend to use their own EASI driver system where possible. ASIO and ASIO II also support soundcards with multiple inputs and outputs, so they aren't limited to stereo audio handling. If the sequencer you're using is compatible with ASIO II, and the audio hardware (whether this is a soundcard or an audio interface) comes complete with ASIO II drivers, the two should run together quite happily.

# EASI

EASI is eMagic's driver system for handling audio data transfer between Logic's sequencer and any external hardware that runs with an EASI driver. The eMagic engineers claim that EASI doesn't put as much of a load on the host processor as ASIO, as it can take advantage of audio accelerators found on the audio interface (where applicable). As with Steinberg, eMagic are making EASI available to third-party developers in the hope that it will become an industry standard.

# the ADAT interface

These standards are wonderful things, which is why the recording industry has so many of them! One such is the ADAT optical, eight-channel audio interface that was first developed for the Alesis ADAT digital eight-track tape recorder. This interface can send up to eight audio tracks in one direction only, so multiples must be used on those occasions when 16 or more channels are needed. Alesis has licensed the technology to a number of other manufactures, who use it to provide audio interface inputs and outputs, digital mixer inputs and outputs and so on. Although the ADAT optical interface carries both audio data and the timing clock, it doesn't carry audio sync information, so if it proves necessary to transfer audio data with sample-accurate sync, the ADAT nine-pin sync cable is also required. Some interfaces come equipped with this facility but others don't. If ADAT sync isn't used, the accuracy with which information can be transferred over the ADAT optical link depends on the alternative sync method used, which is usually MTC (MIDI Time Code). This is accurate enough in most applications, although the precise positioning of the audio may drift by a few milliseconds. You should keep in mind that, although the ADAT optical connector and cable looks the same as that used to transfer optical S/PDIF stereo information, the two data systems are not compatible.

# TDIF

TDIF – or the Tascam Digital Interface, to give it its full title – is Tascam's alternative to the ADAT audio connection protocol. Like ADAT, TDIF can carry eight tracks of audio, but it uses multicore cable rather than an optical system. Separate hardware converters are available to convert TDIF to ADAT and vice versa. Like the ADAT interface, TDIF has been licensed to a number of hardware manufacturers.

# RBUS

Recently introduced, RBUS is Roland's proprietary eight-channel digital audio interface for interconnecting Roland equipment. Converter boxes must be used to translate this to ADAT or TDIF.

# this latency business

Latency is an issue which manufacturers tend to skirt around, and often users don't understand its full implications until they try to use their systems to do some serious work. If you're not familiar with the problem, latency is a short but significant delay that occurs between the time at which sound is fed into a computer-based recording system and the time at which the same sound emerges via the audio outs. On a well-designed system, this latency may only be a few milliseconds, in which case few people will even notice its playback in such an environment. The computer uses memory buffers, which act like reservoirs, keeping the audio flowing when the computer is doing something else, and the larger the buffer, the longer the latency.

The best analogy is that of someone filling a leaky bucket with a cup. As long as the bucket never runs dry, the leak will continue steadily; but if the guy with the cup can't keep up, the bucket will run dry and the flow will stop. Exactly the same thing happens with audio data, and the bigger the memory buffer (the bucket), the less chance there is of a glitch as the computer fails to keep up the supply of audio to the buffer. The problem is that there must always be a delay between the time that the water is poured into the bucket and the time at which that same water has leaked out of the bottom of the bucket. In the memory buffer, latency is caused by this delay. Further delay occurs when audio data is fed into the computer, routed to the CPU, processed and then output from the soundcard. This can take anything from just a few milliseconds in a well-designed system to over half a second. Fortunately, there are solutions for situations where high latency poses a problem.

# tackling latency

There are both hardware and software approaches for minimising latency, notably ASIO II drivers with software and soundcards with *thru monitoring* with hardware. The original ASIO driver format couldn't help out with latency issues, but with ASIO II, when you're recording audio, the monitor source (in other words your soundcard or interface audio output) is fed directly from the input signal, rather than from the input, after it has been routed via the CPU and the computer's internal bussing system. Some buffering is still used to provide an uninterrupted flow of audio, but working in this way the monitoring latency is usually small enough to be considered negligible.

What's the catch? Because the audio is being routed directly to the soundcard output by the shortest possible route, no real-time VST effects can be added to the monitored signal, and so if you're one of those people who need to hear reverb before you can sing in tune you'll need to find another way of adding it. One possibility is to use a soundcard or interface with built-in digital effects, such as the Yamaha SW1000XG card or the Lexicon Core II system with MP100 reverb.

Of course, you may have a system that doesn't support ASIO II drivers, or your software may but your hardware may not. Alternatively, you may just be one of those people who are very sensitive to timing, and for you even minimal latency is too much. What then? Fortunately, there is a solution, if you have a mixer.

# the hardware solution to latency

Unless you have an extremely simple system, on which you rely on the same soundcard to provide synth sounds and audio recording, you're going to need a mixer to combine the output from your soundcard with the outputs from your external synths, samplers and drum machines. Furthermore, unless you're going to entrust VST plug-ins or similar computer-powered virtual devices to carry out all of your audio processing, you'll also need a recording pre-amp with an integral compressor so that you can even out your vocal levels during the recording stage.

Assuming that you have these things, it's possible to set up a simple system in which the output from a recording pre-amp is split to feed both the mixer and the soundcard input. At it's simplest, this could be done with a Y-lead (it's always OK to split signals this way but not to mix them!), but you'll find that a lot of recording pre-amps have two outputs anyway, often one on a jack and the other on an XLR. If this is the case, you should feed the jack output to the soundcard and then make up a balanced-XLR-to-balanced-quarter-inch jack lead to feed into your mixer's line input. You might get away with having an XLR lead plugged directly into the mixer's mic input, but only if your mixer has a pad switch and plenty of range (in the negative direction!) on the input gain trim.

If you don't have a recording pre-amp, you may be able to use one of your mixing channels instead, provided that it has a direct output (or insert send) with which to feed to the soundcard input. You can even use a pre-fade aux send if you don't need this for anything else, and this will allow you to monitor overdubs directly through the mixer when recording. However, you'll need to mute the output from the track being recorded within the software or you'll hear both the direct monitor signal and the delayed signal. Most sequencer packages have a thru monitoring on/off switch for this purpose. After recording, you may want to mute the mixer channel that was used for monitoring the recording pre-amp to prevent your live mic from still feeding into the mix. Other than that, you're in business.

As I pointed out earlier, because you're bypassing the computer while monitoring your overdubs you won't be able to hear the effect of any VST plug-ins until after the track has been recorded. If you need reverb to help you sing better, you can still hook up a regular hardware effects unit to your mixer and add as much monitor reverb or echo as you like – it won't be recorded. The set-up needed to achieve zero-latency monitoring is shown in Figure 3.5.

If you're performing a punch-in recording to patch up a mistake, using thru monitoring as described above means that you won't be able to hear the original track, because it will be turned down or muted. One practical way of working around this problem is to record the punch-in part on a new track and then paste it onto the original track once you've got it right. However, this doesn't help with virtual instruments, where a sub-10ms latency system is they only real solution. A possible compromise is to record parts while playing a regular synth sound and then switch the track to a virtual instrument for playback.

# hard drives

You'll need a fast computer if you want to use it for MIDI-plus-audio recording, one ideally fitted with a separate internal or external hard drive for audio (although you can get away without one if you don't need too many tracks running at once). SCSI drives are significantly faster than the EIDE or Ultra DMA drives used inside most current Macs and PCs, but they're also around three times more expensive. If you only need a handful of audio tracks, an EIDE drive will probably work fine, although you should be aware that, unlike SCSI, which has its own microprocessor to handle disk activity, EIDE drives rely on the host computer to do most of the work. The fastest SCSI drives are know as *fast, wide SCSI* drives, and you should take note that there are at least three different types of SCSI connector currently available. Adaptor cables are also available to connect devices that have different types of SCSI socket. The higher the sustained rate of data transfer that is quoted for a drive, the more tracks you're likely to be able to play back at once.

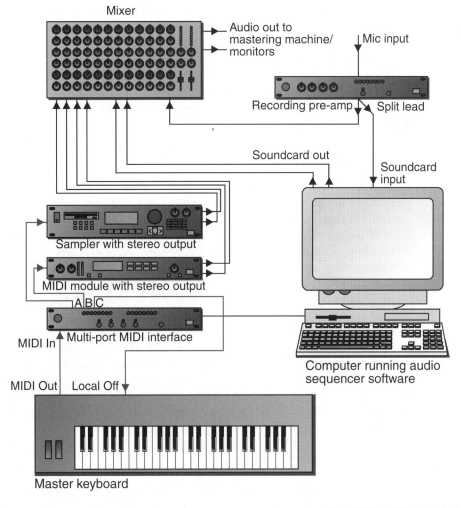

Figure 3.5: Zero-latency monitoring

A maximum of seven devices may be hooked up to a basic SCSI system, one of which is the computer itself. Each SCSI device needs to be set to a different ID number, usually by means of a simple switch on the rear panel, and the last device in a SCSI chain should be terminated, either with a plug-in terminator or with the device's own termination facilities, if provided.

# FireWire

It is likely that even faster FireWire drives will replace SCSI in the near future, and all new Macs (other than entry-level models) already come with a FireWire port as standard. It is hoped that FireWire will also become a standard for PCs. FireWire is essentially a high-speed computer data interface that can be used for networking applications and for connecting high-speed peripherals, such as hard drives. Yamaha are also pioneering a derivative of FireWire for transmitting MIDI, sync information and multiple channels of audio. This is knows as MLAN (Music Local Area Network). Their aim is to persuade other manufacturers to support it so that it becomes a standard in the same way that MIDI did. For audio use, try to leave at least ten per cent free disk space at all times.

# disk fragmentation

Computer drives don't necessarily record audio in one continuous stream. If many files have been written to a drive and then later erased or edited, the drive will become fragmented. A fragmented drive tends to have sections of different files scattered around in different places throughout it, and although it generally manages to join them up seamlessly the speed of the disk's operation can be slowed down noticeably, which will result in a reduction in the maximum number of audio tracks that can be played back at the same time without incurring glitching or dropouts.

To combat this, you should not only use a separate audio drive for storing your audio files but also defragment it fairly regularly, using a program such as Norton Utilities. (Windows has a defrag option built in.) It may also help matters to clear the drive occasionally (after backing up information to CD-ROM, or whatever your favourite medium is) and then reformat it.

# USB

USB (Universal Serial Buss) is a computer peripheral interfacing system designed to replace the older serial and parallel connectors used by previous generations of PCs and Macs, and is intended to be used for connecting things like keyboards, mice, scanners, printers, digital cameras and some types of storage devices. In theory, USB can address up to 127 connected devices, and unlike previous systems (ie SCSI) you don't have to power down to plug in or remove devices. USB hubs provide the multiple USB connections required for larger systems, and the system is supported by both Macs and PCs. At the time of writing, there are some timing issues relating to USB, which means that the manufacturers of MIDI and audio interfaces have to pull some pretty clever tricks in order to prevent audio glitching or MIDI timing drift.

USB can support up to four channels of audio in one direction or stereo and bi-directional, although for more serious applications interfaces that hook in via a PCI computer card must still be used. A number of interesting USB products are emerging for desktop audio use that combine audio and MIDI interfaces with hardware control knobs for the purposes of MIDI mixing, using mic pre-amps and so on. Currently, there's talk of an introducing an improved USB II interface that will address some of the teething problems of the original USB system.

# connecting MIDI interfaces

As stated earlier, for this you'll need a MIDI interface (unless you're using only soundcard or software synths, or a hardware synth with a "to host" connection), as well as suitable sequencing software which supports your MIDI and audio hardware. MIDI interfaces may connect via PC serial ports, USB ports or parallel ports, depending on the model and the support software that comes with them, while older Macs (ie those that came out before the coloured G3 iMacs) used the serial printer or modem ports. Newer Macs use USB, although third-party serial-interface adaptor cards are available for use with legacy hardware. Not all work with MIDI, however, so it's best to check out the software company's web site for more information before you buy anything.

As a rule, it's best to choose a MIDI interface with at least six output ports if you intend to use external synth modules, because you always end up acquiring more synths than you think you will initially. If you're using USB for your MIDI work, I recommend that you use one of the more sophisticated interfaces that uses intelligent buffering in order to avoid MIDI timing problems. eMagic have released the AMT-8 and Unitor 8 MkII interfaces for use with Logic Audio, whereas Steinberg have their own interface optimised for Cubase. Mark Of The Unicorn also produce a range of interfaces that work with most leading sequencing software, although Opcode's OMS is sometimes needed when working with USB interfaces.

# OMS

OMS (Open Music System) is a standard Mac-based system for routing MIDI information. It was developed by Opcode, but is supported by a number of other manufacturers. It works by directing the flow of MIDI data to and from your MIDI interface and between OMS-compatible applications, such as sequencers and patch librarians. OMS also looks after timing data, such as SMPTE, MIDI timecode or MIDI clock, and can also act as a centralised source of timing for different applications.

Because OMS is an industry standard, it is usually supported by third-party manufacturers of MIDI interfaces in order to allow their products to be used with all OMS-compatible MIDI sequencer software. After installing OMS, you'll need to create a single document called "OMS Studio", which will tell the program which devices you have and to which MIDI ports these are connected. If you add a new device to your studio, you simply have to update this document and all of your applications will then know where to find this new device. As a rule, Mac USB MIDI interfaces that aren't designed specifically to work with the host sequencer software generally require OMS to make them work.

In addition to handling routing tasks, OMS can also store names of synth patches and make them available to you between applications via a folder called "Factory Names". It can even help you to extract the patch names from any synths that you have connected to the system. Part of the software known as the Galaxy Name Provider allows OMS to read patch names directly from Opcode's editor/librarian program, Galaxy.

# the music computer

Because of the complexity of music software and the potential for conflicts to spring up between software and hardware, the setting up of a desktop studio isn't always as simple as it might appear at first. If you're planning to buy a PC system but you're not sure what to choose, check out the FAQ (Frequently-Asked Question) sections on the various music web sites, including the extensive one in the "Forum" section of the *Sound On Sound* site at www.sospubs.co.uk. Even when you've decided what to buy, I'd still advise those with limited computer experience to buy a complete, preconfigured system from one vendor, especially if the computer is a PC.

It's not as difficult to choose a Mac as it is a PC because there's a limited range of models, whereas with PCs there's an infinite permutation of components. You should note, however, that all new Macs use the USB serial interface for the connection of peripherals such as MIDI interfaces, although there are serial converter boards available which will be able to connect you to older serial MIDI interfaces. Newer Macs also don't have built-in SCSI, so if you want to use the latest and fastest SCSI drives to record your audio you'll also need to fit a SCSI PCI card, just as your PC counterpart has to. I'd always recommend that you contact the relevant technical support department for your sequencing software before you buy a SCSI card – or a MIDI interface, for that matter – just to ensure that there are no known problems with your potential purchase.

If you don't need many audio tracks then a slower (but cheaper) internal EIDE drive may be adequate, although I'd still recommend that you buy a separate drive for audio file storage rather than use your boot drive. Most Macs have space inside them for a second drive, but if you absolutely must use the same drive for audio and everything else you should at least create a separate partition for your audio work. The newer and faster FireWire drives appear to be the best bet for the storing of audio data on both Macs and PCs in the future, but at the time of writing unfortunately I haven't been able to test one. However, most music software offers little FireWire support.

You should note that, from the coloured iMac onwards, Macintosh machines don't have a floppy drive, although it's possible to buy an external drive that takes regular floppies as well as high-capacity, removable disks. Check with your software vendor to make sure that this doesn't complicate the installation of the software or frustrate the copy protection system in any way. For more information on this subject, see the section on copy protection in chapter six. Pace-protected software requires an enabler file, which can be downloaded from www.paceap.com.

# audio timing

Most people can get by with the resolution of MIDI, but it's extremely frustrating when you have some audio material that refuses to stay in time with the MIDI tracks. There are several reasons why this can happen. Latency is something which many users have to accept when monitoring while recording, and if it gets too bad it can be minimised by monitoring the input signal via a hardware mixer. However, once the audio has been recorded onto a computer hard drive, the playback timing may still wander around to an unacceptable degree if the computer is short of RAM, if it's slower than at least twice what the manufacturers claim to be a minimum specification for the operation of their program, or if the software drivers are not up to date. This latter consideration is important, as a poorly-written driver may allow the playback latency to vary, and this will have the effect of making the timing of the audio drift. You should visit the web site of the manufacturer of the soundcard and/or interface regularly, as well as that of the maker of your sequencer software, as you'll not only find up-to-date drivers and software revisions there but also forums where users help solve each other's technical problems.

To get the best audio performance, you may also need to check your driver settings, adjust RAM buffer sizes and fine-tune your playback delay settings. The manual that came with your sequencing software should explain how to do this, although many soundcard manufacturers provide recommended settings to be used with the more common software packages.

# preventative measure

It may not be a good idea to have audio playback starting on the first beat of a sequence because, when the Start button on the sequencer is pressed, a certain amount of activity goes on behind the scenes (buffer filling, and so on) before the audio can start to play back. If the audio comes in on the first beat of the song, there may be a short delay before everything gets sorted out. It's better to give the sequencer time to prepare for playback by placing a couple of empty bars after the count-in and before the song starts.

# audio and clocks

When audio is recorded into a computer, the audio data is usually synchronised to a crystal clock on the soundcard or interface, and although crystal clocks are very stable they don't all run at exactly the same speed as each other. This means that, if you have a system with two or more soundcards, you will have to be careful when recording via one soundcard and playing back via another, as the playback speed on each card may be slightly different. The situation should improve if each track is replayed via the card that recorded it, but things can still go wrong in a system if you want to sync all of your audio to an external clock for the purposes of digital timing. Because the external clock may not run at exactly the same speed as the clocks on your soundcards, the playback speed may again drift slightly, and with longer audio tracks the drift becomes worse the further you get into the track. If you intend to synchronise all of your cards on playback, sync them while you're recording as well, as this will minimise the chances of drift occurring. Some manufactures endeavour to provide proper sync between multiple cards, while others seem to leave it to chance.

If you're using multiple soundcards in order to have more individual audio outputs at your disposal, it's also unwise to split stereo pairs of signals between two separate cards because even the slightest difference in timing will cause an unpleasant flanging effect. Wherever possible, record stereo material as a stereo audio file; in this way, the two halves can't drift. In the case of multiple cards that can be linked to run from the same clock, these concerns should not arise.

## external sync

What happens when your audio is stable but you decide to sync the sequencer to an outside source that's less than perfectly stable, such as a tape recorder or a similar device? If the master device runs a little slow then the tempo of the MIDI sequencer will drop in order to match it, as it should, but the audio may still carry on at its original rate, causing the MIDI and audio to drift apart. The better sequencers are equipped with something called *continuous audio resync*, which changes the speed of the audio clock in order to match that of the time code coming from the master machine.

## timing workarounds

If the stability of audio timing is still inadequate, despite your best endeavours, one of the most effective workarounds is to divide long audio tracks into sections, each just a few bars long. Each section will then trigger independently, so although there may still be a small amount of drift within each section the effect won't be cumulative.

Cubase VST provides a priority setting in its System Set-up page. This defaults to Normal, which gives equal priority to both audio and MIDI timing; but if you work mainly with audio, you can change this to High or Highest, which will give priority to audio data processing. If, on the other hand, you work mainly with MIDI, reducing the audio priority setting to Low will ensure that MIDI has priority. If you're working with VST, it's also important to have the correct setting for System Pre-roll (located in the Sync menu). Normally, this should be set to the same value as the soundcard's latency. Trade-offs between MIDI and audio timing are usually only an issue with older, slower computers.

When it comes to creating audio loops within your sequencer, a lot depends on how slick your sequencer is at retriggering the same piece of audio. If you find that there's a slight timing discrepancy as the sequencer jumps back to the start of the audio segment, you may be able to make a small change in the tempo (usually a very small fraction of a beat per minute) to compensate. In the event that you can't find a satisfactory cure, perhaps the best way out of trouble would be to return to entrusting your drum loops to an external sampler, although a computer that's fast enough will usually handle audio loops with no problem.

Ultimately, a lot comes down to what we can realistically expect from our desktop systems. MIDI and audio are a given, but we also expect computers to be able to deal with mixing, EQ, VST real-time effects and even virtual synthesis. Unless you have the most powerful computer, you may find that many of your problems simply stem from having an underpowered system. Manufacturers don't help, either, as the minimum specifications that they quote on software packages are usually hopelessly inadequate.

You should ensure that your computer has plenty of memory, ideally double the minimum specified requirement or more, and you may also need to spend some time checking manufacturers' web sites to find the latest drivers and set-up information for your hardware. After you've contacted the support help lines for the relevant software, user groups are probably the best place to start looking for answers to any problems that you still can't resolve. Buying a pre-configures system avoids much of this detective work.

# drive maintenance

If you have a separate hard drive for your audio data, you'll be able to defragment or even reformat the drive regularly without disturbing your program files. Defragmenting software such as Norton Utilities collects up the various sections of files that have been scattered around the disk and rewrites them in contiguous sections. This process optimises the rate at which data can be read on and off the disk – a badly fragmented drive can produce audio glitching or can reduce the number of tracks that can be played back simultaneously. The faster the drive, the more tracks you'll be able to play back, although very fast drives may need a special SCSI interface card in order to enable you to make the best of their capabilities. You should avoid moving or jarring drives while they are operating, as this can cause serious damage.

# guitars and computers

One problem that most guitarists come up against is that computer monitors interfere badly with guitar pickups, producing a nasty buzz on the recording. Some humbucking pickups are reasonably good at rejecting this buzz, as long as the guitarist doesn't sit too close to the monitor while recording, but single-coil pickups tend to be very badly affected, especially if overdrive is used. This problem can be solved cheaply by switching off the monitor just before recording and using keyboard commands to start and stop the recording process.

If you can't switch off the monitor for some reason, the guitarist should sit as far away from it as possible when recording and rotate his position in order to find the null point, where the buzz is least obtrusive. You might also use a noise gate pedal in order to keep the guitar quiet between phrases. Flat-screen LCD monitors are becoming cheaper, and they both save space and eliminate the electromagnetic interference generated by the scan coils of a typical CRT monitor. If you record a lot of guitar music, or are short on space, one of these could be a good investment.

## fan and drive noise

Physical noise is also a problem when miking instruments or voices in the same room as the computer. If possible, turn off any unnecessary external drives, CD-R burners and other peripherals as these often make more noise than the main computer. You should set up the mic (ideally a cardioid model) as far away from the computer as possible and improvise an acoustic screen between the mic and the computer, using a duvet or a sleeping bag. Also, it's important to make sure that the surface at which the mic is pointing is absorptive rather than reflective. It's best if you work as close to the mic as you can without compromising the sound, and always use a pop shield when recording vocals. All of this will be easier if you use a sound-deadening computer cabinet, but if you do then don't forget to provide the necessary ventilation for your computer.

## keep it clean

Most computer audio systems run best if you get rid of any superfluous software, such as screensavers and games. Also, you should make sure that you have no more drivers (extensions, for Mac users) than you actually need. The cleaner the system, the less likely you'll run into problems. Check the web sites of manufacturers to make sure that you have the latest drivers, as improvements are coming onto the market all the time. If you must run other software, consider employing the afore-mentioned dual-boot system, in which two completely different sets of the operating system, along with the relevant programs, are used on two different hard drives. In this way, you can start up from one drive when you're working with music and from the other drive for everyday work or for playing games. Mac users can create different extension sets for music and other tasks by using the Extensions Manager control panel.

It's also wise to carry out some tests in order to determine how many tracks and plug-ins your machine can run without running into trouble. Once you've done this, try to work with no more than half to two thirds of this amount. Most sequencers include some kind of CPU activity monitor to help you, but the problem is that the demands on your CPU aren't constant. Your disk drive will also slow down as it fragments, so try to allow for this; you can't be expected to defragment it after recording every track.

# lightening the load

Both MIDI and audio timing can be optimised by making sure that the computer isn't doing any unnecessary tasks in the background. Scrolling screen displays usually take up more processing power than those that jump when the cursor gets to the end of the screen, so try turning off scrolling if you think that you're pushing your computer's capabilities. You can also go one better than this by zooming in on the song before you play it back so that it all fits into a single page, as this will avoid scrolling and screen redrawing.

Macintosh users should also consider using the Extensions Manager control panel to disable any of their system extensions that aren't needed for music operation, and screensavers are definitely something to avoid. Setting the monitor resolution to 256 colours will also reduce the processing burden. Finally, you should note that some audio software can be disrupted by the energy-saving routine that cuts in if you haven't touched any of the computer's keys for a while. If at all possible, you should disable this, or at least set a very long time period, so that it doesn't cut in while you're recording or processing an album-length sound file.

# microphones

If you already have a good-quality dynamic live vocal mic, this should work fine for recording vocals, drums or electric guitars and basses, although a capacitor microphone will work noticeably better in the recording of quieter acoustic instruments or acoustic instruments that generate a lot of high-frequency detail. Furthermore, capacitor mics are the preferred choice for recording vocals in most studios, and so, even though a dynamic model can provide good results, a capacitor mic is likely to produce a more open and detailed sound. Large-diaphragm capacitor models (with a diaphragm diameter of one inch) are better for vocals, as they produce a full, flattering sound.

All professional mics are low-impedance and balanced models, although they can also be used unbalanced if a suitable lead is used, unless they require phantom power (as do all true capacitor models). If the mic has an XLR connector built into its handle and comes with a separate lead, it's almost certainly low impedance and balanced. You should note that some soundcards have a mic input jack socket, but these usually produce less-than-optimum results with studio mics. If you're recording anything but the most basic demo, you'll need either a hardware mixer or a separate mic pre-amp.

Capacitor mics require phantom power at 48V, which a recording mixer or serious mic pre-amp will provide. This voltage is required to run the internal electronics of a capacitor microphone and is supplied along a regular, balanced mic lead. You need to do nothing other than plug in the mic and switch on the phantom power at the mixer or pre-amp. If you don't have a pre-amp or mixer equipped with phantom power, use a good back-electret mic which has its own internal battery. These can perform as well as true capacitor mics, although the models that can run on battery power tend to be less sensitive.

# DI boxes

DI (Direct Injection) boxes are essential pieces of equipment when it comes to recording because they allow signals from either instruments, pre-amps or power amplifiers to be used as recording sources without having to risk impedance mismatch or hum induced by ground loops. In general, a DI box is used when line-level signals need to be recorded which would normally be incompatible with a mixer or a soundcard line input for reasons due to level or impedance. A DI box performs two important roles: it provides electrical ground isolation between input and output and it also matches the impedance of a source signal to that of the load. For example, a DI box with a high input impedance and a low output impedance may be used to match an electric guitar or a bass to the input stage of a mixing console.

DI boxes fall into two main categories: passive (with transformers) and active (with active electronics), although there are some active electronic models that also include transformers. Passive DI boxes require no power, while active models need either phantom power or batteries.

# transformer DI boxes

Used extensively in both live sound and studio applications, the transformer DI box has the advantages of being simple to use, providing excellent electrical isolation between the input and output, and enjoying a lack of dependence on a power supply. Good-quality transformers are expensive, which is why most cheap DI boxes are active.

When a transformer DI box is used to match a guitar to a mixing desk, the output side of the transformer is required to deliver a higher current than that of the original signal source, which means a significant drop in signal voltage. To overcome this, the DI box needs to be be plugged into a console mic input, where sufficient gain is available to restore the signal level. Such a transformer DI box usually comprises a single transformer with a centre-tapped secondary winding in order to provide a balanced output. The unbalanced input is completely isolated from the output, although the input ground can be connected to the output ground by means of ground lift switch (in the off position). The input connection often has a thru socket so that the DI box can be used to take a feed from an existing signal path without breaking the signal flow. This is useful in live recording applications.

# active DI boxes

Most active DI boxes dispense with transformers altogether, although some include both active components and a transformer output stage. A typical transformerless DI circuit has a "floating" output, where the input and output signal grounds are independent of each other. However, unlike the transformer DI box, there is no true electrical isolation. Ground lift switches and thru sockets are generally fitted.

The main advantage of the active DI box is that it can produce power gain. In other words, the input-to-output voltage ratio can be made independent of the impedance ratio. Many models include switches which enable the user to choose the output level or input sensitivity.

Power for an active DI box can come from internal batteries, but most professional models will also operate from phantom power, which means that they must be plugged into a console or a pre-amp mic input with the phantom power switched on. Some models can use either batteries or phantom power.

# speaker DI

Occasionally, it's necessary to take a DI feed from the speaker output of an amplifier. Both active and passive DI boxes can do this, provided that they are fitted with an input designed to accept speaker-level signals. Speaker outputs carry signals of several tens of volts, while line-level signals are usually of only around a couple of volts, and so plugging a speaker signal into a line-level input would overload it massively. Mic inputs are designed to accept signals that are typically only a few thousandths of a volt in amplitude, so the effect of plugging in a speaker signal would be even more serious. DI boxes with speaker input jacks should also have thru connectors, allowing connection to either the original speaker or to a dummy load. The DI output signal will be at either mic or line level, and can be fed to the appropriate console, pre-amp or audio interface input.

# speaker emulation

Guitar amplifiers are special cases for DI purposes because the sound of a guitar is affected by the characteristics of the guitar amp's loudspeaker cabinet. The sound is filtered in a complex way because of the restricted top end of a typical guitar or bass speaker, and so in order to get an authentic DI sound the DI'd signal needs to be filtered in a similar way. A circuit that does this is known as a *speaker simulator*, and both active and passive models are available. Passive models combine the elements of a DI box with those of a speaker simulator, but unless the speaker simulator also contains a dummy loudspeaker load it's also necessary to connect a loudspeaker to the amplifier via the thru connector of the DI box. Failing to do this will leave the amplifier running into a virtual open circuit, which may affect the sound or even cause damage to your equipment, especially tube amplifiers.

# headphones

While headphones aren't ideal for mixing critically (you should double-check mixes on loudspeakers), they're useful for working when making excessive noise would be antisocial, and they're essential for monitoring performers while overdubbing. Don't skimp on headphones; even a really good pair will cost significantly less than a decent pair of nearfield monitor speakers.

# open phones

Open or semi-enclosed hi-fi headphones usually sound more natural than enclosed phones, but they tend to be "bass light" in comparison. However, they are more comfortable for long periods of use, and you can still hear what's going on outside if you need to speak to somebody. High-quality headphones are particularly useful for working on MIDI compositions at times when monitoring over loudspeakers would be antisocial, and they're also good for scrutinising mixes and making sure nothing's been overlooked.

# enclosed phones

When overdubbing, it's better to use enclosed headphones because they don't allow much sound to leak in or out. Some of the better enclosed headphones are accurate enough for checking mixes, so if your budget only stretches to one pair of phones then a good enclosed pair might be the best option. However, try as many pairs as you can and check how the sound compares with what you hear over loudspeakers.

## chapter 4

# audio and sequencing

Audio data can be recorded into a computer-based sequencer via a suitable soundcard or external audio interface, where it is stored on a hard drive as digital data. Audio may also be imported directly from other disks containing audio data, including (with appropriate extraction software) audio CDs. Given that a lot of sampled drum loops are available in audio CD format, this latter consideration can be important.

As explained earlier, although you can sometimes get away with using the same hard drive for audio and for all your other programs and data, it's not a good idea if you want to be able to play back more than a handful of audio tracks at the same time. Internal drives tend to be EIDE models (sometimes known as Ultra DMA), and, although they're fast enough to handle between ten and 20 tracks of audio material under optimum conditions, this figure is likely to be compromised if the disk becomes fragmented, which will happen if the same disk is used for all computing tasks.

A better option is to use a separate SCSI drive, for which you'll need to install a separate SCSI PCI interface card (unless you're using a beige Power PC Macintosh or G3, which have SCSI interfaces built into them). However, FireWire drives may have become more popular and less expensive by the time you read this book, in which case these should be used instead, provided that they are compatible with your sequencing software. Check with your sequencer's technical support line or their web site if you're in any doubt.

A quick SCSI drive can normally provide over 32 tracks of audio, which should be enough for most users. The track count will fall slightly if 24-bit audio is being used rather than 16 bit, and this figure will be halved again if you work at a sampling rate of 96kHz rather than at 44.1kHz or 48kHz. If your final product is to be an audio CD then I'd suggest that you record either at 16 bit/44.1kHz, for pop music that has a limited dynamic range, or at 24 bit/44.1kHz, for acoustic music or for other forms of music that may require a wide dynamic range. Even though the final CD will still only use 16 bits, you can maintain the highest audio quality if you record, mix and master at 24 bits and then use a noise-shaped dithering system to reduce the final stereo file to 16 bits. This subject will be covered in more detail in the section on mastering.

# recording levels

With all digital recording systems it's best to optimise input signal levels at source because soundcards don't usually have an analogue gain control between the input and the analogue-to-digital converter. Some systems provide digital gain controls after conversion, but if your input is at a level that's too low then resolution is still lost even before the signal reaches the gain control, because the peak signal level isn't using up all of the available bits. Using software gain control can bring the level back up to normal, but any noise and distortion caused by recording too few bits will also be increased by the same amount.

For the lowest distortion and best signal-to-noise ratio, the best approach is to use the level metering provided in your software and to try and keep peak levels just a few decibels below the point at which clipping occurs. Use an external analogue mixer or pre-amp to get the signal at the right level before converting it. Regardless of whether you have 16-, 20- or 24-bit recording capability, the ultimate quality of your recording will be determined at source, and in most cases the dynamic range of a 16-bit system will exceed the dynamic range of the analogue signal being recorded.

For the recording of vocals, you should consider buying a voice channel/pre-amp type of device that combines a good mic amp with EQ and compression. The compressor is useful for preventing peak signals from overloading the analogue-to-digital converter. The same voice channel will be useful when miking acoustic instruments, and some models also feature an instrument DI input, which is suitable for use with bass and clean electric or electro-acoustic guitar. Alternatively, you could use the mic pre-amp of a mixer that you know is suitable for recording.

# random access

On a computer – unlike on a tape machine – you don't use up valuable recording space on a track during those sections that you wish to leave silent. For example, the vocal track will probably be silent during an instrumental solo, and if recorded on a tape machine, that unused section of the vocal track would be so much wasted space. With a computer-based recording system, however, any unfilled disk space can be used for any audio track. Furthermore, if you decide to use some material twice, such as a section of backing vocals, you can make a copy of this section in the Arrange page of your sequencer and paste it to the desired location, which in effect uses the same section of audio twice. If you tried to do the same thing on tape, you'd have to record the part twice and use up twice as much recording space. However, you should be aware that, if you copy sections of audio and then perform a destructive edit on the original material, this edit will affect every instance in which that section is used. In this situation, you should make a duplicate copy of the file that you with to process.

# the virtual mixer

All MIDI/audio sequencers are equipped with a mixer section, which is more or less a representation of the hardware mixer that would be required to do the same job, and if your experience of hardware mixers is limited to simple "something-into-two" models, the virtual mixer can sometimes seem quite daunting. This section deals with the role of the virtual mixer, with particular emphasis on configuring plug-in effects and processors.

Most MIDI/audio sequencers are capable of recording more tracks than the maximum for which hardware mixers can provide physical outputs (many basic soundcards have only stereo outputs). This means that it's necessary to have some way of mixing the tracks inside the computer, which is why MIDI/audio sequencers come with a virtual mixer section. At its simplest, the mixer will combine the audio outputs from the different tracks and mix them down to a stereo pair, although, if the hardware has multiple outputs, some means of routing channels or submixes of these channels to the various outputs will also be included.

As with a hardware mixer, the user has control over level and pan. However, you'll find that most virtual mixers don't provide EQ on every channel as a matter of course. This is because EQ uses up a lot of processing power, so it makes sense to use EQ only when it's needed. Each sequencer does this slightly differently, but you should know what to look for if you read the manual. If more comprehensive EQ is required for a particular task, it may be possible to use an EQ plug-in instead of – or in addition to – the basic channel EQ. Another important difference between a virtual mixer and a hardware mixer is that some virtual mixers allow you to get rid of any channels that aren't currently being used in order to make better use of the available screen space.

Usually, sequencers with virtual mixers also either support third-party plug-in effects (such as VST, or some other format), or they may come with effects built in. Many of the better models do both, and it's pretty standard for them to be able to perform some level of mix automation as well. What's more, since people have started to talk about surround sound with a little more conviction, its becoming increasingly commonplace for software manufacturers to build in facilities to allow the user to produce this, although to be quite honest few project studios have adequate monitoring set-ups to handle surround mixing effectively.

# monitoring and latency

When you first make a recording, you'll probably be singing or playing along to some MIDI parts you've recorded previously. When you monitor what you're recording, you may notice a slight delay in your headphones, although if you have a fast computer and an audio interface that works with ASIO II drivers, or some equally sophisticated driver, this latency may well be too low to notice. The causes of latency are covered in the section 'This Latency Business' in chapter three.

The only really serious problem is the monitoring delay that occurs when you record or play virtual instruments, because if this is more than around 10ms it can seriously throw off your timing. Using modern software, a fast computer and well-written drivers will minimise latency to a point at which it become negligible, but if you can't get it down to a manageable figure with your own system then there is still a workaround that should help. Try monitoring the input signal, rather than the soundcard output for the track being recorded, with a little simple repatching. To do this, you'll need to use an external mixer, where the source of the audio being recorded (the output from a voice channel, for example) is fed directly into the mix to which you're listening (in effect, your monitor mix). It's normally possible to turn off monitoring while recording in the sequencer's Audio Preferences, which avoids the situation in which you hear both your direct monitor source and the delayed version through the computer at the same time.

This simple set-up will allow you to monitor the audio that's being recorded into the computer at the same time as the existing audio and MIDI instruments are played back from the computer. The only drawback of monitoring in this way is that you won't be able to hear any computer-generated effects while you're recording, such as VST plug-ins, even though you can use them when you play the audio back. A full explanation of how to set up a zero-latency monitoring system can be found in chapter three.

Soundcards and interfaces that are fully compatible with the ASIO II driver standard can automatically provide thru monitoring of the input by routing the audio that is being recorded directly to the audio out of the soundcard during recording or overdubbing. This means that, while you can't apply any VST effects to the monitor signal while the new track is being recorded, you can still add them later. In other words, you'll only lose the ability to hear VST effects on the track as you're recording it, because you're actually monitoring the input signal before it reaches the CPU, where the effects are generated.

# mixer layout

In a conventional studio, the balance of the audio tracks already recorded is set by using a mixer, and it's the same in a desktop computer system. The main difference is that virtual mixers tend to have "all-input" formats rather than separate input and monitor channels. You don't have to worry yourself here about split or in-line console formats; all of the channels are arranged side by side, in a row.

Most software designers try to make their virtual mixers look as much like conventional mixers as possible, right down to being able to drag level faders up or down using the mouse. Rotary controls can usually be adjusted by clicking on them with the mouse and then either moving the mouse left/right, up/down or around in circles – it all depends on which method the software designer chose to use. In most instances, a separate virtual mixer channel is used for each audio track on the sequencer, and this can be routed directly to the main stereo outputs or via a subgroup, just like on a real mixer.

# effects and processors

Before patching them into a mixing console, whether it's real or virtual, it's best to consider effects and processors as falling into two distinct categories, each of which must be handled differently. There are those devices that treat the whole signal and those that add a proportion of treated signal to the unprocessed signal in order to create their effect. Even though strictly speaking both types are processors of some kind, it's fairly common to use the term *processor* to describe those devices that treat the whole signal and *effect* for those which use a mixture of processed and unprocessed sound.

Examples of processors include gates, expanders, compressors, limiters, equalisers, enhancers and distortion devices, and all of these are characterised by having no mix control (with the exception of enhancers, on which the mix control determines the depth of the effect produced).

Meanwhile, examples of effects include reverberators, digital delay lines, chorus units, flangers, ADT units and pitch shifters. All of these usually have a mix facility, enabling the user to blend the processed and unprocessed sound within the unit. However, by setting the mix control so that only the effected signal is output, mixing can be (and generally is) performed within the mixing console. Most effects involve some kind of delay, even if it's a very short one, as in the case of chorus and flanging.

An effect may be used either in conjunction with the auxiliary send circuit (in which case mixing is performed by the mixer) or via an insert point (where the unit's own mix control is used). A processor, on the other hand, is normally used via an insert point. Any attempt to use it via the aux send system is likely to yield unpredictable and undesirable results. At best, the resulting sound will be diluted by the addition of the untreated portion of the signal, and at worst phase differences within the circuitry may completely spoil the tonality of the signal.

# using virtual effects

VST plug-ins are used inside the Virtual Audio Mixer section of a sequencer, and there are three main ways in which these plug-ins can be deployed. Each channel on a VST-compatible virtual mixer has one or more insert points into which an effect can be plugged. When more than one plug-in is loaded at the same time, the signal will flow through the topmost plug-in first. Normally, these plug-ins are chosen from a pull-down menu that will show all of the virtual effects and processors available. Placing an effect or a processor in a channel insert point means that everything fed through that channel will pass through the effect.

If the same effect is needed elsewhere, you can open another copy of the same plug-in and place it in the insert point of a different channel. However, it's important to understand that, even though you may be using the same plug-in, if you use it in two different places it will take twice the processing power. This drain on computing power is the only serious limitation you'll encounter because, once a VST plug-in or similar virtual effect has been installed, you can use it in as many insert points as you like, with different settings for each usage. You should note, though, that, for those effects used in insert points, the effect level is set using the mix control on the plug-in's own control panel rather than by any of the mixer controls.

A more economical way of using a plug-in is to place it in the insert point of a group or buss channel (terminology varies a little between sequencers) and then route any channels that need processing to that group or buss. In conventional mixing terms, this equates to creating a subgroup, which may usually be either mono or stereo. The output of the group or buss is then routed to the stereo mix, as shown in Figure 4.1. This means that, although you only have to use the effect once (and if you're processing a stereo submix this will have to be a stereo version), everything fed via that group will also be treated with the same type and level of that effect. This method can be useful for parts such as backing vocals, where every voice must have the same reverb or delay treatment.

The third method is to use aux sends, just as you would on a hardware console. While you can use either effects or processors in insert points,

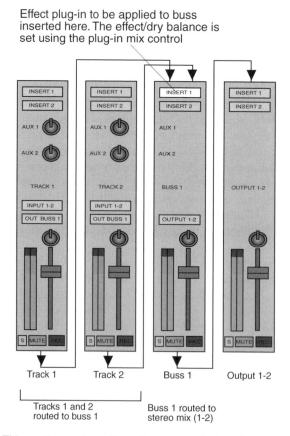

Figure 4.1: VST effect in group insert point

Aux sends are only suitable for use with delay-based effects, such as reverb, delay or chorus/flanging, rather than with processes, such as EQ, compression or gating. In most cases, the aux sends would be used to add a different amount of the same effect – such as reverb – to the tracks in a mix. The way in which aux sends are handled varies a little depending on which sequencer software you're using, but both Logic Audio and Cubase VST work in essentially the same way, despite some differences in terminology. (With Logic Audio, the effect is used in a buss insert point, whereas in Cubase there's a virtual effects rack.)

With Logic Audio, all of the aux sends are routed to a buss, although if necessary it is still possible to have a number of sends for each channel and you can feed these to multiple busses when you're in a situation where you want to combine several effects. For example, all of the aux send As would feed one buss, all of the aux send 2s another buss, and so on. One or more plug-ins are opened in the buss insert points, and the buss "object" output is then routed back into the main stereo mix (or to any other available buss if required). In traditional mixer parlance, the buss insert is comparable to the effects send/return points in a hardware mixer, with the buss controls replacing the aux return level and the routing functions.

In Cubase VST, the aux sends feed the virtual effects rack, which can contain up to eight plug-ins. The output from the effects rack may then be routed back to the stereo mix, but there's currently no way of placing the effects in series. The individual aux send controls on each channel will then set the effects level for that channel. Other packages may offer a slightly different approach, but the most important thing is to know that this mode of operation exists in the first place, so that you can look it up in the program manual. Note that, when you're using aux sends in this way, the mix control on the plug-in should be set to maximum so that it produces a signal that's all effect, 0% dry. This will enable the channel aux controls to regulate the overall amount of effect that is added to each channel. Figure 4.2 shows the aux routing for Logic Audio.

# mix automation

Another key feature of virtual mixers is that it's possible to automate their controls so that parameters like EQ, pan and mix level will change during the course of a mix without the engineer needing a perfect memory or needing to grow several extra pairs of hands. Indeed, mix automation is pretty much essential on a computer sequencer because, if you're using a mouse, there's no way in which to adjust more than one control at

Aux send 1 controls routed to buss 1 (or Effects Rack in Cubase). These controls may be used to adjust the amount of effect added to each track

Effect to be applied to aux send 1 inserted here. Effect set for 100% mix

Dry signals from channels are combined with the effect output at the main output

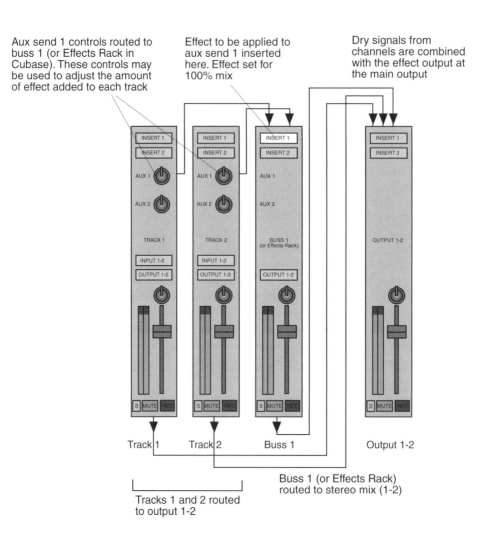

Track 1    Track 2    Buss 1    Output 1-2

Tracks 1 and 2 routed to output 1-2

Buss 1 (or Effects Rack) routed to stereo mix (1-2)

This system is effectively the same as in a traditional console when the post-fade aux (effect) sends are being used in conjunction with the effects send/return loop

Figure 4.2: Using a plug-in with an aux send.

once. If you want to use hardware knobs or faders to control the channel levels on the mixer, and so on, there are numerous hardware boxes on the market that can do this via MIDI, but most users seem to get by with using nothing more than the mouse and the keyboard. If you do choose to use a hardware controller, all that you need to do is set up the MIDI control messages sent by the device to match those that are expected by your sequencer.

Mix automation can usually be used in two ways: snapshot or dynamic. Snapshot automation allows you to save the current state of the mixer as a snapshot, which may be saved and referred back to later. In this way you can create snapshots for every section of a song and then have the automation system call up the desired snapshots as the song plays back. Snapshots are static, and so can contain no moves used by dynamic automation, such as fades.

Dynamic automation, on the other hand, provides you with the ability to record all fader and rotary control moves so that fades and gradual changes in level can be recreated on playback. Dynamic automation can usually be applied to settings of level, pan, EQ, aux sends and even effects.

If you haven't used mix automation before, you may be wondering how it works. The knobs or faders on your virtual mixer generate MIDI data when they are moved, and when you're recording automation moves (which is done in Write mode) this data is stored by the sequencer in much the same way as it would store any other MIDI data. You can put one or more tracks into Write mode and then just move the controls around when needed. This process can be repeated as many times as you like, until all of the necessary automation has been added to all of the tracks that need it. As with other MIDI information, you can also edit mix data after the event.

It's unlikely that you'll get the mix right the first time, so there's always an option that will allow you to rewrite sections of a mix. There may also be an Update or Trim mode available, similar to that on an automated hardware console, with which new fader movements combine with earlier fader movements rather than replacing them. This is very useful when your original automation pass is nominally OK but just needs lifting or dropping in level in some places.

Software mixers also usually have graphic displays of the automation data, comprising a series of points joined by straight lines. The points indicate the locations at which controls were moved, but you can also edit the mix automation in this graphic mode by adding new points (usually by clicking on the line where you want to create a new point) or by dragging existing points to new positions. In many instances, this is a more precise way of fine-tuning automation moves, and I know some users who do all of their mixing in the graphic editor without ever touching the virtual faders, other than in order to establish an initial level. Similar graphics are used to display other control information, such as pan position.

The degree to which your mix can be automated depends on the software you're using, but most provide automation of level and pan at the very least. More advanced packages allow you to automate just about every knob and switch available to you. Most VST plug-ins can also be automated in a similar way to any other mixer parameter, so if you want the reverb decay time to change between verse and chorus it's a simple matter to arrange it.

You should note that some sequencing software (specifically Logic Audio) comes with its own built-in effects that are accessed in exactly the same way as VST plug-ins are, but these aren't necessarily compatible with VST. These can be used within the program just like conventional VST plug-ins, but they can't be shared with other audio software.

# waveform editing

Being able to record multitrack audio directly onto a computer is wonderful in itself, but some of the editing features that sequencers provide will allow you to do things that would never have been possible if you were recording onto tape. All of the major MIDI/audio sequencers have a Waveform Edit page (although it isn't always called that), on which it's possible to view sections of audio material as a waveform and perform various operations on this. The most basic feature – but also one of the most useful – is the ability to select and silence sections of audio. This is perfect for removing short-duration noise that occurs before or after the sounds you want to keep, and it's quite easy because you can actually see them onscreen.

If background noise is a problem, you can often improve matters by manually silencing all of the gaps between words and phrases. This doesn't take as long as you might think, and can really improve the quality of a recording, especially where there are multiple audio tracks. A noise gate plug-in might enable you to do the same thing, but if the job is done manually it's often more accurate.

Waveform editing is particularly useful for silencing unwanted finger noise between notes in guitar tracks. You may often end up with a take that's almost perfect but with perhaps too much squeak or finger noise between notes, or maybe you caught the next string just after bending a note. You can use the Silence function to surgically remove these little errors, although you may end up with a more natural sound if you leave squeaks intact and instead reduce them in level by between 6dB and 20dB. You can also silence page turns, coughs and other noises on vocal parts, and you can do some very creative things, such as adding fade-ins to guitar parts in order to simulate the action of a swell pedal. Figure 4.3 shows a typical sequencer Waveform Edit page.

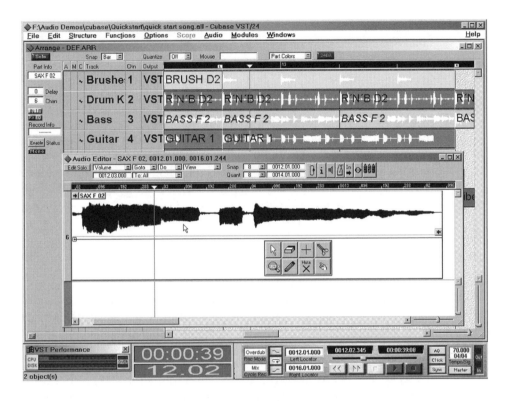

Figure 4.3: Waveform Edit page in Cubase (above) and Logic Audio (below)

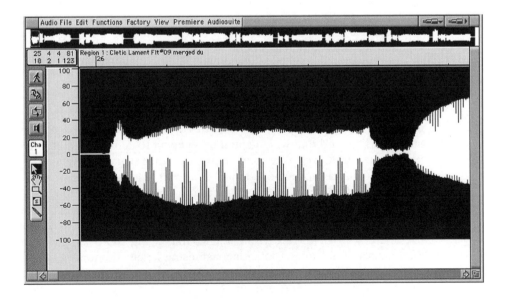

Other common functions available on Waveform Edit pages include the ability to change gain and even to reverse whole sections of audio for that genuine "backwards tape" sound.

To give you the greatest possible flexibility when it comes to adding effects in a mix, try to record all of the parts dry. In particular, don't add reverb or delay at source unless you really have to. If you need to hear reverb in order to create a good performance, add it at the monitoring stage but don't record it. In this way you'll be able to edit tracks without cutting holes in the echo or delay effects that you've added. Furthermore, if there are any edits that are a bit close for comfort, adding the necessary delay or echo afterwards will help to disguise the edit points, making the recording sound more natural.

# computer power

As with any other software, plug-ins always take up a certain amount of the available computing power, so if you want to add the same delay or reverb-based effects to several tracks it's most efficient to use a single plug-in configured as an aux send processor rather than using a separate insert plug-in on every track.

Don't try to force your software to do everything for you just because it can. Very often you'll find that you can get a better sound with discrete outboard devices, and of course these won't burden your CPU at all. Even if you don't have a multi-output soundcard, you can still compress signals as you record them, ideally by using a voice-channel-type device as described earlier. The same applies to EQ; only the best digital EQs sound as natural as good analogue equalisers.

# time and pitch manipulation

There are lots of tricks that you can pull by using the audio manipulation facilities provided by your sequencer or by plug-ins, and many of these will extend beyond that which you might expect to achieve with a simple multi-effects unit. For example, there are some very powerful filters available that can process sounds in order to make them appear synthetic, and there are devices that can distort sound in interesting ways. Built-in facilities vary from one software package to another, but pitch changing and time stretching facilities are supported by most machines, facilities that are invaluable for massaging audio sample loops. You may also find other tools for maximising levels, de-noising, and so on. Some of the more processor-intensive processes work offline, so you can use them even on a slower machine.

# pitch to MIDI

Pitch-to-MIDI conversion is also fairly common, and allows a monophonic recording of an instrument to be analysed in order to produce a MIDI track that mirrors the note and pitch-bend information of the original audio recording. This is useful when it's necessary to have a MIDI instrument playing along in unison with a real instrument that's just been recorded. Some software even offers the quantisation of audio tracks, enabling the timing of things like drum parts and guitar riffs to be tightened up. In my experience, this can work well as long as you don't process sections that are too long at once, and as long as the original audio material isn't too complex. You'll need to experiment to see what will work and what won't.

# audio timing

Most people can get by with the level of resolution used by MIDI, but audio material that refuses to stay in time with the MIDI tracks is extremely frustrating. There are several reasons why this can happen. Again, latency is something that many users have to accept when monitoring while recording, but if it becomes too bad it can be ameliorated by monitoring the input signal via a hardware mixer, as described in chapter three. However, once audio has been recorded onto the computer's hard drive, playback timing can still wander to an unacceptable degree if your computer is short of RAM (ie slower than at least twice what the manufacturers claim as a minimum specification), or if the software drivers aren't up to date. This latter consideration is important, as a poorly-written driver may allow the playback latency to vary, and this will have the effect of causing the audio timing to drift. You may also need to have a look at the pages listing driver settings, adjusting the amount of RAM buffering and playback delay settings to coax your system into behaving properly. As pointed out earlier, many manufacturers of soundcards provide the recommended settings of their equipment so that they work with the more common software packages. Because of the frequency with which software is updated, internet access becomes increasingly important.

# audio in arrangements

Unless you're editing waveforms surgically, or performing off-line time stretching, you'll probably spend most of your time on the Arrange page of your sequencer. Here you can can split audio sequences, copy and move parts and so on, and you might find a few more useful functions, depending on your sequencing software, such as the ability to set up a crossfade between adjoining audio regions. Long crossfades are usually employed for artistic reasons, but shorter crossfades can be used to prevent clicks or glitches from occurring at the point at which two sections of audio data are joined. A crossfade of between 20ms and 50ms is generally adequate for this purpose.

When an audio or MIDI part is dragged to a new location in the Arrange window, it will probably snap to the nearest beat rather than land exactly where you want to put it, so it's important to familiarise yourself with the key commands that allow you to drag MIDI and audio sections around in such a way that they snap to finer increments (such as the currently-selected quantise value) and the ones that allow them to be moved completely freely.

# managing audio files

Unless you're very careful, you can end up with a hard drive full of audio files that are identifiable only by their numbers, so it's best to study your software manual and determine the best way of bringing some order to this potential chaos. One way is to create a new folder on your audio drive for each new project and name this so that it relates to the song on which you're working, then set up the Audio Record Path so that all of your audio files are recorded into this folder. Even so, you'll probably find that, unless you get everything right the first time, you'll end up with many more files than you actually need. Some programs have a function that allows you to erase audio files that aren't being used in the song that's currently open, but I have an instinctive distrust of anything so final!

As a user of Logic Audio, I have the ability to add colour to MIDI and audio sequences in the Arrange page. These colours then also appear in the page that lets me see all of the audio files associated with the project. This provides a useful way of double checking things because all of my wanted files contain some coloured regions, whereas any unused files show up completely grey (the default colour). If the program says that a file isn't needed, and it's grey, then I feel fairly safe in discarding it, as long as it isn't needed in another song or another version of the song. Clearly not all software works exactly like this, but there's usually a similar strategy that can be applied. In any event, storing files related to particular songs in separate folders seems to help to keep things organised, and if you have the patience to rename them so that they also relate to their audio content then so much the better.

# VST instruments

In order to play a VST instrument from a keyboard, the audio part of your system will need to have a very low latency or you'll hear the lag between playing and hearing the sound. High latency makes normal playing impossible, especially with sounds that have a fast attack, such as pianos. One (not entirely satisfactory) way around this problem is to record the part over a regular synth or soundcard, so that no latency arises, and then switch the track to the VST instrument after it's been recorded. However, you should note that the computing power that a VST instrument needs tends to relate to the number of notes or voices being played at once, so the more voices you use, the fewer VST plug-ins you can run at the same time. Most software will let you record a finished virtual instrument track as audio, which conserves CPU power.

# recording with microphones

Choosing appropriate microphones is fundamental to any recording project, regardless of whether you're recording onto tape or onto a computer. As a rule, dynamic mics are good for miking drums and electric instruments, whereas capacitor mics are better for high-quality vocal and acoustic instrumental work. Large-diaphragm capacitor mics tend to be more flattering than small-diaphragm models, especially on vocals, although there are some exceptions. Now that it's possible to buy a good capacitor mic for less than a quarter of the cost of a typical computer, there's little excuse for compromising your work by using something cheap and unsuitable. If by using a cheap mic you end up with a bad sound, there's not much that you can do about it. There are various programs available that purport to be able to remodel recordings, so that they sound as though they were made with a different mic, but in reality these systems work much better when you start out with a good mic and then try to change the sound to that of a cheaper model rather than vice versa.

# the proximity effect

All cardioid-pattern mics exhibit a proximity effect, producing more bass when used very close to the sound source, thanks to a side-effect of the pressure-gradient principle on which they operate. Most fixed-pattern mics used in project studios use a cardioid pattern, as this helps reject unwanted sound coming from behind the mic. A good vocalist can use the proximity effect to his or her advantage, using it as a kind of real-time tone control, but inexperienced singers may find it a problem. Singing at six inches or more from the microphone should be enough to avoid these problems.

Another reason not to work too close to a vocal mic is that any variation in distance, caused by the singer moving about, will affect the signal level as well as the proximity bass boost. On the other hand, moving too far away will result in a greater proportion of the room reverb being recorded, often resulting in a boxy sound. (A distance of six to twelve inches is generally fine for solo vocal recording.) If you're recording at home in an untreated room, hanging up sleeping bags or blankets on either side of and behind the singer will help to create a more neutral recording environment, absorbing unwanted reflections.

It's unwise to record vocals without using a pop shield between the mic and the vocalist, thus preventing bumping noises on B and P sounds. A nylon stocking stretched over a wire hoop or wooden ring is cheaper than a commercial model, and works just as well. Place the shield halfway between the singer's mouth and mic and your popping problems should disappear without the sound of the mic being compromised. External foam pop shields are notoriously ineffective at preventing popping.

A surprising amount of low-frequency vibration reaches the mic if a hanging cable is accidentally knocked or kicked, so take care to secure loose cables. Taping or clipping the cable to the mic stand will help, but leave a loop of cable at the mic end to allow for further adjustment. This loop will also absorb some of the remaining vibrational energy travelling along the cable. The low cut filter on the mic or mixer may help to reduce very low-frequency vibrations, but always try to produce as clean a signal as possible at source before switching these in. Also, you should be aware that the low cut filters on some mics work at quite a high frequency, and if you're working several inches from the mic then the resulting sound may be too thin.

# capacitor care

It's not a good idea to either plug in or remove capacitor mics while the phantom power is switched on because some older, less robust models could be damaged. Some of the components in a mic amp can also be damaged by this action, and even though they may not fail immediately they can become noisier over time. After switching off the phantom power, it's best to wait for around 30 seconds before unplugging the mic so that the phantom power supply can discharge.

Balanced dynamic mics can be plugged into a phantom powered mic input with no problem, but unbalanced mics won't work properly when phantom power is applied and they could be damaged. As a general rule, avoid applying phantom power to any input that doesn't need it.

Capacitor mics are delicate pieces of precision engineering, so avoid dropping them or using them in excessively humid environments. If condensation occurs within the mic, the sound quality and sensitivity will suffer. If this happens, placing the mic in a warm place for a while should restore it to normal operation. A pop shield will help to prevent condensation from the singer's breath, causing problems.

# using microphones

The mic placements shown in textbooks can only ever be approximate, so a little experimentation often pays off in obtaining a better sound. One way to find the best mic position is to wear fully-enclosed headphones so that you can hear the output from the mic as you move it. As the performer plays the material, you can then choose the best mic position by ear.

Few instruments, if any, produce all of their sound from one point, which means that, if you place the mic too close to the source, you'll capture only one element of the sound. Rock music is exempted from this rule, as electric guitar cabinets are often miked very close, but in that case the aim is to obtain an impressive sound, not necessarily a natural one.

When working with instruments such as acoustic guitars that have soundholes, try not to aim the mic directly at the hole itself; it may produce a large and apparently healthy signal, but it's also likely to sound too boomy or boxy. Pull back the mic and move it to the side of the soundhole until what you hear in the headphones seems even and natural.

For recording sound sources that are less well documented, I've devised a simple (if approximate) rule that should enable you to obtain natural-sounding results. You should first estimate the length of the section of the instrument that produces the sound and then use that as an initial distance at which to position the mic. For example, most of the sound from an acoustic guitar comes from the body, so the mic distance should be at least same distance away as the length of the body. Similarly, a mic recording a piano should be around a piano's width away. The same theory also applies to wind instruments. In this case, don't put the mic too close to the noisy end; if you position it a little farther back, this will allow all parts of the instrument to contribute to the overall sound. You can then use your headphones to fine-tune the mic position.

## EQ and microphones

Before adding EQ, try moving the mic or changing to a different type altogether. Even the best EQ units won't compensate for a poorly-chosen or -positioned mic. Unless you're close miking, you should also keep in mind that the room acoustic will have a significant influence on the sound reaching the mic, and so improvise screens if necessary, using blankets. Also, avoid working with mics located too close to walls or corners.

# mic patterns

Cardioid-pattern mics pick up less off-axis spill than omni-directional mics (those that pick up sound equally from all directions), but off-axis sounds may appear slightly nasal or coloured. In some situations, using an omni mic and accepting a little more spill will produce a noticeably more natural result, especially if room reflections are contributing to the sound in a constructive way. Even with on-axis sounds, omni mics tend to produce a more open, natural result, because they don't use the same acoustic labyrinth design employed by cardioids, which they need in order to achieve the desired polar pattern. Even so, most pop studio work is recorded with cardioid mics. However, don't be afraid of using an omni just because you think you'll pick up lots of unwanted sounds. In practice, the difference between the spill picked up by an omni and a cardioid mic is fairly small.

# cables and connections

It's important to buy good-quality mic cables, ideally those with gold-plated connector pins, and these must be cleaned from time to time – using Deoxit or a similar non-greasy contact cleaner – in order to avoid pops and crackles. Mic signals are very small when compared with line signals, which means that the effect of noisy connectors can be very noticeable. Most connector problems are due to a film of oxide or dirt building up on the pins, resulting in a higher-than-usual contact resistance, which varies whenever the connector is moved.

Some mic cable is itself microphonic because of the way in which the spacing between the conductors changes when the cable is bent or subjected to vibration. In extreme cases, this results in an audible crackling or crunching noise whenever the cable is moved or bent. Good-quality cable designed specifically for use with microphones should be quiet, so if you experience this problem you should use the cable for something less demanding and buy yourself a new mic lead.

# miking electric guitars

Although there are now many guitar pre-amps that sound perfectly good when DI'd, there are still occasions when an amp sounds best. To mic up an amp, place a cardioid mic (generally a dynamic model) close to the speaker grille and point it directly into the speaker. It's very tempting to hang the mic from the cabinet handle, so that it dangles in front of the speaker, but this means that the most sensitive part of the mic will be pointing at the floor rather than at the amp. Of course, you can dangle an omni mic in this way because they pick up sounds from all directions.

# background noise

When recording quieter instruments, try to be aware of what other sounds the mic will be picking up in addition to the music. For example, I've heard quartz watches ticking away on acoustic guitar tracks, and you should also listen out for wall clocks, central heating systems, computer drives and fans, and other external noises. The best way of checking is to use enclosed headphones. Background sounds are largely hidden in some types of music, in which case you needn't be too obsessive, but exposed solo instruments need to be recorded very carefully.

Where a number of mics are being used to record separate sound sources, it's important to minimise crosstalk into them or the overall sound may be compromised and you'll have less control over the individual instruments when it comes to mixing. The general rule to is to try to space mics at least five times further apart than the distance between the mic and the instrument. (This 5:1 rule doesn't apply to stereo-miking set-ups because the intention there is for both mics to pick up the same sound, albeit from a slightly different perspective.)

Drum miking is covered in some depth in my earlier book *Creative Recording II* (also published by Sanctuary), but essentially the secret is to make sure that the drums sound good before you start recording. General-purpose dynamic mics are OK for snare and toms, but you should use capacitor mics for overheads and choose a mic for the kick drum that is specifically designed for the purpose. (Most vocal or instrument mics roll off the low bass that you need to capture intact.)

Snare and tom mics may be placed around two inches from the head and two or three inches in from the edge of the drum, while the kick-drum mic is usually positioned inside the shell, at around six inches from the point at which the beater impacts with the head. This requires a hole to be cut in the front head (which most drummers do anyway), and damping can be achieved by placing a folded blanket in the bottom of the drum. Remember to observe the 5:1 rule wherever possible when setting up the mics in order to minimise spill between the drums. If you're using cardioid mics, these may also be angled away from each other to further reduce spill. A stereo pair of overhead mics should be positioned at least three feet above the cymbals, spaced apart by roughly the width of the drum kit.

# warmth

You'll hear recording engineers talking a lot about equipment or mics that sound "warm". This is a difficult description to pin down, but in general it means that something sounds solid and transparent at the low end without being harsh at the high end. Warm vocal mics also have a tendency to flatter the chest resonances of the voice to some extent, which makes the performer sound larger than life.

As a very general rule, large-diaphragm capacitor mics (with a capsule diameter of three quarters of an inch or greater) tend to produce a warmer, more flattering sound than the more clinical small-diaphragm models, although this is at the expense of a less-accurate off-axis response. Well-designed valve mics also tend to have a warm character that doesn't sound unlike mild compression. Even so, you don't have to buy a valve mic in order to obtain a warm sound; a valve pre-amp or some other valve processor used in the signal chain may create the same effect, as may using some compression. The converters used in some soundcards and interfaces – while producing perfectly good technical specs on paper – can sound a little cold or thin, and so if you use a mic/line pre-amp or voice channel that includes some valve circuitry, you should be able to help balance this. Photo-electric compressors (ie those that use a lamp and photo-resistor to control the signal gain) can also sound very flattering on vocals.

In reality, any respectable mic will provide you with a good vocal sound, if used properly, so if you're having serious problems it's unlikely that a better mic will bring about the improvements you're after. Always suspect the room acoustics first if you're getting a boxy sound, and remember to keep the mic away from those noisy computer drives and fans.

## chapter 5

# choosing your system

Basic MIDI sequencing systems don't place too many demands on the host computer, but life gets more complicated when you want to add audio. Not only do you have to budget for a faster computer but you also have to make decisions concerning the audio interface or soundcard that you'll be using. For example, should it be 16 bit or 24 bit? Do you need multiple ins and outs, or will stereo suffice? Do you need digital I/O? And, if you're working with digital consoles or ADAT recorders, do you need an interface with ADAT compatibility? There may also be other technicalities to consider, so it may be helpful to refer back to chapter three if you're unsure of any of the terms that you come across.

Systems that are based around a simple interface leave the computer to do all of the hard work involved with audio routing, recording, playback and mixing. A more elaborate system may also include virtual (sometimes called native) effects and virtual instruments, also powered by the host computer. Although modern computers are fast and powerful, there comes a point at which they can't perform any more consecutive tasks. In practice, this limits the number of audio tracks you can record or play back simultaneously, and/or limits the number of virtual effects that you can use at once. If you're using virtual instruments, the general rule is that the more voices that are playing at once, the more processor power is used. As long as you're realistic with your expectations, a native system can function very effectively, but if you're looking for more power, there's another route that you can follow.

One way of lightening the load on your computer is to use audio hardware that includes its own DSPs (Digital Signal Processors) for handling things like digital effects and mixing. The most famous of these systems on the Mac is probably Digidesign's ProTools, while Soundscape offers similar functionality on the PC. At a lower level, the Yamaha SW1000XG card can provide up to twelve tracks of audio recording and mixing, with multi-effects and a very respectable GM/XG synth, without taxing the host processor, and Lexicon's Core II package – complete with a reverb expansion effects board – can also handle audio, mixing and effects. Other DSP-based systems are available from companies such as Creamware and Soundscape, but one point to bear in mind at an early stage is that few (if any) of the systems that use their own DSPs to power effects plug-ins allow you to use VST plug-ins. Instead, they tend to have their own proprietary format of plug-in which is designed to work with their specific DSP architecture.

On the plus side, the more serious DSP-assisted audio systems are generally free from latency problems (for all practical purposes, at least), and because they don't tax your host computer in the same way as native systems you don't have to keep on upgrading your computer whenever you find yourself needing more power. High-end systems such as Soundscape and ProTools also tend to be more stable than native systems. Latency is explained in some depth in chapter three.

# the Mac/PC debate

If you haven't yet decided on which computer system to use, you'll need to choose between buying either a Macintosh or a PC, as they're really the only two options worth considering for serious audio work. Even before making this choice, though, you'll need to decide which software you want to run. If you need to perform a specific task, for which only one piece of software is appropriate, and if that software runs on only one of the two major platforms, then your choice is already made for you. For example, if you just have to have Cakewalk then you're going to have to work on a PC. The other top sequencing packages – Logic Audio, Cubase VST, Digital Performer and StudioVision – are all available in both Mac and PC versions, but there may be other audio software to consider, such as an editing package.

Macs tend to be easier to set up and manage than PCs, and audio latency seems less of a problem, especially on G4s and above. Apart from some laptops, Macs also have basic 16-bit stereo audio ins and outs as part of the basic hardware configuration, whereas a PC requires a soundcard or some other kind of audio interface to achieve this.

The disadvantage with Macintoshes is that they are more expensive than their PC counterparts (although just comparing processor speeds doesn't tell you the whole story), and they have fewer expansion slots in which to add things like audio cards, SCSI interfaces, multiple monitors and so on. Most models have only three available slots, while the iMac and G4 cube don't have any at all.

Macintoshes are also less easy to upgrade than PCs. SCSI – which used to be fitted to all Macs – is no longer a standard attachment, and the serial ports (which were once used for connecting printers, MIDI interfaces and modems) have now been replaced by the USB (Universal Serial Buss) connector. Third-party adaptors are available which can provide old-style serial ports on new Macs, but unless you have a lot of legacy hardware to accommodate you're better off buying USB-compatible hardware and software with USB dongles where applicable. Most Mac users feel that the additional expenditure is worth it.

PCs are relatively cheap, they can be pulled apart and upgraded as necessary, and peripherals for them are usually cheaper than those for Macs. They usually have more free slots than Macs, and most new models are equipped with USB as well as with legacy PC connectors.

You'll need to buy a separate soundcard in order to transfer audio data into and out of the computer (although most come bundled with a basic audio/games card), and, because of the number of permutations of hardware devices that can be used to build the average PC, you may run into problems when handling audio. This is one reason why I strongly recommend that you buy a complete, ready-configured system, if you go the PC route.

## other considerations

Once you've decided on the computer platform with which to entrust your musical future, you'll need to think about the extra bits and pieces you'll need to make your choice of machine work in a musical context. For example, I've already explained that the EIDE drives used in standard Macs and PCs aren't really fast enough if you need to maximise the number of audio tracks that you can play back at once, so if you want the best possible performance you'll need to include a suitably quick SCSI card and external SCSI drive as part of the basic specification. However, a SCSI drive may cost you three times as much as an EIDE drive of equivalent size. Hard drives are now appearing on the market which connect up via the USB connector, but these are much slower than even the most basic implementation of SCSI and are therefore best suited to backing up data.

FireWire drives are also becoming more popular, now that all modern Apple computers are fitted with FireWire ports, and there's a good chance that FireWire will take over from SCSI in the near future.

## video cards

Macs come with a built-in video capability, whereas with PCs you get a choice of which video card to use. It's important to choose a card that is known to work well with audio systems, because some of the fastest cards break a few programming rules in order to achieve their speed. This usually doesn't affect games or word processors, but it can cause glitches in audio playback. If you're in any doubt, you should visit the web sites of the sequencer manufacturer for their recommendations.

Both Macs and PCs running Windows 98 or later can have a second video card fitted with which to drive a second monitor. This can be very useful when working with a sequencing package that's based around a large number of windows.

# computer speed

It usually pays to buy the fastest computer that you can afford, unless you've decided to stay a year or two behind everyone else and save money by buying a used machine (which isn't always a bad idea!). Don't be fooled by clock speeds alone, though, because a 400MHz G4 Macintosh can perform just as much work as a Pentium III PC running at around twice the clock speed. At the time of writing, buying anything from new that's slower than a Mac G4 400 or a Pentium 500 would probably be inadvisable for music applications, although a used G3 266MHz Mac or a Pentium III 300 MHz PC can still do an awful lot if you're working on a tighter budget. If you intend to use mainly hardware synths or soundcard synths, as opposed to the software equivalent, you won't necessarily need a computer quite this fast, but remember that, the slower your computer, the sooner it will be hopelessly out of date!

# audio and MIDI hardware

Your choice of MIDI and audio hardware depends mainly on the scale of what you're trying to achieve. For example, if you have three or four hardware synths, each of which is multitimbral, then a multiport MIDI interface is advisable. My own preference is to use a Mark Of The Unicorn or eMagic interface where possible, as the newer USB compatible models from both these manufacturers have very good MIDI timing and are supported by the main sequencer packages. Note that some MIDI interfaces have to be supported via Opcode's OMS (Open MIDI System) MIDI routing software when used with a Mac computer's USB ports. (OMS is normally provided with any piece of equipment that needs it.) eMagic's AMT series interfaces will work directly with either the PC or Mac versions of Logic Audio without the need for any further software.

# choosing the right digital I/O

In addition to stereo ins and outs, some soundcards also provide digital connections. With budget machines this may simply be an S/PDIF co-axial output, but with a little more money you should be able to buy a card that has an S/PDIF input as well. S/PDIF I/O is particularly useful if you're mastering directly from your soundcard to a DAT machine, or if you have an external digital mixer with an S/PDIF input. By the same token, an S/PDIF input will enable you to load in material from DAT, MiniDisc or CD-R for future editing, as long as your source machine has an S/PDIF output. Inexpensive converters are available for changing optical S/PDIF into co-axial S/PDIF and vice versa.

For more professional applications, or for use in systems that have external hardware with word clock facilities, it may be advisable to choose audio cards or interfaces that have word clock connectors fitted. By using word clock to sync the various elements of a system, it's usually possible to obtain lower levels of jitter, which in turn produces cleaner-sounding audio with better stereo imaging. Jitter occurs when the sample clock driving a converter varies or jitters in frequency rather than remaining perfectly stable.

# driving hard

The EIDE drives that are used in standard Macs and PCs are fast enough to allow you record between ten and 20 tracks of audio, but it's important to understand that they are controlled via the host processor, and so they have a tendency to slow down if there are a lot of edits involved in the piece or if the audio is fragmented. A SCSI drive is recommended for more serious work, and with the new Macs and all PCs this will mean having a SCSI interface card fitted. There are several incarnations of SCSI that have different speed capabilities, but if you're setting up a system specifically to perform audio work then you should use a separate UltraWide SCSI 2 drive with a spindle speed of at least 7,200rpm. This will ensure that you have an adequate number of tracks, even when the going gets tough, and because SCSI has its own sub-processor to handle data data transfer to and from the disk you won't waste any of the power of your host processor.

# RAM requirements

At one time, RAM (Read Only Memory) cost more than the computer into which it was plugged, but these days the prices have fallen drastically and are now a little more sensible. Most serious audio requirements require around 128Mb of RAM or upwards, and if you're thinking of using a software sampler that uses the host computer's RAM then the sky's the limit. As a rule of thumb, you should determine what the manufacturer of your sequencer software recommends as a sensible amount of RAM and then double this figure!

# bits and pieces

Most audio hardware now works at both 16- and 24-bit resolution, so you can choose which is best for your projects. However, some hardware is limited to a sampling rate of 48kHz, while others support rates of 96kHz. My own view is that 96kHz sample rates only provide an audible advantage in a world-class studio environment, and in any event working at this rate gobbles up processor power and disk space exactly twice as quickly as working at 48kHz.

Working at 24 bit/44.1kHz or 48kHz seems a sensible compromise when working with acoustic instruments, or with music that has wide dynamic range, while 16 bit/44.1kHz is perfectly adequate for most pop or dance music with a limited dynamic range.

# a basic system

The most basic audio system uses the stereo analogue ins and outs of a games-style soundcard, as shown in Figure 5.1. The sound quality depends on the specification of the card, and you don't have to spend a fortune to buy something that sounds respectable. The audio output will be mixed with the sound of any MIDI instruments, either virtual of generated by the soundcard, so if you don't have any external synths you can still get by without a mixer. Nevertheless, it's unlikely that you'd want to record via the mic input of a typical soundcard, as these are invariably rather basic, and the level control is usually handled by software after the input has been digitised. If your mic signal is too low, boosting it with a software gain control won't improve your signal-to-noise ratio.

A much better way of working is using a dedicated voice channel, a piece of outboard gear that combines a mic pre-amp with a compressor and maybe an equaliser as well. If you use a voice channel with one of the excellent low-cost capacitor mics that are currently available, you should have no problem with making clean recordings. The system shown in Figure 5.1 includes a voice channel and microphone, although most voice channels also provide line- and instrument-level inputs for recording other sources.

A system of this type is clearly restricted to recording no more than one or two tracks at a time, so it's best suited to the person who works with both MIDI and audio and who builds up the audio tracks one or two at a time. Because the output is in stereo, any mixing must take place within the computer, which means that effects must either be added during recording or created within the computer using plug-in effects (or

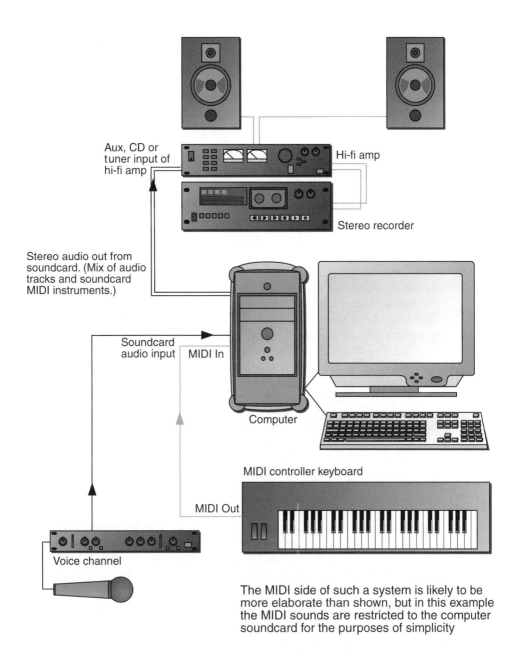

Aux, CD or tuner input of hi-fi amp

Hi-fi amp

Stereo recorder

Stereo audio out from soundcard. (Mix of audio tracks and soundcard MIDI instruments.)

Soundcard audio input

MIDI In

Computer

MIDI controller keyboard

MIDI Out

Voice channel

The MIDI side of such a system is likely to be more elaborate than shown, but in this example the MIDI sounds are restricted to the computer soundcard for the purposes of simplicity

Figure 5.1: A basic stereo soundcard system

hardware effects, if provided by the soundcard). If you add effects to the signal as it comes out of the soundcard, the same effect will be added to everything in the mix, which isn't usually desirable.

You should note that, if you're working without a mixer, you won't be able to combat latency by monitoring overdubs via the mixer rather than monitoring everything at the soundcard output (a technique which is described later). This shouldn't be a problem, as long as you use a low-latency soundcard and a fast computer, but the best solution is if both card and software support ASIO II drivers, because ASIO II provides the user with the option of thru monitoring, where the signal being overdubbed is sent directly to the soundcard output rather than being routed via the CPU. One drawback of this system is that you then won't have the opportunity to add native effects to the monitoring signal as you record, but at least you'll be able to hear your overdubs in time.

Computers are physically noisy, especially their fans and drives, and conventional monitors also generate a significant amount of electromagnetic radiation, which will interfere with guitar pickups if you get too close to them. Ideally, you should record in a separate room to your computer, but unless your system is particularly noisy you'll probably get away with working at the opposite end of the room. For more critical work, you should consider buying a sound-deadening cabinet for the computer, and if you do a lot of work with electric guitars you could either use humbucking pickups or budget for a flat-screen LCD monitor. Most audio/MIDI sequencers need a monitor of 17 inches or larger in order to allow you to make sense of the multiple windows that these programs usually flash up onto the screen, although a 15-inch flat-screen monitor will provide almost as much viewing area.

# upgrade paths

As long as you have a fast enough computer, you can upgrade by adding extra VST plug-ins to enhance your virtual mixing environment, and you could also load in some virtual instruments or samplers. All of this can be done without upgrading your audio I/O, provided that your computer is powerful enough to do everything that you want it to. You may also wish to add external hardware synths, in which case you'll also need a separate mixer.

# multiple out systems

You'll also need an external mixer if you wish to use a soundcard that has multiple analogue outputs, as illustrated in Figure 5.2. Note, however, that, although the example shows a soundcard-based system, the

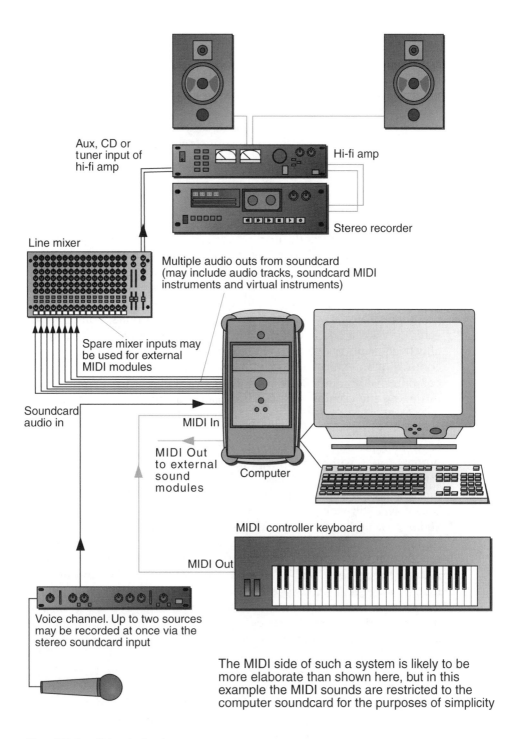

Aux, CD or tuner input of hi-fi amp

Hi-fi amp

Stereo recorder

Line mixer

Multiple audio outs from soundcard (may include audio tracks, soundcard MIDI instruments and virtual instruments)

Spare mixer inputs may be used for external MIDI modules

Soundcard audio in

MIDI In

MIDI Out to external sound modules

Computer

MIDI controller keyboard

MIDI Out

Voice channel. Up to two sources may be recorded at once via the stereo soundcard input

The MIDI side of such a system is likely to be more elaborate than shown here, but in this example the MIDI sounds are restricted to the computer soundcard for the purposes of simplicity

Figure 5.2: A multiple output system

diagram applies just as readily to a system that uses an external interface box. The same connection regime is also applicable to systems that have their own DSP-powered effects. You should also note that, although many musicians use external MIDI modules, such as synths, samplers and drum machines, these have been omitted in order to avoid overcomplicating the diagram. The chapter on MIDI illustrates how hardware MIDI instruments can be connected.

Although it's possible to do all of your mixing inside the computer, it's sometimes useful to be able to keep some of the signals separate, as this will allow you to use the hardware mixer EQ rather than the digital EQ within your software (presuming that the analogue EQ sounds better). More importantly, however, it also allows you to use external effects and other outboard processing. For example, good-quality native reverb plug-ins tend to be very power hungry, and yet you can buy a better-sounding dedicated hardware reverb unit for little more than the cost of a software plug-in, which won't use up any of your CPU power. Similarly, if you already own multi-effects units, compressors, gates or enhancers, it will provide you with a means of using these effectively. Many people also find it much easier to mix with the physical controls of an external mixer rather than making all adjustments on a computer, although the clear advantage of doing at least some of the mixing on the computer is that most software packages allow the mix levels and other parameters to be automated.

Most multiple-output soundcards offer no more than around eight outputs (often with two inputs, plus S/PDIF digital I/O), although some can be used in pairs to double up the I/O capability of the system. In practical terms, this means that, unless you limit your number of audio tracks, you still won't be able to allocate one physical output to each audio track, and so some internal mixing will still be required. This won't be a problem in most instances because most sounds fall into logical sub-groups that can be mixed and then treated together, and when sounds within a subgroup require different treatment you can still use your plug-ins. For example, a percussion submix that requires more reverb on one particular sound might be treated with one of the more basic, less power-hungry reverb plug-ins. A shorter but better-quality reverb could then be applied to the overall percussion mix.

You may also decide to allocate your main vocal and main lead instrument their own outputs in order to allow yourself complete freedom over their treatments. However, you'll find that things like backing vocals, pad keyboards and percussion can often be submixed without sacrificing any flexibility.

A system such as this one is still best suited to those who build up their compositions a track at a time but who also demand more flexibility when it comes to mixing their material. These users may already have a mixer and outboard effects which they wish to continue to use. If your requirements are more ambitious, however, and you need to record either multiple inputs at the same time or you want to integrate a digital mixer into the system, your choice of audio interface will be quite different.

# hardware assistance

Combined with the right software, a powerful desktop computer will do amazing things without requiring any external hardware other than a monitoring system, a MIDI keyboard and a mic pre-amp. However, even a fast computer has its limits. What can you do if you routinely need to perform more operations than your computer can cope with? Faced with this scenario, you have the option of either using specialised DSP-based computer expansion cards to take over some of the more labour-intensive functions, or you can start adding external hardware synths, samplers, effects boxes and mixers to your system rather than expect your computer to do everything. These alternatives were outlined back in chapter one, but now it's probably time to look at them in more detail.

If you choose to use DSP cards, you'll find that at the top end of the market there are some DSP-based systems available, such as ProTools, which handle all of the hard-disk recording, mixing and plug-in activity via their own DSPs, and there are also more affordable solutions on the market, such as the Yamaha SW1000XG and Lexicon's Core II, which combine hardware-mixing facilities, audio I/O and digital effects on a single card. The only thing that you need to watch out for is how well these will integrate into your existing system. For example, you need to find out if the hardware can be accessed via your existing sequencer package or whether it comes with its own support software, which may restrict you in some way. Most MIDI-compatible hardware can be controlled from a mixer map set up in your own sequencer package, but this isn't always as seamless as the manufacturers would have you believe. The most satisfactory system is one in which the hardware is supported directly by your sequencer software, as is the case with ProTools or Digi 001 hardware that is used from within Logic Audio or Cubase. An equally valid alternative is to use an external digital mixer, as these devices combine mixing, routing, dynamics processing and effects all in one box, complete with a hardware user interface and, more often than not, mix automation.

# digital mixers

A typical digital mixer provides the practical benefits of a physical user interface and also shares some of the workload normally undertaken by your computer's CPU. Most digital mixers provide on-board EQ, dynamics processing and effects, as well as routing and automated mixing (both dynamic and snapshot), and by removing this load from your computer you'll find that your system runs more smoothly, leaving you with plenty of power in reserve for those special plug-ins or software-driven virtual instruments that you may need to use later.

In order to take full advantage of a digital mixer, you'll also need a soundcard or interface with multiple outputs, and if you want to record several musicians playing at the same time you'll need multiple inputs too. Clearly, you wouldn't be taking full advantage of your digital console if you were to connect it to your soundcard entirely via analogue cables; a multichannel digital audio interface will preserve your signal quality and will also relieve you of the chore of matching your audio I/O levels with those of your mixer. The most common digital audio formats are currently ADAT and T/DIF, both of which carry eight channels of audio. Roland has its own system, R-BUS, which also handles eight channels of audio per connection, but at the time of writing R-BUS is only supported by Roland's own equipment.

ADAT uses a lightpipe to transfer information, while T/DIF uses multicore cable. If you need to transfer more than eight channels at once, you'll need an interface with more than one ADAT or T/DIF port, and similarly your mixer will need to be equipped with a suitable number of digital ins and outs, usually via an optional interface card. Mark Of The Unicorn's 2408 interface is popular in achieving this, as it provides up to 24 channels of digital I/O as well as eight analogue connections. Few project studio systems support more than 24 channels of digital I/O, in any case.

Although I said earlier that connecting a digital console via analogue cables isn't really the best way of getting signals from A to B, sometimes circumstances force you into working in this way. For example, the popular Yamaha 03D mixing console can only be expanded to eight channels of digital I/O (in addition to its stereo S/PDIF I/O), so if you need to mix 16 tracks you may end up with eight tracks fed in digitally and a further eight fed in via the analogue inputs. Although not a technically ideal situation, this set-up does offer some advantages, because transferring data by analogue means will allow you to insert other analogue signal processors in the signal chain. As most affordable digital mixers have few or no insert points in the digital input path, this can be a useful workaround. If a normalised patchbay is used between the audio interface and the mixer, this job is a lot easier.

Figure 5.3 shows a desktop system connected to a mixer that has eight analogue channels and eight digital channels. In this example, the signals being recorded are still being fed in via a voice channel, but if you have a mixer with sufficient channels there's no reason why you shouldn't record via your mixer and route your signals to the audio interface's digital input.

In those situations where you want to work with a number of musicians or bands, you'll need to be able to record several channels at the same time, as well as have a low-latency system in order to allow smooth and accurate punching in and out. It's still possible to use separate mic amps or voice channels to feed the various inputs, but a more conventional solution is to use a digital mixer that is designed with recording in mind and that has a built-in means of monitoring what's already been recorded. Mixers such as (but not limited to) the Mackie d8b or Yamaha's 02R are well suited to this purpose, and can be expanded to offer more digital I/O than smaller consoles. Once your soundcard or audio interface has been set up to use its multichannel digital connectors, signal routing to and from the computer is handled by your mixer in exactly the same way as it would be if you were working with a tape machine.

# submixing

If you're working with a lot of audio tracks on your computer, you may still end up with more tracks than you have mixer I/O to accommodate them, which means that you'll have to submix some tracks inside the computer. As pointed out earlier, this isn't too limiting, as there are often backing vocals, keyboard layers or percussion parts that can be pre-mixed without compromising the flexibility of your mix too much, and if you find that you require different EQ or effects settings on the various parts prior to submixing, you can still set these up by using plug-ins as you submix. In most instances, submixes will be in stereo, which means that you'll use up two channels of digital I/O and two mixer channels for each submix.

When it comes to mixing, there's no reason why you shouldn't use the automated mixing capabilities of both your mixer and your computer, although you'll need to feed MTC (MIDI Time Code) or SMPTE to the mixer so that it can sync to your song. If you plan your submixes carefully, you should be able to set up your virtual mixer section so that it has to do very little by way of automation, enabling you to do almost all of the mixing on your hardware mixer.

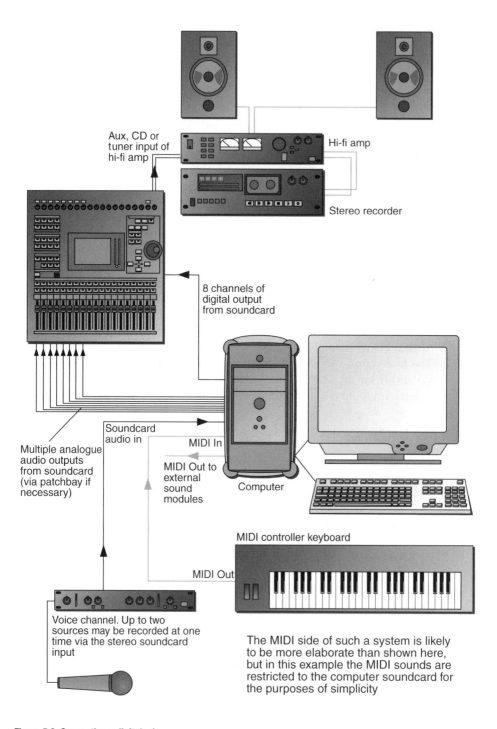

Aux, CD or tuner input of hi-fi amp

Hi-fi amp

Stereo recorder

8 channels of digital output from soundcard

Multiple analogue audio outputs from soundcard (via patchbay if necessary)

Soundcard audio in

MIDI In

MIDI Out to external sound modules

Computer

MIDI controller keyboard

MIDI Out

Voice channel. Up to two sources may be recorded at one time via the stereo soundcard input

The MIDI side of such a system is likely to be more elaborate than shown here, but in this example the MIDI sounds are restricted to the computer soundcard for the purposes of simplicity

Figure 5.3: Connecting a digital mixer

# FireWire

In the near future, FireWire – or one of its musical implementations (such as Yamaha's MLAN) – may take over from existing digital audio interfaces, and a single optical or copper connection should theoretically be able to carry as many audio and MIDI channels as you're ever likely to need, as well as sync information. If the manufacturers take this to its logical conclusion, mixers will be able to interface directly to the FireWire port on the back of a Mac or PC without the need for a soundcard or an external audio interface. This makes perfect sense, because digital mixers already have built-in converters and I/O.

## system components

When calculating your budget, make sure that you've allowed for your monitoring system, your microphones, a CD recorder or DAT machine and any external audio processors and synths that you might wish to use, on top of the SCSI interface, a large external audio drive, a MIDI interface and whatever audio interface you've chosen. It's also false economy to skimp on cables, especially digital interconnects, as these can have a profound effect on audio quality. Poor interconnects can introduce massive data errors.

You may have committed most of your budget at this point, but you should still try to leave yourself an upgrade path. Therefore, if you've decided to buy an external mixer, make sure that the one you choose has plenty of spare inputs in which to accept all of those additional synths and samplers that you're sure to accumulate in the future. If you don't intend to use an external mixer, you might consider adding a hardware MIDI control surface to drive the mixer section of your sequencer. A number of models are available, from those with only a handful of MIDI faders running right up to those with work surfaces similar in size and cost to a regular mixing console.

## software

Choosing the right MIDI/audio sequencing software isn't always easy because, until you've tried it and got used to it, you won't know what its strengths and weaknesses are. If you already have friends who work with a specific software sequencer, you might want to use the same as them so that you can collaborate on projects more easily. Friends are also a good source of free technical support!

My own preference is to use a sequencer that supports VST plug-ins, and in Europe I think that it's fair to say that eMagic's Logic Audio and Steinberg's Cubase VST are the most flexible and sophisticated packages around. In the US, however, musicians tend to favour Digital Performer, Studio Vision and Cakewalk. Because these sequencers are very sophisticated, they come with a pretty frightening learning curve, so it's a good idea to spend a few hours with someone who already knows the system, even if you have to pay for it. Once you can find your way around, you'll probably find that you only use a few per cent of the available features at first, but the important thing to know is where those essential features are. When you become more familiar with the software, you can try out some of the less familiar functions, and if you can discipline yourself, it's good experience to try out one new feature every session, even if you can't think of an immediate use for it.

The criteria for choosing monitor loudspeakers is covered in chapter eight, while the key points of the different types of microphones are outlined in chapter four. More in-depth information on mics, monitoring and acoustic treatment can be found in my book *Creative Recording II*, also available from Sanctuary Publishing.

## chapter 6

# plug-in effects

## software plug-ins

Over the past few years, many of the traditional recording and signal-processing tasks, which were once the sole domain of specialised hardware, are now available in software form, and can be either used with the native processing power of desktop PCs or running on DSP cards that have been optimised for audio applications. The turning point, as far as the home recording musician was concerned, was when the major sequencer manufacturers added audio recording, mixing and signal-processing capabilities to their systems, which use only the native processing power of the host computer. This opened up the world of recording to those musicians who previously might only have been able to budget for a basic MIDI sequencing system. Plug-in effects and processing software is now available from a number of third-party suppliers, which means that the functionality of the host software (an audio-plus-MIDI sequencer, for example) can be extended in many ways. However, different versions may be required, depending on whether the host system runs on a Mac or PC and on whether you intend to run the effects on the native processor or on a DSP system. The various types of plug-in formats are described in chapter three.

Software plug-ins can provide all of the common studio effects, along with some rather more esoteric functions, including the ability to correct tuning problems. More plug-ins are being designed each month, but even standard effects can be confusing if you've never owned the hardware version before. For that reason, this chapter presents an overview of the most commonly-used studio effects, along with a few tips concerning their use.

## the plug-in interface

One obvious advantage of using software is that computers are able to provide an optimised graphic interface, as well as controls and meters. In the context of plug-ins, these often provide dynamic graphs of things like compressor slopes or EQ curves, which would be impractical to include in the hardware version. Even so, designers still seem to like to emulate the appearance of hardware, and so many plug-ins come with nicely-drawn 3D front panels, knobs, faders and LEDs. One piece of software I saw recently could even be "turned around" so that you could see how the cables plugged into the back of it!

# reverberation

Reverberation is probably the most important effect in the studio, but it is also one of the most processor hungry, due to the complex nature of the calculations involved in its creation. Reverberation occurs naturally when sound is reflected and re-reflected from walls and other obstacles within a large room or acoustic space, and an electronic reverb unit mimics this effect by generating thousands of reflections electronically. Figure 6.1 shows the pattern of decaying reflections created by a typical digital reverberation unit. Reverb can be used to create the impression of sound produced in a real room, but it may also be used to create new effects that have no obvious counterpart in nature. As a rule, rooms with hard surfaces produce a bright, lively reverb sound while more absorbent rooms produce a warmer sound with much less high end.

The quality of a reverb plug-in is proportional to the amount of processing power that it consumes, which is why some designers offer a choice of reverb qualities, allowing you to opt for a less refined effect (with generally fewer reflections per second) if you're short on processing power. In general, the better reverb algorithms sound smoother and more natural than the more basic ones, and reverb quality tends to show up most on vocals and drums.

Most musical applications require a fairly short reverb time of between one and three seconds, although digital reverbs can also emulate much larger, reflective spaces with decay times of ten seconds or more. Plate settings are popular for general use, especially on vocals and drums. The term *plate* refers to the mechanical reverb plate which was used in studios before digital reverb units were invented.

All serious reverb units have stereo outputs because in real life both ears pick up slightly different patterns of reverb reflections. In a natural situation, these inter-aural differences provide the brain with stereo information that is used to estimate the size and character of the space. Digital reverb units process a mono input in order to produce two different sets of synthetic reflections and thus create a convincing stereo effect. These two sets of reflection patterns are very chaotic and are only loosely related to each other so that, if the reverb outputs are summed to mono (as they are when played back on a mono radio), the sound quality isn't affected too badly.

# reverb parameters

The main reverb parameters available for user control are the pre-delay time, the early reflection pattern and level, the overall decay time and high-frequency damping. Pre-delay determines the time between the original sound and the first reflection, and provides a simple way of creating an illusion of room size. Longer pre-delays can sometimes sound effective when treating vocals.

The user will normally select from a handful of stored patterns simulating various rooms, halls, chambers, plates or small-room ambience. The overall reverb decay time (the time it takes for the reverb to die away) affects how we perceive the environment – longer reverb times suggest large, reflective spaces, whereas short decay times may be used to simulate smaller rooms or heavily-damped spaces. Meanwhile, high-frequency damping allows the high-frequency decay time to be made shorter than the overall decay time. The greater the high-frequency damping, the more the reverb sounds like a room with soft furnishings or carpets.

By selecting the appropriate pattern for the environment you wish to simulate and then adjusting the other parameters, the effects available to you can range from fairly dry rooms to cathedrals. Most of the musically-useful reverb treatments have a decay time below three seconds but longer reverb times are useful for creating special effects.

Some algorithms allow you control the size of the room, adjusting several

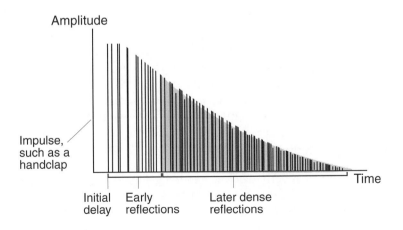

**Figure 6.1: Reverb decay pattern**

**Figure 6.2: Using pirated software is not a good idea! Note the Snapease hackers logo**

of the parameters simultaneously to give the impression of a larger or smaller space. This saves time and makes it easier for those with less experience in fine-tuning effects to set up the equipment. Unlike most hardware reverbs, plug-ins often provide some form of graphic illustration to show how the reverb is affected when the parameters are adjusted. These are often more decorative than functional, but there are some that provide useful information. Note that, although it may be tempting to obtain free pirate plug-ins via the internet, it is illegal and also leaves your system vulnerable to viruses. Pirated software often includes a hackers logo, such as that shown in Figure 6.2.

# gated reverb

Hardware reverb devices generally include gated and reverse reverb, although in the virtual world these are sometimes offered as separate plug-ins. Gated reverb features an abrupt cut-off rather than a smooth decay, and is created by burst of closely-spaced reflections that stop abruptly after around half a second.

Reverse reverb is similar to gated reverb, but the level envelope of the reverb starts off low and then increases steadily, producing the illusion of a tape being played backwards. As with gated reverb, the main parameter is the time it takes for the reverb to build up and cut off.

# delay and echo

Delays and echoes use up a lot of RAM but actually demand less processing power than most other plug-ins. The effect produced by these is the electronic equivalent of an old tape echo unit, and by feeding some of the delayed sound back into the input it's possible to set up repeating echoes. The time it takes for echoes to die away is set with the feedback parameter.

Modern multi-effects units often include multi-tapped delay programs, which generate multiple echoes at different delay times. It may also be possible to pan the individual delays from left to right in the stereo field in order to create interesting spatial effects. Most of the simple delay plug-ins are less sophisticated than this, although more elaborate effects are available if required. These are generally fine for creating mono or stereo delays with variable feedback, and it's also common for the delay time to be set in relation to the tempo so that, if the song includes a tempo change, the delay time will automatically change to match it.

# modulated delay

If you take a basic delay and use a low-frequency oscillator to modulate the delay time, it's possible to generate effects such as chorus, flanging, vibrato and phasing. Some modulation effects, such as phasing, use such short delay times that no delay is perceptible, while chorus and ADT use a slightly longer delay time to produce a doubling or thickening effect.

Chorus can be created using a short delay of around 70ms, gently modulated at three of four cycles per second. An equal mix of the delayed and unprocessed sound creates an effect rather like two instruments playing the same part but with slight differences in timing and tuning. If the modulation depth is set too high, the sound takes on an unnatural warbling characteristic.

ADT (Automatic Double Tracking) is similar to chorus but uses a slightly longer delay time in order to create a more obvious doubling or "slapback" echo effect. ADT is often used to process vocals to make it appear that the same singer has performed the part twice, on different tape tracks, again to obtain a thicker sound. The amount of modulation should be so slight as to be only just noticeable.

# phasing

Phasing is produced by setting up a fairly short delay of between 1ms and 10ms and then modulating the delay and mixing it with the original dry sound. This creates a a moving comb filter (a filter with deep notches in its response), which sounds not unlike mild tape flanging.

# flanging

Flanging is a process similar to phasing, but it works by combining slightly longer delay times (up to 50ms) with feedback in order to create a richer, more dynamic effect. The more the feedback control is advanced, the stronger the effect. As a rule, the faster the modulation rate, the less depth you need.

# vibrato

Vibrato is a modulation of pitch similar to that produced manually by a guitar or violin player, and is created by using only the delayed sound and none of the original. The delay is kept to just a few milliseconds so as not to affect the timing of the performance significantly, while the modulation depth sets the vibrato intensity. A modulation rate of between two and seven cycles per second is typical.

# pitch shifting

A pitch shifter can change the pitch of the original signal without changing the speed of the sound, and usually has a maximum range of at least an octave above and below the original pitch. It works by breaking up the sound into very short segments, which are then sped up or slowed down and then either looped or truncated (depending on whether the pitch is being moved up or down) before being joined back together. Simple pitch shifters impart a strange timbre, which is caused by the regular modulation of the looping processes, but if mixed with the original sound this side-effect can be disguised. There's also a slight delay incurred by the looping process, but this can be as short as just a few milliseconds.

Smaller pitch shifts sound very similar to chorus effects, albeit without the regular modulation of chorus. Combined with a short delay, such de-tuning treatments are often used to double or thicken vocals.

Rather than use a real-time plug-in for pitch shifting, it may be better to use your sequencer's off-line pitch-shifting facility, if it has one, as these are often able to examine the audio file prior to processing, after which they optimise their processing to suit the material. As a result, the quality of the shifted signal is likely to be better than that from a real-time plug-in, but still expect some discrepancies if you're shifting the pitch a long way away from the original. Adding an audio track to a copy pitch-shifted by around five to seven cents can be effective.

# autopanners

An autopanner will pan a mono signal from left to right in a mix, usually under the control of a low-frequency oscillator or external trigger. Used in time with the tempo of a track, panning can be quite subtle. Stereo autopanners are also sometimes available, and on these devices the panning effect causes the two signals to move in opposite directions.

# amp/speaker simulators

While keyboards tend to work best through a sound system with a flat frequency response and minimal distortion, guitar and bass amplifiers are *voiced*, which means that their frequency responses are shaped to suit the instrument rather than flat. Furthermore, the loudspeakers and enclosures used in guitar and bass amplifiers usually have a very limited frequency response, which provides them with the ability to filter out the rougher-sounding components present in amplifier distortion. Guitar pre-amp plug-ins based on physical modelling can sound particularly authentic.

Although hardware solutions may be more convenient, the primary advantage of being able to use software guitar amps and speaker simulators is that you can record the guitar part clean while monitoring via the plug-in, thus allowing you to change the amp sound after recording. Such amp simulators are also useful for warming up digital synths, where a fatter, more analogue sound is desired, or for grunging up drum loops.

# distortion

There are various plug-ins available which distort sound in a more general way, either by emulating analogue saturation and clipping or by reducing the bit depth of the original audio signal. These are popular in dance music circles for creating lo-fi sounds, and are often applied to drum loops. There are also some more sophisticated distortion plug-ins (such as Steinberg's QuadraFuzz) which split the audio data into separate frequency bands and then distort each band independently. This approach produces a more tightly-controlled sound than that produced by basic overall distortion.

# filters

In addition to parametric and graphic EQ, there are also plug-ins available which can emulate the swept-resonant filters used in synthesisers. These may be controlled via an LFO, via the level of the input signal, or sometimes via their own MIDI-triggered envelope. Any audio signal can be treated, from basic keyboard sounds to drums and vocals.

# MIDI control

Most of the current MIDI-plus-audio sequencers can use MIDI information to automate certain plug-in effect parameters, provided that they are are designed for MIDI control in the first place. The specification of the VST II plug-in has a provision for MIDI control, although exactly which parameters are available is down to the designer of the plug-in.

# effects patching

Effects such as reverb or delay may be either fed from a post-fade send control (effects send) or used in channel, group and master insert points. You can feed a reverb unit from a pre-fade send if you want to fade out the dry signal while still leaving the reverb audible, but most of the time the post-fade send is used so that the effect level varies in proportion to the dry signal as the channel level fader is adjusted. The advantage of using the aux send system is that it will allow the same effects device to be shared among all of the mixer channels while still allowing you to have different amounts of effect on each channel.

# processors

Processors – which include exciters, equalisers, compressors, limiters, gates, expanders and autopanners – can't normally be used in the aux send/return loop, so you'll need to load them either into your channel insert points (where only one channel can be processed at once with the plug-in) or a group insert point (so that the process can be applied to a complete submix).

# compressors/limiters

Compressors are used to even out excessive peaks in signal level that occur in vocal or instrumental performances by automatically changing the gain of the signal path depending on the level of the signal that passes through them. The threshold is determined by the user, and signals which fall below this level remain unchanged while higher-level sounds are subjected to gain reduction. The degree of gain reduction applied is set by the Compression Ratio control: the higher the ratio, the more the signal level is squashed if the input exceeds the threshold level. The input/output graph of a compressor is shown in Figure 6.3.

When the ratio is set very high, the compressor's maximum output is maintained at the threshold level and is effectively prevented from going beyond it, and this process is known as limiting. Limiting is used in

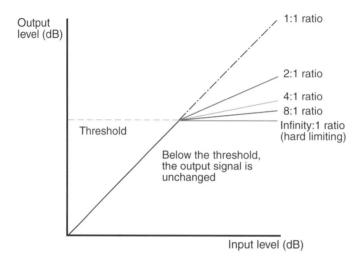

Figure 6.3: Graph showing the response of a compressor

circumstances in which it would be undesirable for a signal to exceed a specific level (for example, to prevent clipping on a digital recorder).

A compressor's Attack parameter determines how quickly the circuitry responds once a signal has exceeded the threshold, while Release determines the time it takes for the gain to return to normal once the input has dropped back below the threshold. Some compressors have Auto-Attack and -Release settings, which respond to the dynamic character of the input signal. Auto-Attack is very useful for processing signals with constantly changing characteristics, such as vocals, slap/pull bass guitar or complete mixes.

Compressors designed for use with stereo signals are fitted with two separate signal channels, which have their side-chain circuits linked so that both channels are always compressed by the same amount. This is necessary in order to prevent the image from appearing to move to one side or the other when a loud sound appears on only one side of the mix.

Compressors essentially increase the level of quiet sounds while also controlling the levels of peaks, so any low-level noise present in the input signal will also be boosted by them. To combat this problem, some hardware compressors come with built-in gates, so that the signal may be silenced during pauses. When using a virtual mixer, the best way of doing this is by patching a gate or expander plug-in directly before the compressor.

# gates

Whereas compressors control the levels of signals that exceed a threshold, gates control the levels of signals which fall below a threshold. Their purpose is to silence the signal during pauses, when any background noise will not be masked by the presence of a signal. If the threshold level of the gate is set just above the background noise, the gate will operate whenever there is a pause in the signal. It must be understood, however, that gates only remove noise when there is a pause in the wanted signal – they can't help with noise that's audible over the top of the programme material.

Expanders are very similar to gates, except that they close down gently, more like a compressor in reverse. Most gates have attack and release times that can be adjusted to produce the most natural-sounding results on the material being processed. As a rule, rapid attack sounds require a fast gate attack setting, while slowly-decaying sounds need a slow release setting so that the end of the wanted sound isn't cut off abruptly.

# equalisers

Equalisers are essentially tone controls. Most virtual mixers have EQ built in, but it's often useful to have a better-quality equaliser plug-in on hand that can be used on those occasions when more precise control is required. Parametric equalisers are the most versatile, but they also take the most time to set up properly. Because a sophisticated equaliser takes more processing power than a basic EQ, it's best not to use more EQ than is strictly necessary.

# shelving equalisers

The simplest equaliser is the shelving equaliser, a device which applies cut or boost, rather like a volume control, but only to the frequencies above or below the cut-off point of the equaliser, depending on whether the equaliser is based around a high-pass or a low-pass filter.

As its name suggests, a low-pass shelving filter passes all frequencies below its cut-off frequency but attenuates all frequencies above this. Similarly, a high-pass filter passes all frequencies above its cut-off frequency but affects all frequencies below. Figure 6.4 shows the frequency response graphs of a typical treble/bass EQ using both high- and low-pass filters. It's important to note that the filter graph shows a slope at the cut-off point. It's neither possible nor desirable to have a filter with an infinitely sharp response. The steeper the slope, the sharper the filter response. Simple shelving filters typically have a slope of 6dB per octave, so that their influence is felt more progressively, although it's still possible to have much steeper slopes that this if required. The gentler the slope of the filter, the more frequencies outside its range will be affected.

# bandpass filters

A filter that passes frequencies between two limits is known as a *bandpass filter*. On a typical sweep equaliser, the bandpass filter will have variable cut and boost, and it will also be tunable, so that its centre frequency can be altered by the user. Figure 6.5 shows the frequency

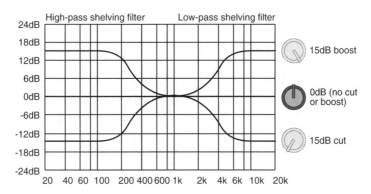

Figure 6.4: Frequency response of a shelving equaliser

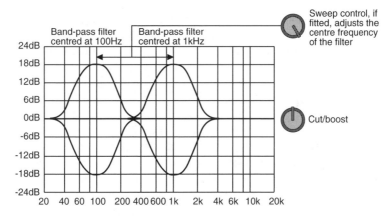

Figure 6.5: Frequency response of a sweep equaliser

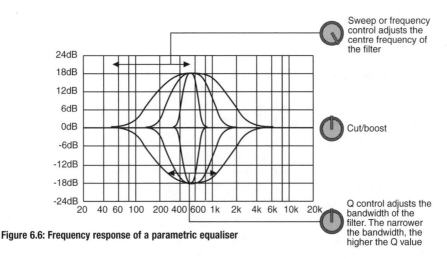

Figure 6.6: Frequency response of a parametric equaliser

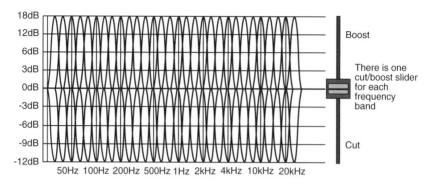

**Figure 6.7: Frequency response of a graphic equaliser**

response of a typical bandpass filter, including its Sweep Control function. Sweep equalisers are more specific than shelving equalisers in that they can be tuned to the exact frequency range that needs cutting or boosting.

# parametric EQ

A parametric EQ is very similar to a sweep EQ, with the exception that a third control is added in order to allow the user to adjust the width of the filter response. The width of a filter response is sometimes described as its $Q$ value, where Q is the filter frequency divided by the bandwidth of the filter. A high value of Q corresponds to a very narrow filter, whereas a low value of Q corresponds to a wide filter. High Q values are useful for picking out sounds that occupy a very narrow part of the audio spectrum, whereas lower Qs produce a smoother, more musical sound. Figure 6.6 shows the frequency response of a typical parametric equaliser.

# graphic equalisers

A graphic equaliser can be recognised by the row of faders across its front panel, with each fader controlling its own narrow section of the audio spectrum. For example, a 30-band graphic equaliser provides independent control over 30 different bands, spaced a third of an octave apart.

Other than the highest and lowest faders, which usually control shelving filters, each of the filters in a graphic equaliser is a fixed-frequency bandpass filter. Boost is applied by moving the fader up from its centre position and cut is achieved by moving the fader down.

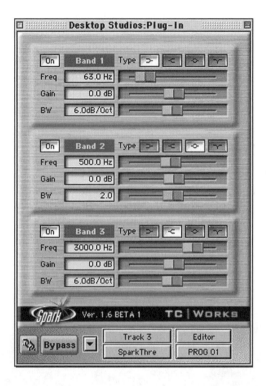

Graphic equalisers are very easy to set up, but unless they are very well designed they can have an adverse effect on the sound, unless used sparingly. They are also less flexible than the parametric equaliser, which can be exactly tuned to specific frequencies. The range covered by each fader is fixed, and the width of each individual band of a third-octave equaliser is actually rather wider than a third of an octave, allowing a smooth overlap between bands. Figure 6.7 shows the frequency response of a typical graphic equaliser.

Some EQ plug-ins provide multiple bands of adjustment, like a hardware graphic EQ as well as displaying a frequency response curve, so that the combined effect of the various filter controls can be clearly seen. A further refinement is the parametric EQ, on which each band of a multiple-band equaliser has full parametric controls. Functionally, this is the same as a multi-band parametric EQ, but usually with the addition of a graphic display of the overall EQ function.

# exciters

Also known as enhancers, exciters are devices that add synthesised high-frequency harmonics to a signal to make it sound brighter and more intimate than the original sound. The process was developed and patented by Aphex, and is different to equalisation, which can only redistributes the harmonics that already exist. Exciters are used to push sounds to the front of the mix, or to create clarity and space in crowded mixes. Various plug-ins are available to achieve this purpose, and the best thing to do is to use them sparingly, as it's easy to make sound harsh by overprocessing it.

# Auto-Tune

AnTares' Auto-Tune is, in my view, one of the few truly innovative musical developments of the past couple of years. It's available as both a hardware box and a software plug-in, and it provides a practical answer to the very real problem of pitching imperfections. Other companies are already developing their own pitch correctors.

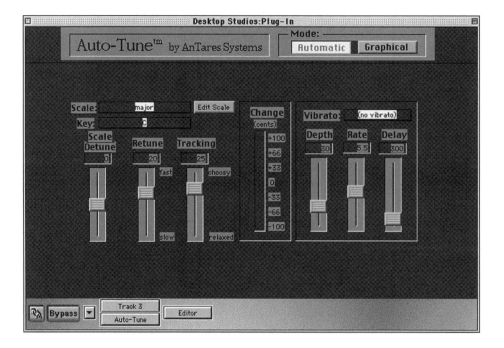

The main purpose of Auto-Tune is to tighten up vocal pitching, but it can also be used to produce creative effects and to improve monophonic instrument performances. Auto-Tune needs to be able to calculate the pitch of the incoming signal, so that it can only work with monophonic sources. Then, once the pitch has been detected, Auto-Tune uses real-time pitch-shifting techniques to change the pitch of the original sound to match the nearest note in a user-definable scale. It is possible to leave Auto-Tune set to a chromatic scale, but then it's likely that the pitch of a badly-sung note could go to an "illegal" note. A slider adjusts the rate at which correction takes place, and so, by slowing down the reactions of the program, natural bends and vibrato are allowed through unaltered. Even sounds like fretless bass, cello and theramin can be tightened up without losing their essential character.

When that distinctive vocoder effect appeared on Cher's single 'Believe', it turned out that Auto-Tune had been used in a rather unorthodox way to create the effect, simply by setting the pitch correction rate to its fastest rate, setting up a suitable scale and going for it. The result is an aggressively pitch-quantised version of the voice that has an interesting, almost robotic quality. Tuning correction plug-ins are processors, and so must always be patched in via an insert point to treat a single sound source.

# bass enhancement

Most domestic hi-fi equipment can't produce the lowest fundamental frequencies of bass guitars or some electronic sounds, but they still sound punchy because the higher harmonics of the bass sounds are reproduced reasonably accurately, and the human brain has a tendency to compensate for the missing fundamental. A relatively new digital process has been developed which enhances the apparent bass energy of sounds destined to be played back through smaller speaker systems, and this is achieved by extracting the harmonics from the bottom octave or so of the original sound and then doubling their frequencies. The same system also allows the very low end of the original system to be adjusted by reducing its level to reduce the stress on small speakers. By reducing the real low bass and increasing the level of the newly-generated bass harmonics, the sound can actually be made to appear as though it has more bass energy when played back over small speakers, even though the actual low-frequency energy may have decreased. Bass enhancement plug-ins are processors, and so may be used via insert points, although they can be used to treat complete mixes as well as single sound sources if used via a buss insert point.

# stereo enhancers

Most enhancers work on the frequency spectrum of the sound being processed, making it sound brighter or more punchy. However, there's another type of enhancer available, which is designed to increase the subjective stereo width of a mix by using regular stereo speakers. The

success of their operation depends on the sound being processed, but in general they allow sounds to be positioned so that they appear to originate from outside the stereo speakers. In some cases, sounds can even appear behind you.

The best-known commercial 3D enhancement systems are probably Q Sound, Roland's RSS system and Spatializer, all of which work in similar ways. All rely on the fact that the human brain works out the direction of the source of a sound by comparing the sounds that arrive at both ears. Small differences in arrival time and tonality are unconsciously analysed and tell us the location of the original sound. The difference in tonality is caused by both the shape of the outer ear and by the way in which the head masks sounds coming from the opposite side, but the software mimics this by using filters and delays

A number of 3D software emulations are available as plug-ins, and some of them can position sounds outside the speakers very convincingly. These effects are generally used to treat only specific elements within the mix, because the spectral changes and inter-channel delays needed to create the effect compromise the mono compatibility of the sound being treated. For this reason, the main elements of the mix are best left as conventional stereo, with spatial enhancement being reserved for sound effects and incidental instrumentation.

# power shortage?

One way around the need for a powerful processor is to use a non-real-time plug-in. These generally allow the user to audition a short section of audio while adjusting the various parameters. The audio file (or section) is then processed off-line. Unlike a real-time process, which doesn't actually change the source audio file, off-line processes are destructive, in that either the original file is changed or a new file reflecting the processing changes is created. Similarly, tracks using real-time plug-ins, such as VST, can be "bounced" to a new track alon with their effect.

# other types of plug-in

Virtually any effect or processor that can exist in hardware form can be implemented in software, even vintage analogue processors. In addition to the more obvious processes, plug-ins can also handle de-noising, de-clicking and other high-level tasks, such as azimuth correction of analogue tape masters made on improperly-aligned machines. There are even plug-ins which deliberately add noise and crackle to a recording in order to simulate vinyl reproduction. These latter devices are fashionable for making new recordings sound like vintage vinyl samples, and include such parameters as record speed, recording age, amount of surface damage and so on.

Processes like surround sound mixing and encoding are becoming increasingly available through the use of plug-ins, enabling a multi-channel audio workstation to handle sophisticated TV and film sound mixing. There are also numerous multiband dynamics processors available, which allow the bass, mid range and high frequencies of a sound to be processed independently. If used properly, multiband compressors and limiters produce fewer audible side-effects than their full-band equivalents, which makes them idea for use in critical mastering applications.

The plug-in environment also allows a few more off-the-wall ideas to flourish, such as multiband fuzz boxes, unusual dynamic equalisers with user-adjustable compression curves and frequency points, and various interesting metering systems for viewing things like stereo image, phase and frequency content, among others. Another interesting development is the plug-in that allows the user to analyse the spectral content of commercial recordings and then automatically EQ his own recordings to have the same spectral composition.

Perhaps one of the most fascinating areas is the ability to emulate real recording environments by analysing a recording of a special test signal made in a real acoustic space, which could be anything from a concert hall to a canyon. By recording the room's influence on a special test signal, it's possible to build up a model of how that room behaves and emulate it. This process is known as *convolution*, and may be extended to emulate some items of analogue processing equipment.

# software copy protection

Software piracy is a major problem in some sectors of the industry, and so music software tends to be protected, which can be inconvenient for the legitimate user. However, it prevents unlawful copying of the software, which in the long term should mean better product support and lower prices for the end user. Protection comes in several forms,

with the two most common being hardware keys (dongles) and disk-limited installations.

Dongles plug in series to a computer port, such as the keyboard buss on older Macs or the USB ports on newer machines. PCs can use one of the mouse ports, although USB is likely to become more common there, too. The user can make multiple back-up copies of the software if required, but the copies will only run on a machine that has the correct dongle plugged into it. This is a generally a good system, although things can get messy if you have multiple dongles hanging from the back of your computer. Also, the introduction of USB has complicated issues slightly.

Some plug-in manufacturers issue a single dongle, which will authorise whichever of their plug-ins that you have bought, and this usually works with some kind of password system. When you've paid for the plug-in, you receive a password which effectively upgrades your dongle to run the new plug-in, as well as those that you already have.

A number of companies are making extensive use of the Internet, not only to sell software but also as a medium for providing passwords to registered users and providing updates to their software. Where a dongle is needed to run the software, the latest versions of all of the company's products can be made freely available to all registered users with no risk of piracy.

# disk-based protection

Copy protection based on a limited number of disk installations uses an uncopyable master floppy disk, from which the software is installed. The master disk usually allows the software to be installed twice, and after each install a counter on the floppy is decremented. When there are no more installs left, the only way to get the master disk to work again is to uninstall the software (again using the master disk), which increments the counter on the master disk and allows an additional installation. The disadvantage of this system – other than the risk of damaging your master disk – is that, if you need to change computers or reformat your hard drive, you first have to uninstall all of your copy-protected software, and this can be a long job if you have a lot of software. On newer computers that don't have internal floppy drives, it's sometimes possible to use external drives to install the software authorisation. However, in some cases you will need to obtain an additional program in order for the external drive to work in the same way as an internal drive. If in any doubt, you should consult your software supplier. Note that running pirate software sometimes corrupts the key disks of legitimate software.

# CD copy protection

A more recent and less intrusive system of copy protection involves the use of an uncopyable CD-ROM as the master disc. The software is installed from this CD-ROM in the normal way, but on random occasions (usually when starting up the program up) the user is asked to insert the master CD-ROM before being allowed to continue working. This is clearly a better system for those computers that are no longer fitted with floppy drives.

Once you've installed a lot of software, being asked to find master CDs at random intervals can become tiring. Luckily, there's yet another system of copy protection, known as *challenge and response*. Once you've installed your software, a string of words, numbers or characters is generated that is unique to your computer system. These are e-mailed or faxed to the software manufacturer, who will then issue you with another set of codes to type into your computer. Once this has been done, the software will run only on that computer, not on any other machine.

## summary

Effects and signal processors are essential to modern recording, with reverberation being the most important effect of all. Because good reverb takes a lot of processing power, I'd still advocate using a hardware unit if possible, or a soundcard with built-in reverb. If this is impractical, just be careful about how many plug-ins you use, and try to pick the reverb algorithm that best suits the material you're processing. For example, some non-percussive sounds work well with low-power reverbs, while percussive sounds demand considerable levels.

When recording into a digital system, it's still quite common to use outboard analogue mic/line pre-amps (sometimes called voice channels), which include compression and equalisation. These often provide the most convenient way of transferring a high-quality signal into a computer-based digital recording system. The main thing to do is to add slightly less compression than you think you might ultimately need. Then, if you need more, you can always use a plug-in to add the final touches.

## chapter 7

# the creative process

At the risk of sounding seriously boring, I'm going to suggest that, before you start recording (and especially before you call the technical support helpline), you should read the manual for your sequencing software. The book you're reading now can never be a substitute for a software manual, because every program approaches things slightly differently. However, this book does provide an overview of the process that will enable you to locate the important sections of the manual quickly. If you've used sequencing software before, you may be able to hack your way around a program reasonably well by just checking out the menus to see what's on offer, but even the experienced software user can miss out on a lot of advanced functions in this way. I'd recommend that you read the "Getting Started" part of your manual thoroughly, at least, and if you're new to making music on computers you should spend some time mastering the MIDI aspects of the program before moving on to audio.

Once you've learned you way around the basics, there's no better way to learn than to try and put a song together. Once you become familiar with the program, and gain more experience, you'll develop your own unique approach to composing and mixing, but until then the method described here is as good as any.

## getting started

In most instances, it's easiest to start by laying down the main MIDI tracks before starting with audio, and for both pop and dance music it's a good idea to lay down a repeating rhythm loop which you can then build on. Once you've got the rhythm, bass and chord parts down, you will have established the rhythm and the basic structure for the final composition, although of course you can change the arrangement later if you wish to – that's the great thing about software composition. At this point, it will help you to set up a balance that's somewhere close to what you think you might need in the final mix, as the overall sound tends to affect the way in which you play subsequent overdubs. In most cases, you'll probably find that you adjust the mix as you record new parts, so that, by the time all of the parts are recorded, the mix is pretty close to the way it will finally sound. You should familiarise yourself with the MIDI and audio facilities concerned with automation on your mixer, as these are very important. (You'll usually find that there are several ways of doing the same job, but most people choose the one they like best and then use that most of the time. For example, I know a number of people who prefer to use the graphic editor to draw in automation envelopes for level and pan rather than move virtual faders in real time.) Try them all and then use what suits you best.

When using mix automation, bear in mind that an automated level or pan position will always stay at its last position unless it receives new information telling it to change. For example, if you've used the graphic editor to create a fade-out at the end of a track, but you haven't automated the start of the track, the next time you play the track from the top the track level will stay turned down, because the track wasn't told to turn itself back up. For this reason, you should automate the start of the track in order to bring its level up to the desired level before the audio or MIDI data in that track actually starts playing.

This effect can be even more confusing if you've created a short sequence with a fade-out, or some other set of automation moves, and you then copy this part so that it's used several times. Modern programs will copy automation data along with MIDI or audio parts, but again, if you've created a fade-out without automating the start of the sequence, the part will fade out the first time it is played back, as planned, but it will still be silent the next time it's supposed to occur in the song. You can avoid this type of confusion by using automation throughout the whole track on which automation is required, rather than trying to get away with automating only those parts at which there are changes.

If you're not using automation, the track level and pan information is set up via the track level and pan parameters that establish how that track begins. If no changes are made, these levels prevail throughout the track. However, once you've created automation data, the initial track parameters are changed as soon as the first automation event comes along. If you want to adjust the overall level of an automated track, it's no good trying to do this by adjusting the track parameters, as the automation data will simply take over and impose its values as soon as the song starts. Instead, look in your manual and find out how your software increases or decreases the overall level of automation data. If your virtual mixer has the facility of being able to emulate the Trim or Offset mode on a regular automated mixing console, this will provide you with a way of doing what you need to do.

# logistics

The musician working from home often works alone, which can be a problem with computer systems as it's sometimes necessary to set up the mics quite a distance away in order to prevent the noise of the computer's fans and drives from compromising the quality of the recording. At the same time, it's necessary to be close enough to the computer to be able to reach the controls and read the display. Most people settle for putting the sequencer into Record and then walking over to the other side of the room to make the recording. It can also help to use keyboard and mouse extensions to get the CPU box away from your recording area, although though they don't solve the problem of CRT radiation.

CRT-type displays radiate a lot of magnetic interference that can affect any electronic equipment that uses magnetic pickups or sensitive audio transformers. Guitars with single-coil pickups are the most susceptible to interference, especially when some form of overdrive effect is being used, as these effects bring up low-level gain in much the same way as a compressor would. If you don't want to change your guitar pickups for low-noise models, the only solution is to work as far away from the monitor as possible, or to invest in a solid-state display.

Chapter three looked at a practical way of avoiding the adverse effects of latency experienced during overdubbing by arranging to monitor the signal being recorded directly rather than monitoring the track output, which is often delayed by several milliseconds because of the way in which audio data is handled by the computer. Although this precludes the ability to monitor an overdub with virtual effects, it's generally a better option than trying to play with a delay in monitoring. If your system includes an external mixer and one or more hardware effects, you'll be able to add reverb or delay to your sound as you record or overdub. The effect doesn't have to be recorded, it's just there to make you feel comfortable while you're playing, so you're still free to use a different type and amount of effect when you mix, if you want to. Again, editing will be much easier if you record everything without any delay or reverb added at source, and adding these effects at the mixing stage will help to hide any slight discontinuities caused by the editing process.

# latency

If you're fortunate enough to have a system that can run with a very low latency (10ms or less), the chances are that you won't notice it at all unless you have a particularly acute sense of timing. In this case, the choice of whether to monitor directly or via the recording software depends on whether or not you need virtual effects to help you feel more comfortable when overdubbing.

Latency tends to be a more serious issue when you're dealing with virtual instruments, especially when the selected sound has a rapid attack time, like a piano. The solution that was suggested when monitoring audio tracks obviously won't work for instruments, so if excessive latency is giving you problems it may be better to record the part using a hardware or card-based synth sound as a guide and then change the instrument prior to playback, so that the virtual instrument is used instead of the guide sound. Latency isn't a problem during playback, because the program will be able to introduce the necessary offsets in timing in order to bring the audio, MIDI and virtual instrument tracks into proper alignment. (Sometimes, when the system is first configured, this will need to be adjusted by the user, although some software is able to optimise its own parameters.)

# handling audio

Generally speaking, recording audio is simply a matter of setting recording levels and then playing. However, if you decide to redo a part, it's worth making sure that the program you're using automatically erases the unwanted take from disk, or you'll end up with a drive full of short, unwanted files that are confusing and a waste of space. If your software simply removes deleted takes from the screen, and still leaves them on the drive, you'll have to delete them manually. When you delete parts during the editing process, the audio file invariably remains intact so that, if you later decide that you need to restore the deleted part, it can be re-imported into the song, usually via the Audio File menu. Most audio editing performed that relates to the positioning of audio data within a song is non-destructive, so even though you may have chopped an audio part into sections and then duplicated, moved or deleted some of the sections, the original file will remain unchanged. Even when you move audio onto a new track, or even split it between several tracks, the original file remains unaltered. The only way to get rid of audio permanently is to deliberately delete the file from your disk, but before you do this you should make sure that you don't need other parts of this file elsewhere in your song, or even in other songs. If possible, add colour to your audio tracks or regions in the arrange window once you've decided to keep them. Then, if a file shows up coloured or contains some coloured regions when viewed in the window that shows all of the audio files associated with the song, you'll know it's one that you've used and it shouldn't be deleted.

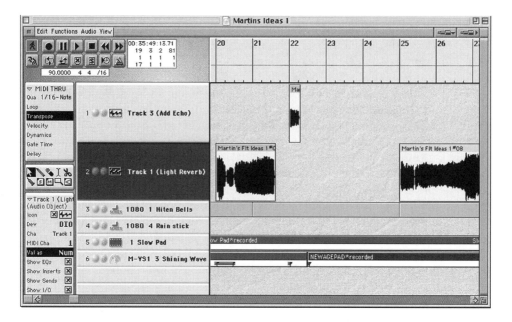

**Figure 7.1: Dividing a track for processing. (Moving words to a new track in order to add echo)**

One useful technique I've discovered is the trick of splitting a piece of audio over two or more tracks when I need to apply different effects to different parts of the audio. For example, if you have a vocal line on which only certain words need delay added to them, it's generally quite simple to divide the audio into sections so that the desired words are isolated, after which you can drag these onto another track. You can add delay to the track to which you've moved the words to be effected but still leave the rest of the audio on the original track, either untreated or treated using a different effect. The whole process is illustrated in Figure 7.1, where the uppermost track has a delay plug-in applied to it.

Another trick I've found useful on occasions involves copying a short section of audio onto a new track to create echoes, as shown in Figure 7.2. By copying audio rather than using a plug-in effect you can create a precise number of repeats of a single word, phrase or sound, and by using the graphic editor to set the level of the repeats you can have them decay in level with each repeat, have all repeats the same level, or even have the repeats increasing in level. It's also easy to use the graphic editor to automate the pan position of the individual echoes. If you need the delays to overlap, you'll need to use two or more separate audio tracks for the repeats. This method of setting up occasional echoes is precise, simple and easy to control, and you won't need to waste processing power on setting up an extra plug-in delay effect.

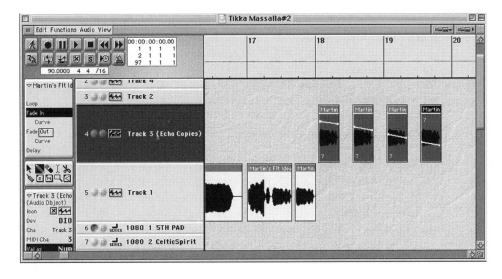

Figure 7.2: Creating echoes by copying

# the science of mixing

Once you've recorded all of your MIDI and audio parts and edited them to your satisfaction, it's time to set up your mix. The way in which you'll go about this will depend on the type of system you're using, but the end result will be a stereo recording. You may need to process this further at the mastering stage before it's compiled onto an album along with other tracks you've recorded. If you have an external DAT or MiniDisc recorder, you can mix straight to this, either from your soundcard output or from an external mixer. The external mixer will provide you with more flexibility if used in conjunction with a multi-output soundcard, or if you have hardware synths, but if you're working with a soundcard that provides a single stereo mix of your audio and MIDI tracks then there's little advantage in using a mixer. In fact, in terms of signal quality, the best results are obtained by taking the digital output from your soundcard (if you have one) and feeding this directly into your digital recorder's digital input. Once your mix has been recorded onto DAT, MiniDisc or CD-R, you will then be able to feed it back into your computer at a later date when you want to compile your album. At this point, it should be pointed out that most common mastering recorders operate at 16 bits. If you have been working at 20- or 24-bit resolution and wish to produce the best possible master recording, you'll need to mix down at the same bit depth as the original recording, which means that you'll have to find a suitable mastering machine or mix back to two spare audio tracks in your sequencing software. This latter approach is an excellent way of preserving quality but it doesn't offer the convenient archive format of DAT. The final reduction in bit depth necessary to produce 16-bit/44.1kHz files ready for CD production should come right at the end of the mastering process, after all EQ, level and dynamic changes have been made. If a suitable dithering program is used, much of the dynamic range of the original 20- or 24-bit recording will be preserved.

Some systems will allow you to mix your stereo file to disk without it ever leaving the computer. This should be possible with any system that uses software-based synthesis, and where the synth can be routed via the same software mixer as the audio tracks (for example, using Steinberg's ReWire with software synths). Similarly, a few soundcards provide a shared mixing environment for the audio and on-card synth sounds, in which case you should also be able to record your final mix to disk within the computer. Once again, it's important that you read the manual for your soundcard and sequencing software thoroughly, as there are now so many different systems that it's impossible to describe a general procedure which will be correct in all situations.

What you should be looking to achieve is either a separate stereo sound file for each song, or a single audio file containing all of your songs, which you've marked into regions with your audio editing software. These files and regions may then be compiled within the playlist of a CD-burning program to create an audio CD album.

The way I work, once I've set up a mix (usually by using the automated MIDI and audio mix automation within my sequencing software), I save a copy of the song file and all of its associated audio files into a single folder located on a separate hard drive to the one on which I've been recording the data. This provides me with a little security, as it's unlikely that two hard drives will go down at the same time. When I've completed several songs, I burn their folders to a CD-R, which provides me with a cheap and reliable back-up that is easy to reload if I ever need to perform any further work on the songs. If the work is really important then I'll make at least two CD-R back-ups. It makes sense to check that these will reload into your machine without any problems before you finally commit to wiping the original files from your hard drive.

# the art of mixing

Technically speaking, mixing is the process of balancing and processing the parts that have been recorded in order to produce a final stereo track. Mixing is often the most satisfying part of the whole process, as it's here that all of the different elements come together to produce a finished result.

A good mix starts with a good recording. Don't be tempted to think that you can rely on clever plug-ins to dig you out of trouble. These can help with some minor problems, such as fine-tuning pitch or levels, but if a sung or played part is sonically or artistically wrong it's best just to do it again.

Similarly, it pays to mix onto the best possible stereo format in order to preserve your work at the highest possible quality. If you don't have a hardware recorder, record back to two of the audio tracks of your sequencer, set up as a stereo pair. The results will be as good as the quality of the converters on your soundcard or interface, as long as you're careful with your recording levels. You should always record at the highest possible level that doesn't result in clipping when using any form of digital recorder.

## track sheets

A professional will always keep a track sheet with him that will tell him which instrument is recorded on which track, along with performance and mixing notes. To some extent, a desktop system does away with the need for writing all of this down on paper, provided that you name your tracks after they've been recorded, but sometimes it's useful to keep notes to remind you of actions that will need to be taken during mixing. An engineer might write on a track sheet something like "Use the first half of guitar solo from track one combined with last four bars from track two", and you can do the same thing by finding the notepad facility of your sequencer (or, if it doesn't have one, the computer's own notepad system) to jot down important production notes and reminders. Even if you think it's too simple to write down, you may miss something if you need to remix the song again in a year's time.

If you have a separate mixer, make sure that you don't have any redundant channels routed either to the groups or the left/right buss. Also, take advantage of the subgrouping facilities and group logical batches of sounds (such as percussion sections) under the control of a single fader where possible.

Unless you've been setting up mix automation and effects as you go along (which most people do as soon as they've gained a little confidence), you should set the pans to central, bypass any EQ and effects plug-ins and then just listen to what you've got. Listen carefully for tuning or timing problems that need to be addressed, and display all of the MIDI notes from all of the tracks (except for the drums) at the same time on the piano-roll editor, if you have the facility to do so, because it's easy to pick up any timing problems in this way and to spot sections with discordant notes. Scrutinise individual audio tracks carefully, and if you find long periods of silence with audible background noise in them you should use the waveform editor to silence them. Similarly, you should also take out (or at least reduce in level) those annoying guitar squeaks or noisy breaths. In theory, you could do all this with the automation of the mixer, but it's often simpler and more precise to trim things in the waveform editor, as there you can see (and audition) exactly what you're erasing or dropping in level.

At this point, there are two possible approaches to setting a balance: you can either start with the rhythm section and build up (which is a good method for those with limited experience), or you can just push up all of the faders and then start to balance everything in relation to everything else. Professional engineers working to tape tend to do this a lot, although in a software environment it may be easier to work on a few tracks at a time and keep other tracks muted until you need to work on them.

If your audio recordings are clean, it should be possible to set up a workable balance fairly quickly without resorting to EQ. Don't worry about panning the sounds until a reasonably good balance has been achieved. If your recording is a mix of audio and MIDI parts, you may discover that some of the MIDI parts don't quite fit, in which case now is the time to either choose different patches or to edit the ones you already have. If you're using hardware synths, you may also be able to EQ them on your hardware mixer, and often simply using shelving filters to tame the high end or low end will help to make the sounds sit better in a busy mix. Acoustic guitar often needs EQ for the same reason – what sounds right as a solo part may have too much low mid to work properly in the context of a busy mix – so you can use EQ here to thin out the sound a little.

Once a reasonable balance has been achieved, you can then think about panning sounds, adding EQ and effects. However, don't spend too much time on trying to EQ individual tracks in isolation because they'll almost certainly sound quite different when all of the other tracks are playing. Try to arrive at a ballpark level of EQ fairly quickly and leave the fine-tuning until the whole mix is playing.

It's inadvisable to feed sync signals via a hardware mixer because of the danger of bleedthrough onto the audio tracks. If you hear a background noise a little like a fax machine, it's probably time code crosstalking onto your audio.

# more on balance

As suggested earlier, it's often easiest to balance the drums and bass first, as these form the foundation for the whole track, particularly in dance music. Once the rhythm section is sounding good, you can think about adding the other instruments and the main vocal. With most musical styles it's important to leave space for the vocal, and many engineers add some compression to the vocals while they're recording and then add more when mixing in order to even out the level. If noise is in any way a problem, putting a gate plug-in before the compressor at the mixing stage may help, although again you can also silence noise by using the waveform editor.

A useful way of compressing vocals is to choose a fast attack combined with a release time of half a second or so and a ratio of between 2:1 and 5:1 if you want to use the compression purely for control, or a higher ratio if you want a more obviously compressed sound. Unless you're after a really obviously compressed effect, you probably don't need to aim for more than around 10dB of gain reduction on signal peaks, and less if you've already added some compression during recording. The most important thing to ensure is that the vocals sit evenly in the mix. Remember, you don't have to do all of the work using compression; you can also use mix automation to change levels if some words or phrases still sound too loud or too quiet.

# pan position

Once the mono balance sounds about right, you can then work on the stereo panning. Bass drums, bass guitars, bass synth lines or any other predominantly low-frequency sounds should be left panned to the centre, because these sounds carry most of the energy, and this will ensure that both speakers in a stereo system share the load. Vocals are normally positioned at the centre because that's where we expect to hear them, but you can move them to one side or the other for artistic reasons if you wish.

Other instruments, backing vocals and effects can be spread out to create an illusion of space. Reverb returns are almost always added in stereo, in order to provide the maximum sensation of space and depth. Most reverb plug-ins will accept a mono signal and will generate a stereo output, and so usually work best if used in the aux send/return loop. No matter where the original signal is panned in the mix, its reverb will come equally from both sides, a situation that mirrors what happens in nature. However, you should be aware that, although reverb increases the sense of space, it can also dilute the perception of the placement of a sound, making it more difficult to locate. For this reason, some engineers will occasionally use reverb in mono (via an insert) in order to clarify the position of a sound.

The pragmatic way of looking at conventional stereo reverb is to think of it as trading off a degree of stereo localisation for a sense of stereo space. Adding a short reverb to a panned mono sound is probably the most effective way of making something sound as though it exists in a natural environment.

# panning for effect

The way in which a traditional pop mix is set up is generally based on the way in which you might hear the musicians onstage, with the drums, bass and singer close to the centre and the other instruments and backing vocals spread around the stereo soundstage. It can be tempting to spread things out too much in the stereo mix, but this can lead to an unnatural sound, especially if you do things like spread stereo pianos and drum kits over too great a width. A narrower spread will sound more natural, and the use of stereo reverb will provide an adequate illusion of width.

The same is true of dynamic panning. Using the automation functions of a sequencer, both MIDI and audio can be panned from side to side as fast and as often as you want. However, as with any other effect, restraint usually works better than excess. Panning effects returns rather than the original signal can be both effective and subtle, and in most cases regular pans that are in sync with the tempo of the song work better than those that aren't.

# adding depth to your mix

Sound exists in three dimensions, not two, but in conventional stereo everything comes from just two speakers. The early reflections produced when a sound occurs in an enclosed space have a profound influence on how near or far the sound appears to be from the listener, which is one reason why reverb is such an important effect. Small-room or closely-spaced patterns of reflection seem to create a sense of closeness or intimacy, while large-hall reverbs mimic what happens in a large space in real life, where reflections start life more widely spaced. The better reverb algorithms also simulate the way in which natural reverb behaves when sound bounces back from a large distance, which is why the better reverb boxes and plug-ins sound more three dimensional than more basic ones. By using a reverb algorithm that conveys a sense of distance, you can use it to treat sounds that you may wish to place at the back of your mix.

For a sound to appear closer to the listener, it usually needs a lower level of reverb added to it, and it also helps if the sound is made slightly brighter. For vocals, using compression to stabilise the level is a good tactic, and this should allow you to place your sound right at the front of the mix without the sound seeming too loud.

## mix problems

Until you've gained a bit of experience, you may find that, by the time you've added all of your tracks to a mix, it sounds rather overcrowded and doesn't have the same sparkle as commercial records. The problems that you'll be facing can be categorised as those that occurred at the recording stage (tuning, timing or the inappropriate choice of sounds, for example) and those that are associated with blending the sounds together. Sometimes these latter problems can be resolved by mixing, but on other occasions you may find that the fault lies with the arrangement. There are also technical problems, such as excessive noise or distortion, and in virtually all cases it's easier to sing or play the part again rather than try to fix it in the mix. Nevertheless, a modest amount of noise can be cured with the use of either gates or, better still, dedicated de-noising software.

## EQ as a tool

The first rule of EQ is that you can only boost frequencies that are already present in the original sound. For example, overdriven electric guitar contains no really deep bass because the fundamental frequency of the bottom string doesn't go that low, while the top end rolls off sharply above 3kHz-4kHz, because of the limited response of a typical twelve-inch guitar speaker. To make any significant change to the sound, such a guitar track needs to be EQ'd mostly in the 150Hz-3kHz range. However, you can also apply this rule in reverse and use EQ cut below 150Hz to reduce unwanted hum while not affecting the bass end of the sound too much, and you can use high-frequency cut at above 3-4kHz to bring down hiss without blunting the sound excessively. You'll need to experiment in order to find the exact frequencies and amounts of cut and boost that work best, but the improvements can be worthwhile. It may also be possible to use shelving EQ cut at the high and low ends of a sound's natural range in order to squeeze it into a narrower range. This is a valuable technique for getting sounds to co-exist where they naturally overlap into each other's areas of the audio spectrum. By narrowing the amount of overlap, you'll often end up with a clearer mix, and it's particularly important to make sure that nothing conflicts too strongly with the mid-range element of the lead vocals.

In more traditional times, it was common for engineers to try to reshape guitar and keyboard sounds using EQ, playing the tracks back through guitar combos and remiking them. The amps and speakers act as filters, radically changing the basic sound. Of course, you can still do this with a computer workstation, but it may be more convenient to use an amp simulator plug-in to do the job. The main point is that, if you have a plug-in like this that is designed for use with guitars, try it out on basses and keyboards as well. Some people even use them to thicken and distort vocals.

# more on EQ and processing

I know that some engineers like to EQ virtually everything, but I prefer to leave natural sounds alone as much as possible and only use EQ for fine tuning. In this respect, if you can solve a problem using EQ cut rather than boost it will probably sound more natural. Bass and electric guitars, however, can often benefit from quite aggressive equalisation because they were never inherently natural-sounding instruments in the first place. Even so, it's not much use spending hours perfecting a bass guitar sound in isolation because it will sound totally different when you listen to it in the context of the mix. It's better to set up a quick and dirty EQ and then make all of your fine adjustments when the whole mix is playing.

Bass guitars can be tricky instruments to record. A straight DI will produce a clean and detailed sound, but this may become lost when it has to compete with the rest of the mix. I'd be tempted to use one of the new external bass guitar recording pre-amps in order to obtain more of a miked amp sound, which tends to cut through better. That's not to say that you can't get a good DI sound using just a DI box, however; by applying some compression and suitable EQ, you should be able to get a good sound, as long as you started with a decent instrument and a good player in the first place.

Although bass guitars generate a lot of low-frequency energy, their definition comes largely from the mid range. You may need to apply quite a lot of boost somewhere between 2kHz and 4kHz in order to get the right edge on the sound, but it's sometimes necessary to combine this with some shelving cut higher up in order to reduce excessive string and finger noise.

At the bass end, you can add boost at between 70Hz and 120Hz, which will add weight to the sound if you're using a parametric or sweep EQ plug-in. However, you should experiment by cutting and boosting in the 150Hz-1kHz range, as a lot of the bass guitar's audible character is due to frequencies here.

# electric guitars

As with the bass, it's important to start with an adequate instrument and a good player. Traditionally, a guitar amp would be miked close to the speaker cloth with a dynamic mic, but because there are now so many good modelling pre-amps out there it's possible to get just about any guitar sound in a conveniently DI'able format. There are also several good plug-ins out there that will do the same kind of thing. If you use a pre-amp, you won't have to worry about latency (you'll still get the proper guitar tone if you decide to monitor the source signal), and you won't need to ascribe any extra CPU power. On the other hand, a guitar amp will allow you to change your sound as much as you like after you've recorded the basic part, because what's really recorded is clean, DI'd guitar. Interestingly, the most aggressive lead sounds come through without too much distortion. If you use excessive overdrive, the result is often an unfocused sound with poor definition that just muddies up the mix.

Whether you close-mike a guitar amp or use an amp simulator, you'll still need to add reverb in order to make the sound seem authentic. Sometimes the amp or simulator will include a reverb setting, but if you're using a plug-in you'll probably have to follow it up with a reverb plug-in. Try a short, ambient room setting rather than a long wash if you're after a natural room sound, and also experiment with the pre-delay time or add a slap-back echo to obtain a more vintage rock sound. Most of the tonal changes you'll need should be available by using the EQ controls on your amp or amp simulator, but if you need to change the recorded sound try concentrating your EQ efforts in the 150Hz-3kHz part of the spectrum. Cut applied at a higher frequency can be used to smoothe out a buzzy overdrive sound, while clean DI'd guitar can be EQ'd effectively up to 6kHz or 7kHz, because it contains a lot of harmonics.

# vocals

Some engineers reach for the EQ knobs as soon as a vocal track is down, but for natural-sounding results a good mic and a good singer should actually need very little extra tonal control. Of course, if you want a particularly processed sound (for a dance record, for example), you can do whatever you think the track needs doing to it.

Unless the EQ changes, you need involve only a little general brightening or warming, and for this you should use a parametric EQ rather than a shelving equaliser because it will offer much more precise control. The presence of "character" in a voice can be fine-tuned by cutting or boosting in the 3kHz-7kHz range, while all of the interesting chest resonances tend to lie in the 150kHz-300Hz range. Compression can be applied before or after EQ, but I find that I generally have more control if I compress first and EQ afterwards

Like guitars, close-miked vocals always need reverb to inject a sense of space into the mix, but you don't always need as much as you think. Listen carefully to commercial records and try and determine the type of reverb that they're using. Too much reverb can unfocus the vocals, and you'll find that a lot of commercial mixes use relatively little vocal reverb. It's also important to reserve one of your better reverb units or plug-ins for treating vocals.

This kind of "less is more" philosophy applies just as much to backing instruments as it does to vocals. Rich, bright reverb sounds are popular on pop vocals but tend to emphasise sibilance, so always listen carefully to your vocal sound both with and without effects.

# a crash course in mixing

Putting together what we've learned so far, it's possible to develop a concise strategy for tackling mixing. The following method also works for difficult mixes, but remember that the original performance needs to be right to start with. Minor problems in the vocal pitching can be tightened up by using something like Auto-Tune, but your job is mostly about making a good song sound as good as possible, rather than creating a good record from a bad performance.

Here's the order in which to do things. Don't feel that you have to stick to this, once you've accumulated a bit of experience, because by then you'll be starting to develop your own working methods.

- Check the individual tracks for noise or unwanted pieces of audio and either erase the unwanted parts or use mix automation to mute them.

- Set up a rough mix, initially in mono and with no EQ or effects, and check how it sounds. If you don't feel comfortable doing all of this at once, start with the rhythm section and then build things up a track at a time.

- If the mix seems too busy, first see if you can change the arrangement and make some more space. You may also be able to use different MIDI instrument sounds. EQ can sometimes be used to squeeze recorded sounds into a narrower band to minimise overlap. This is particularly important in the mid range, where the vocals are located.

Use EQ to thin out pad synths, backing vocals or acoustic guitar parts that sound too thick or muddy.

• Pan the sounds, keeping the main vocal and the bass sounds near the middle of the mix. Don't overdo effects, as they can make things sound less immediate. Try using less reverb on up-front sounds to make them drier.

• Let your mix automation do all of the work. Once the basic mix is set, go through it again and use the automation to bring up instrument levels in solos, tame vocal level excesses that the compressors can't cope with, and so on. Unless you're working on fairly abstract music, such as dance music, you may only need to automate a few of the tracks. Both MIDI and audio parts can be automated, but you should avoid changing the levels of the drums or the bass too much as these normally provide the stable reference on which the rest of the track sits. Care must be taken to ensure that the release time of any gates or automation fades are long enough to prevent slowly-decaying sounds from being cut short.

• Enhancers can be useful in adding definition and clarity to individual tracks, or even to whole mixes. Use them sparingly, however, and if you have a process that you'd like to apply to all of the tracks (exciter, EQ, compressor, etc) you should consider leaving this until the mastering stage, because you'll then stand a better chance of making all of the songs on an album sit together comfortably. It also gives you time to put a little distance between yourself and the original mix.

• Finally, when you think the mix is as good as it's going to get, take a break, have a cup of tea, listen to a few records, and then listen to the mix again. Close your eyes and just think about the music – the mix automation will take care of the level changes needed during the mix. If it still sounds good, listen again from the next room with the adjoining door left open, because anything that's too loud or too quiet in the mix becomes instantly obvious. Lots of professional engineers do this, and it's one of the most useful and effective tips I've ever been given. A mix is never complete until it's passed the "next door" test. At this stage, it's also worth making a cassette of your mix so that you can check how it sounds on a car stereo or a cheap music system.

## mix compression

It sometimes helps to compress an otherwise finished mix in order to create the illusion of greater energy. Generally, this is best done at the mastering stage, but you can also do it while mixing by patching a hardware compressor into the left/right insert points of your external mixer. In this way, the compressor will treat both your computer-generated and external-synth-based sounds at the same time.

It can also help to improve the sound by equalising the mix, compensating for limitations in the recording chain, but again this is best left until the mastering stage. A gentle high-frequency boost between 6kHz and 12kHz adds definition to a mix, while some engineers swear by a broadband boost centred at around 15kHz or 16kHz, which adds "air" and transparency to a mix. Boosting the low bass and gently cutting the mid range can also make a mix louder and clearer.

# mix levels

If you're mixing to analogue cassette in order to produce a rough evaluation copy, try adjusting the record level on your cassette recorder so that the loudest signal peaks push the meters at around +4dB into the red. Most professionals prefer to work without Dolby noise reduction on the mastering recorder, but this is largely a matter of personal preference. If you're working with open-reel analogue tape (and some people still do, just to get the sound of analogue tape compression), you can probably afford to push the levels a couple of decibels further still.

Digital recorders, on the other hand, don't tolerate signal peaks in excess of full scale, they simply clip, and unless the periods of clipping are extremely brief and infrequent they are likely to be unpleasantly audible. In most cases, the meters on analogue and digital machines will produce different readings because of the different calibration levels and meter ballistics used, so always go by the meter on the recording device itself. When mixing to DAT, leave around 30 seconds of unrecorded tape at the beginning to avoid experiencing dropouts, and always store the masters away from dust, heat, moisture or strong magnetic fields. CD-R masters should be treated with similar respect, and should also be shielded from bright light.

# mastering

Commercial records are mastered at specialist facilities, and the process involves a lot of expensive equipment and requires a lot of skill. Despite what you may have read, there's a lot more to mastering than compressing everything to make it sound as loud as possible. Nevertheless, if you're making records for independent release and can't afford to have your work professionally mastered, you can get excellent results in a home studio, as long as you have a reasonably accurate monitoring system and you take care with what you're doing. At the bare minimum, the only extra equipment you'll need is a software package suitable for editing stereo audio files and a CD-R burner. It's possible to perform just about any processing function that you might require by using software plug-ins, and most of the recent editing packages also include the necessary functions to allow you to burn an audio CD directly without having to use an additional CD compilation program.

There are a number of quite simple mastering tricks that you can employ to make the tracks sound better than when you mixed them, but mastering is also about making the different tracks on an album sound consistent and arriving at the correct relative levels. The most important tool is the ear of the person doing the job, regardless of the equipment being used, so listen critically to as much music as you can and try to figure out what was done to it at the mastering stage.

The smallest plug-in toolkit that could be used for mastering would include a parametric equaliser and a compressor/limiter, although enhancer-type plug-ins can also be useful. If you have audible background noise on your mixes, de-noising plug-ins will help considerably, but don't expect them to work miracles on hopelessly noisy material.

The most important requirement – apart from your own ears – is an accurate monitoring environment, which means hi-fi speakers or studio monitors with a reasonable bass response. Computer-style multimedia speakers aren't really suitable for any serious musical work, and especially not for mastering. It's also important that the speakers are accurate, rather than flattering, and that they are arranged symmetrically, forming a roughly equilateral triangle around the mixing position. (Monitoring will be covered in more detail in chapter eight.)

When it comes to mastering, it's easy to overdo processing when the track doesn't need it. Don't process a piece of music just because you can or it may end up sounding worse than the original mix.

# editing tasks

One of the first things that you'll need to do when mastering a track is silencing unwanted noise at the beginning and the end. You may also want to fade out the last few moments of the song so that the last decaying cymbal crash ends in perfect silence. Don't start this until the natural fade of the sound is well under way, however, or the track might appear to end too abruptly. A good guidelines is to look at the waveform editor and then, when the last note or beat has decayed to around 5% of its original level, start to fade, making the fade around half to one second long. When creating regions to define the beginnings and endings of songs, another good trick is to include around 250ms of silence at the start of each song so that there's no risk of a slow CD player missing the start of the song. You may not need to do this if your CD-burning software allows you to move track-start IDs.

After creating regions for each song on the album and tidying up the beginnings and ends, assemble the tracks in the order you wish them to appear on the album using the playlist function of the editor. Once you've done this, you can set the gaps between the tracks and also make any level adjustments necessary to get the songs to sit together comfortably on the album. When deciding on the space between tracks on an album, listen to how the first track ends and how the second one starts. Gaps are rarely shorter than two seconds, but if the starts and ends are very abrupt you may need to leave up to four seconds between tracks. Use the pre-roll or fast rewind feature of your digital editor to listen to the transition so that you can get a feel for when the next track should start.

Matching levels doesn't simply mean making everything the same level. If you do that, more restrained material, such as ballads, will seem too loud compared to the stronger songs. There's no clear rule for how to do this, other than by listening and using your judgement. Listening to the vocal levels often provides a good idea of how well matched songs are. Listening through an open door is also a good way of identifying tracks that are obviously too loud or too quiet.

# mastering EQ

Tracks that were recorded at different times or in different studios can sound very different, so you may need to use a little overall EQ to even things out. Listen first to the bass end of each song to hear how that differs, and then use EQ to try to arrive at a similar character. For example, one song might have deep, booming bass, while another may have a tighter, more focused bass with less depth. By using EQ, you can probably get these two sounds to meet somewhere in the middle. Every equaliser sounds different, so you'll need to experiment, but you're looking to apply cut in those areas in which sounds are too strong and boost where they're too weak. If you can, keep the boost gentle and use cut rather than boost when a more radical change is needed. If you need to add top to a track that has little or no natural high-frequency content, try using a harmonic enhancer plug-in. Keep the amount of processing to a minimum, though, as it's easy to make things sound harsh and fatiguing by enhancing them too much. As a precaution, keep a CD player patched into your system and make frequent comparisons between your results and some commercial recordings in a similar style.

You should note that, counter to what logic might suggest, applying EQ cut to a signal that has been normalised (ie brought up in level so the highest peak is at digital full scale) can cause the level to increase further, resulting in clipping. This is particularly evident when cutting low frequencies, because you may cut a frequency that was originally cancelling out another frequency at various points throughout the song, which often results in very audible clipping. I've had experience of mixing sessions where the peak signal level has increased by more than 2dB after EQ cut has been applied. If you find yourself with a low-level track that you need to normalise, either allow a few decibels of headroom and normalise to -3dB DFS (Digital Full Scale) or use an EQ and mastering limiter in combination to take care of any peaks that might result. As a rule, apply any processing that you can before normalising.

# mastering compression

To make a track sound louder when it's already peaking close to digital full scale, use a limiter plug-in that's designed for mastering. In most cases, you can increase the overall level by at least 6dB before your ears notice that the peaks have been processed in any way. However, don't feel that you have to limit everything to excess simply to make it sound loud, as this will destroy the natural dynamics of the music.

Overall compression can also add energy to a mix and can help to even out a track, but as with limiting you should only use it if the track needs it. When making before-and-after comparisons, always make sure that both versions can be monitored at the same level so you're not being fooled by the old "loudest sounds best" effect. Often a compressor will change the apparent balance of a mix slightly, so you may need to use it in combination with EQ. Boosted frequencies are compressed the most if the EQ is inserted before the compressor, while inserting it after the compressor will allow the EQ to work more naturally.

Split-band compressors and limiters are usually better for use in mastering than conventional full-band types, because with these there's less interaction between things happening in different parts of the audio spectrum. For example, if a loud bass sound causes the compressor to cut in hard, the middle and treble won't be affected if you're using a multiband compressor. As a rule, I find that fairly low thresholds and ratios (ie below 1.4:1) work best for mastering purposes as they don't make the compressed mix sound unnatural. Dynamic equalisers that apply EQ cut or boost in proportion to signal level are also useful, as they can be used to add punch or brightness to individual beats without significantly affecting what occurs between those beats.

# de-noising

If you're using a digital de-noising program, you shouldn't expect miracles, because even the best systems produce side-effects if you try to remove all of the noise from a recording that has a very high level of background hiss. The simpler de-noiser plug-ins are effectively multi-band expanders, where the threshold of each band is set by first allowing the software to "learn" a selected section of noise from what occurs between tracks. Because it first has to learn a section of noise, if you know you're going to need in order to use a de-noising plug-in you should leave a little noise before each track for it to sample. This noise may be silenced after the de-noising process is complete, if required.

It should be possible to achieve a few decibels of noise reduction before audible side-effects set in, although the exact amount varies enormously from one de-noising package to another. The problem is that, as low-level signals open and close the expanders in their respective frequency bands, the background noise is modulated in an unnatural way that's reminiscent of "chirping" or "ringing". The best strategy may be to reduce the noise to the point at which there is just enough hiss left to cover up these unnatural side-effects.

# track editing

When editing tracks together from various takes or sections, try to make butt joins just before or just after a drum beat so that any discontinuities are masked by the beat. However, if you need to use a crossfade edit to smoothe over a transition, it may be wise to move the edit a little way from the drum beat in order to avoid the situation in which the drum beat is audible twice during the crossfade. If this happens, you may hear a phasing or flamming effect where the two beats overlap. As a rule, crossfades should be as short as possible and yet still provide a smooth edit. Once you've edited a track, you should resave it as a new sound file, as this will make CD burning easier.

Before burning your CD, listen to the finished master all the way through as it plays back from the playlist and check for errors or problems. It's best to use headphones when doing this, as they tend to show up flaws rather more effectively than loudspeakers. Even when you've burned your CD, don't make further copies until you've played the master on a few different systems to make sure that your mixes sound good elsewhere. Finally, if the CD is to be used as a master for commercial duplication, it will save you money if your mastering software can produce what is known as a Red-Book-compatible, PQ-encoded master disc. This software will create all of the the necessary track start and pause codes, as well as a table of contents in the form used by consumer audio CDs. Other software may well produce a playable audio CD, but it may not be suitable as a production master.

A Red Book disc must be written in Disc At Once mode, rather than a track at a time in order to avoid errors being created between tracks. Check with your CD manufacturer to confirm that they can work from CD-R as a master, and take note of any special requirements that they may have.

When you're ready to burn the CD, load in a good-quality, branded, blank CD-R. Cheap discs can save a few pence, but may not be reliable, and they also tend to produce higher block error rates than reputable branded discs. Always hold the blank CD-R by its edges, as dirt or fingerprints on the surface also causes errors.

# internet audio

In addition to making a CD master, you may also wish to prepare extracts from your work in a form that can be downloaded from the internet. For example, you may want to create a web site to publicise your material at which visitors can hear a short section of your music.

Because the internet – or, more accurately, the telephone system – is too slow to transmit CD-quality audio in real time, the amount of audio data needs to be reduced if the download time isn't going to be excessive. .WAV or .AIFF files are very large, which is why MP3 was invented. MP3 is an audio data compression system that shrinks audio files to less than a tenth of the size of the original, and yet allows them to retain near-CD quality. MP3 files can be downloaded from the internet just like any other file, and can be either played back on the computer or on a hardware MP3 player. Faster internet connections may even be able to play MP3 files in real time. At the time of writing, MP3 seems to be the format of choice for audio that's sold over the internet. As a rule of thumb, one minute of MP3 stereo audio will require something like 1Mb of data, although various compression ratios are available, depending on how much quality you're prepared to sacrifice in the interest of speed.

One alternative to using MP3 is to use one of the so-called *streaming* formats, such as RealAudio. Streamed files are much more heavily compressed than MP3, with a consequent reduction in subjective sound quality. However, they are compact enough for most users to play back in real time (after first loading a small section of the file), and are good enough to provide a basic idea of what the music sounds like. This makes streamed files more suitable for casual browsers among record catalogues or private musicians' web sites. The low subjective quality also makes music piracy less of a concern.

To turn .WAV, SDII or .AIFF files into MP3 or a streaming format like RealAudio, you'll need a piece of encoding software. MP3 encoding is sometimes included as part of commercial editing packages, but streaming software usually has to be bought separately. The person receiving the files can usually download a free player from the software vendor, and so it's common for a download site to include a link to the software vendor's site, so that visitors to your site can obtain the necessary player software without having to search for it. MP3 playback is often supported via plug-ins for existing browser software, such as Microsoft's Internet Explorer or Netscape Navigator.

## chapter 8

# the home desktop studio

A traditional recording studio is a complex and sprawling affair compared with its desktop counterpart, but the basic components are essentially the same. It's just that, in a desktop system, a lot of conventional studio hardware is replaced by software. This saves a lot of money and time spent installing cabling, although you'll still probably find that you end up with more wiring than you initially expected!

Studios are exceptionally greedy when it comes to power points, even virtual studios. You'll most often need to resort to using mains distribution boards with multiple power sockets, and in most cases using those with six or more sockets is tidier and more efficient than stringing together lots of four-way distribution boards. Audio equipment doesn't demand a lot of power, so it's generally quite safe to run a desktop studio system from just a pair of distribution boards fed from a double wall socket. Although we all do it sometimes, it's not a good idea to plug one distribution board into another, because before you know it you'll have a whole string of the things running around the room, so it's best to try to obtain all the power you need from one double wall socket. However, if you find that you need more outlets, use the next one along as well, provided that it's on the same ring main. Of course, the best option is to fit more mains sockets, but this isn't always practical in a domestic situation.

Commercial distribution boards are generally OK for studio use, as long as you avoid the very cheap ones, and wherever possible you should plug things into them and then leave them alone. If you keep plugging and unplugging things then the spring contacts will weaken, and you could end up suffering from intermittent connections that produce difficult-to-find pops and crackles. It's also a wise move to use a mains filter on your computer to help prevent crashes caused by interference on the mains supply.

Don't remove the earth leads from any equipment that's supposed to be earthed, and remember to check your mains plugs regularly, because loose wires are not only dangerous but they will also cause intermittent crackles and buzzes. Plugs need to be checked regularly, because even the best-made connections have a habit of coming loose over time. I've heard some studio owners claim that cleaning the pins of mains plugs with wire wool can result in better sound quality. I'm always a little sceptical of this kind of thing, but keeping a clean, low-resistance ground path still seems sensible.

Your audio interface will provide a means to accommodate sound sources, such as mics, DI boxes or recording pre-amps, but as well as this – along with your MIDI interface and your computer – you'll still need a conventional monitoring system, plus either a mastering recorder or a CD burner, and indeed many users have both. All audio connections should use screened cable, while noisy computer drives should be positioned as far away from the mixing position as possible. Some drives are much noisier than others, so it's worth spending a little more on a computer with a quieter drive, especially if you want to record in the same room as your computer.

Unless you plan to restrict your MIDI sound sources to those that can be generated within the computer, you'll also need an external mixer and some external sound modules, as well as your master keyboard. This will involve a certain amount of wiring, but much less than you'd find in a hardware-based studio. Again, it's vital to use proper screened cable if interference problems are to be avoided. The purpose of this chapter is to examine the layout of the various components in a desktop studio, and also to look at the acoustic environment with a view to making the monitoring system as accurate as possible.

# studio layout

The mixing console is the nerve centre of a traditional recording studio, and the positioning of everything else is in relation to the mixer. In the desktop studio, however, you may have both a computer and a mixer, and so the focal point of your system is both the keyboard and monitor of your computer (it doesn't matter where you put the CPU) and your hardware mixer. You have to be able to operate both without moving from the ideal monitoring position, which usually means having the mixer dead centre, with the computer monitor behind it and the computer keyboard in front. Unfortunately, you'll also need to be close to the computer when you're working on your master MIDI keyboard, so the best solution is often to use a tiered keyboard system. In my own studio, the MIDI keyboard slides out from beneath the computer table when needed, but otherwise the general layout is the same.

If you have more equipment than you can accommodate at the central monitoring/mixing position, think carefully about what equipment you'll need to operate when mixing and set things up to accommodate this. For example, you don't need to have perfect stereo imaging when recording, so your master keyboard could be set slightly off to one side. This shouldn't be a problem, as long as you can can still see the computer monitor and reach the keyboard. Similarly, DAT recorders and CD burners can generally be positioned to one side, as you don't need to reach them very often during a mix.

# the components

For the musician working alone, a combined mic pre-amp and compressor is the ideal tool with which to get a high-quality audio signal into the system, and if you play guitar or bass, one of these that also features line- and instrument-level inputs would be useful. All serious mic pre-amps will provide phantom power for capacitor microphones, and some also include EQ. Most pre-amps are rack-mounted affairs, as are synth modules, samplers and some MIDI interfaces, so it's often best to put all of these in a free-standing rack positioned to one side of the mixing position. The cables between this rack and the mixer can be tied together and hidden in specially-designed split corrugated plastic tubing. Even so, you should avoid having mains leads running alongside signal cables, as this can introduce hum into the system, and you should also keep mains-adaptor-style power supplies away from signal cables.

It's very important at this point to stress that nothing should be placed between the monitor speakers and the mix engineer's head, so if the rack is higher than the bottom of your monitor speakers it should be moved right around to the side.

You'll find a stereo DAT tape machine useful, and although tape is old technology DAT has the advantages of being reasonably cheap and easy to archive. Conventional DAT machines work at 16-bit/44.1 kHz or 48kHz, although some specialist models are now available that can record at 24-bit resolution by running the tape twice as fast. A good cassette deck is useful for creating quick listening copies, which you can try in the car or in your ghetto blaster, while a regular CD player patched into your mixer will help you to compare what you're doing with other recordings quickly and easily. If your computer set-up doesn't include a CD-burner, you should get one as soon as possible, but make sure that it's supported by the CD writing software that you plan to use. These can also go into your equipment rack, and if you have some devices that aren't rack mountable you can always invest in some rack shelves.

My own system is based around a small digital mixer, which includes dynamic processing on every channel, as well as very respectable on-board effects. Even so, there should still be a place for high-quality outboard effects in your system, especially high-end reverb, and in most cases these can be left patched into the aux send/return loop of your hardware mixer. More traditional studios rely on patchbays for plugging in outboard effects and for changing routing options, but it's better if you can configure your desktop system to avoid them. Not only do patchbays contribute to cost and complexity but they also become unreliable once their socket contacts have become tarnished or dirty. They also seem to attract more than their fair share of interference and ground-loop problems. Even so, if you feel that a patchbay would make life easier for you, by making some of your more commonly changed connections more accessible, then by all means use one. My only advice would be to keep it as simple as possible and to cover it up with a cloth when not in use so as to prevent dust from settling in the sockets.

Digital patchbays are now becoming increasingly common tools for handling the optical or co-axial digital interconnects between soundcards or interfaces, digital mixers and recorders. Again, it's worth getting one if you find that you're constantly having to replug connectors, as RCA phono connections don't stand up well to being plugged and unplugged on a regular basis.

# the monitoring system

A practical monitoring system for a home studio would be a pair of nearfield monitors and a pair of headphones. While it's never a great idea to do all recording and mixing over headphones, because of their different imaging properties and the way in which they can misrepresent bass, they are still extremely useful, and are able to pick up small distortions, noise and other flaws that loudspeakers might miss. Think of headphones as your audio microscope.

A stereo hi-fi amp, or a dedicated power amp of at least 30 watts per channel, is probably the minimum requirement for accurate monitoring, because, although you may not mix very loudly, brief signal peaks can often exceed the average signal level by a huge margin. For accurate monitoring, it's essential that your amplifier can translate these peaks cleanly. Distorted signal peaks caused by an under-powered amplifier can also lead to tweeter damage.

If you're using a hi-fi amplifier (as opposed to a studio monitoring power amp), ensure that it has either aux, CD or tuner inputs that you can use to accept the output from your soundcard or interface. You can't use the phono record deck inputs for this purpose because these have built-in tonal correction circuitry for record player cartridges, and they would make your mixes sound completely wrong. They're also not optimised for use at line level.

# loudspeakers

Everything you do in your studio is evaluated over your monitor loudspeakers, so it's important to choose a pair that you can rely on to let you know what's really happening. Choose the most honest-sounding speakers that you can afford, rather than speakers that flatter, and try not to be tempted into buying speakers that are too big for the room in which you're working. Medium-sized, two-way nearfield speaker systems are the best choice, as they tend to be more resistant to abuse than regular hi-fi speakers. When auditioning speakers, take a selection of familiar CDs with you so that you have some sort of reference point. The demonstration material that most salesmen have to hand is chosen purely because it sounds impressive.

I personally prefer to use active loudspeakers (those with separate built-in amplifiers for the bass/mid driver and the tweeter), as they sound tighter and cleaner than passive models of the same power rating. Using active monitors also means that you don't have to worry about choosing a suitable amplifier, and you also don't need speaker cable because the speakers are driven directly from your mixer or soundcard line output, often via a regular XLR mic cable. Whether you use active or passive speakers, you'll still need to pick either magnetically-shielded models or those fitted with low magnetic radiation drivers if you want to use them near a conventional computer monitor. Failure to do this may result in colour distortion at the edges of your monitor display. (Flat-screen LCD monitors are unaffected by magnetic fields.)

# the speaker/room interface

Loudspeakers don't work in isolation, but instead form a symbiotic relationship with the room in which they are used. Small rooms can be very problematic at low bass frequencies because of the relationship between the room dimensions and the long wavelengths of low audio frequencies, so it's invariably best to use two-way nearfield monitors that roll off gently below 60Hz rather than those which generate a lot of really deep bass. Monitor speakers should be placed on rigid stands behind the mixer or computer desk, not on top of it, and stands filled with sand or lead shot give the best results. Speakers that haven't been securely mounted can have a serious effect on the clarity of the sound and the tightness of the bass.

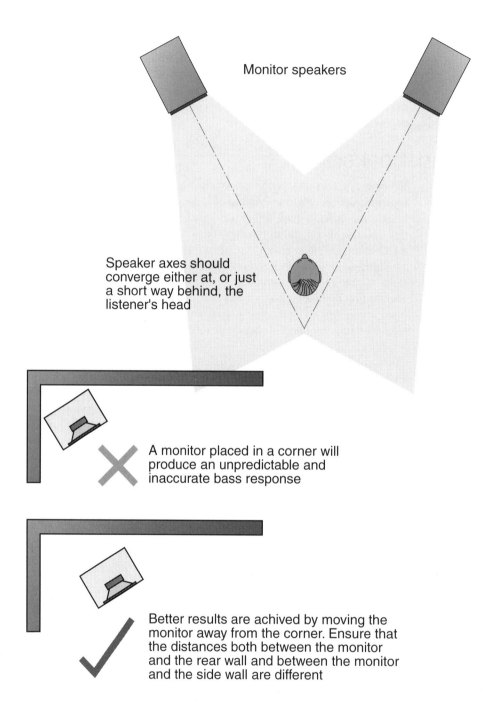

Monitor speakers

Speaker axes should converge either at, or just a short way behind, the listener's head

A monitor placed in a corner will produce an unpredictable and inaccurate bass response

Better results are achived by moving the monitor away from the corner. Ensure that the distances both between the monitor and the rear wall and between the monitor and the side wall are different

**Figure 8.1: Monitor set-up**

It's very important to have the speakers set up symmetrically, as shown in Figure 8.1, or your stereo image will be adversely affected. Not only this but the room should also be as acoustically symmetrical as possible. This is particularly important when it comes to the area near the mixing position, where it's not a good idea to have a reflective surface on one side and an absorbent surface on the other, as this will affect the stereo imaging badly. Positioning the speakers between one and one and a half metres from the mixing position is usually best in a small studio, but it's also advisable to keep the speakers at least half a metre away from corners in order to avoid unpredictable bass boost being caused by the boundary effect.

Simply put, the boundary effect means that sound bouncing off the walls combines with the direct sound from the speaker, and the nearer you are to a corner, the more reinforcement occurs at the bass end of the spectrum. Obtaining free bass by positioning your speakers in the corner may seem like an attractive prospect, but the resulting response is so uneven that you have no idea what you're really hearing. In a rectangular room, it's usually best to position the speakers along the longest wall. Consult the manual that came with your monitors to determine how far away from the wall you should stand them. If you have any leeway in your speakers' position, try to move them a short distance forwards or backwards while playing some known commercial material and find a spot at which the bass end is as even as possible. You should be listening for a position at which all of the bass notes are at nominally the same level.

It's important that you use your speakers the right way up, as specified in the manual. Mounting speakers on their sides may look good but it narrows the sweet spot (the area in which you can sit to hear an accurate mix) considerably, and also compromises the stereo imaging. The optimum listening position is located exactly between the speakers, and in order to ensure that this sweet spot is as wide as possible the speakers should be angled inwards so the tweeters point either at or just behind the listener's head. The monitors can also be tilted if necessary, again so the tweeters point directly at the engineer's head, in both the vertical and horizontal planes, although it's better to choose stands that are high enough to allow the monitors to remain vertical.

# acoustic treatment

A little basic acoustic treatment can improve the accuracy of a monitoring environment significantly. Most monitoring problems are caused by strong reflections from the walls, floors and ceilings of a room, which combine with the direct sound from the speakers to produce an

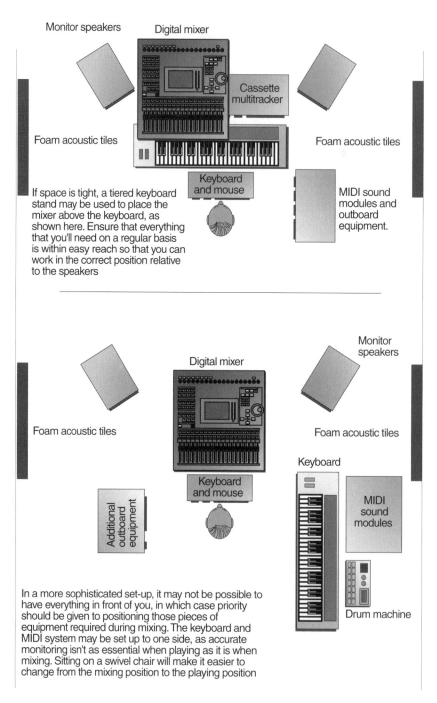

Monitor speakers

Digital mixer

Cassette multitracker

Foam acoustic tiles

Foam acoustic tiles

Keyboard and mouse

MIDI sound modules and outboard equipment.

If space is tight, a tiered keyboard stand may be used to place the mixer above the keyboard, as shown here. Ensure that everything that you'll need on a regular basis is within easy reach so that you can work in the correct position relative to the speakers

Monitor speakers

Digital mixer

Foam acoustic tiles

Foam acoustic tiles

Keyboard

Keyboard and mouse

Additional outboard equipment

MIDI sound modules

Drum machine

In a more sophisticated set-up, it may not be possible to have everything in front of you, in which case priority should be given to positioning those pieces of equipment required during mixing. The keyboard and MIDI system may be set up to one side, as accurate monitoring isn't as essential when playing as it is when mixing. Sitting on a swivel chair will make it easier to change from the mixing position to the playing position

**Figure 8.2: Fitting acoustic tiles**

inaccurate listening experience. Cutting down on excessive reflections helps, although you shouldn't damp your room too much or it will sound uncomfortably dead. Furthermore, it's incredibly difficult to absorb bass frequencies, so any attempt to create a completely dead room will probably result in too much boomy bass and not enough top end. Carpets, curtains and soft furnishings will help damp low frequencies enormously without making the room sound too dead. If you can clearly hear another person talking across the room, it's a good indication that it's damped well enough to mix in it.

One of the benefits of nearfield monitoring is that, because the speakers are physically close to your listening position, you can hear more of the direct sound from the speakers and less of the reflected sound from the room. The fact that nearfield monitors don't produce excessive deep bass is also helpful, as it's the bass frequencies that bring out the worst in a room, particularly a small one.

If the room is excessively reverberant, try hanging a rug or a thick drape on the rear wall and stick two slabs of 100mm-thick acoustic foam tiles of around a metre square on the side walls on either side of your normal listening position, as shown in Figure 8.2. A further area of foam tiles on the ceiling between your listening position and the monitors may also help, especially if you have a large, reflective mixer or computer desk. In practice, though, bedroom studios often work well enough with little or no extra treatment, because the carpets, curtains and bedding provide plenty of absorption.

It should be noted that acoustic treatment is not the same thing as soundproofing. Fixing a layer of acoustic tiling to the walls will change the acoustics of the room but it will do little to prevent unwanted sound leaking in or out. Soundproofing is a completely different kettle of fish, and is explored (along with acoustic treatment and monitoring systems) in my book *Creative Recording II*, which is also available from Sanctuary Publishing.

# audio connections

Most home studios use a lot of unbalanced connections, simply because most synths and pre-amps have unbalanced outputs, as are the insert points on most low- and mid-priced hardware mixers. However, if you have the option to connect using balanced cable, such as from an audio interface that has balanced outputs to a hardware mixer with balanced line inputs, it's always worth doing so. Not only is balanced wiring less susceptible to interference, but you often have to pay a penalty in the

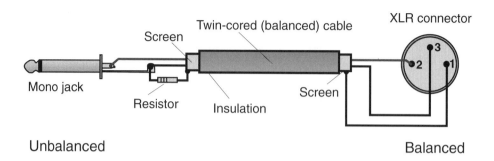

**Figure 8.3: Balanced-to-unbalanced connection**

signal level of between six and twelve decibels when wiring balanced connections for unbalanced operation.

Another useful tip is to connect unbalanced sources (such as many synths and samplers) to balanced mixer inputs using a pseudo-balanced cable, as shown in Figure 8.3. This wiring arrangement helps to prevent background hum and buzzing caused by a phenomenon known as a ground loop, where multiple ground paths exist between various pieces of audio equipment.

Digital connections are very important, as a poor connection can lead to errors, which in turn causes random clicks and pops or even, occasionally, total signal breakdown. Co-axial S/PDIF signals are generally connected by using RCA phono cables, and physically these are interchangeable with many audio cables. Short audio cables often appear to work for the transferring of digital audio material, but it's not wise to use them because the cable will have the wrong impedance, increasing its susceptibility for incurring errors dramatically. Even if the sound seems OK, it could be the case that your error-correction system is working overtime to keep things going. When more errors occur than it can deal with, you'll start to hear pops and ticks. Digital cable for use with S/PDIF should be 70-ohm co-ax, and it's well worth buying ready-made digital cables from a reputable source as they often use better connectors than those that you can buy from an audio parts store.

You might imagine that optical cables would be less problematic, but in reality there are several different grades of cable, and the cheaper varieties are only suitable for transmitting data over short distances. It's also vitally important not to kink optical cables or bend them around too tight a radius.

# coda

On the practical side, leave a little physical room for expansion – few project studio owners rely on their computers to do everything, so the rack of outboard gear is likely to remain a familiar sight for a few years yet, as is the digital hardware mixer. No matter how happy you are with your current system, you'll still come across new bits of gear that you'd like to add, and so the more flexibility you allow yourself the fewer times you'll need to completely strip down your system and start all over again.

A desktop studio can bring a lot of pleasure, and if you use yours with care you'll be able to use it to make recordings that stand comparison with commercial records. However, it's a complex subject, and the old adage "make haste slowly" is particularly relevant. Having a studio inside a PC or Mac may at first appear to be a compact and straightforward arrangement, but all of the complexity of a real studio still exists within them, in virtual form. In some ways, the virtual studio is harder to deal with because, unlike its hardware counterpart, if a signal goes missing it's not a simple matter of checking to see if a cable is plugged in or not. Your best plan is to get to know your system in manageable stages, and even though reading manuals isn't always fun you should still keep them close at hand for reference. I can guarantee that you'll need to consult them from time to time, no matter how experienced you become. I can also guarantee that you'll also learn a lot more about computers than you might have envisaged when you first embarked on this adventure.

# glossary

## AC

Alternating Current.

## A/D converter

Circuit for converting analogue waveforms into a series of equally-spaced numerical values represented by binary numbers. The more bits a converter has, the greater the resolution of its sampling process.

## active

Describes a circuit containing transistors, integrated circuits, tubes and other devices that require power in order to operate and are capable of amplification.

## ADAT

Digital eight--track tape machine developed by Alesis. Also describes the ADAT audio interfacing standard developed by Alesis, which handles up to eight channels per connection. Many soundcards and digital mixers support the ADAT interface. Connection is via an optical cable.

## AES/EBU

Digital interface protocol for stereo audio signals at sample rates of up to 48kHz across balanced cable, normally connected via a standard three-pin XLR connector. Systems for delivering audio at sample rates of up to 96kHz use a pair of AES/EBU cables. Certain consumer "flags" are not recognised by AES/EBU, including SCMS copy-protection data and DAT track-start IDs.

## additive synthesis

System used for the generation of waveforms or sounds by combining basic waveforms or sampled sounds before these are then processed further with filters and envelope shapers.

# ADSR

Envelope generator with Attack, Decay, Sustain and Release parameters. This is a simple type of envelope generator which was first used on early analogue synthesisers and continues to be popular on modern instruments. (See "Decay" for more details.)

# active sensing

System used to verify that a MIDI connection is working, which involves the sending device sending frequent short messages to the receiving device to reassure it that all is well. If the remote device doesn't respond for any reason, the receiving device will recognise a fault and switch off all notes. Not all MIDI devices support active sensing.

# AFL

After Fade Listen, a system used within mixing consoles to allow specific signals to be monitored at the level set by their fader of level control knob. Aux sends are generally monitored AFL rather than PFL (see PFL).

# aftertouch

Means of generating a control signal based on how much pressure is applied to the keys of a MIDI keyboard. Most instruments that support this do not have independent pressure sensing for all keys but instead detect the overall pressure exerted on a sensing strip that runs beneath the keys. Aftertouch may be used to control such functions as depth of vibrato, filter brightness, loudness and so on.

# .AIFF

Audio file format often used by Macintosh-based audio systems.

# algorithm

Computer program designed to perform a specific task within a piece of equipment. In the context of effects units, algorithms usually describe a software building block designed to create a specific effect or combination of effects.

# aliasing

When an analogue signal is sampled in order to be converted into a stream of digital data, the sampling frequency must be at least twice that of the component of the input signal which has the highest frequency. The sampling process will become ambiguous if this rule is disobeyed, because then there will be insufficient points with which to define each cycle of the waveform, resulting in enharmonic frequencies being added to the audible signal.

# ambience

Result of sound reflections in a confined space being added to the original sound. Ambience may also be created electronically by some digital reverb units. The main difference between ambience and reverberation is that ambience doesn't have the characteristic long delay time of reverberation; the reflections mainly provide a sense of space.

# amp

Unit of electrical current. Short for ampere.

# amplifier

Device that increases the level of an electrical signal.

# amplitude

Another word for level. Can refer to levels of sound or electrical signal.

# analogue

Circuitry that uses a continually-changing voltage or current to represent a signal. The electrical signal can be thought of as being analogous to the original signal.

# analogue synthesis

A system of synthesising sounds by means of analogue circuitry, usually by filtering simple repeating waveforms.

# attenuate

To make lower in level.

# anti-aliasing filter

Filter used to limit the frequency range of an analogue signal prior to A/D conversion so that the maximum frequency doesn't exceed half of the sampling rate.

# application

Alternative term for computer program.

# arpeggiator

Device (or program) that allows a MIDI instrument to sequence around any notes currently being played. Most arpeggiators also allow the sound to be sequenced over several octaves so that the holding down of a simple chord can result in an impressive repeating sequence of notes.

# ASCII

American Standard Code For Information Interchange. A standard code for representing computer keyboard characters in binary data.

# ASIO

Standard software driver developed by Steinberg, allowing compatible soundcards or audio interfaces and software to work together effectively and with low latency. ASIO II also provides the option for source monitoring with compatible hardware, which avoids the effects of latency when recording or overdubbing.

# attack

The time it takes for a sound to achieve maximum its amplitude. Drums have a fast attack, whereas bowed strings have a slow attack. In compressors and gates, the attack time equates to how quickly the processor can change its gain.

# audio frequency

Signals in the human audio range, nominally 20Hz-20kHz.

# autolocator

Feature of a tape or other recording device that enables locations to be stored and then recalled at a later time. For example, you may store the start of a verse as a locate point so that the machine winds back the start of the verse after you've recorded an overdub.

# aux

Control on a mixing console designed to route a proportion of the channel signal to the effects or cue mix outputs (aux send).

# aux send

Physical output from a mixer aux send buss.

# aux return

Mixer inputs used to add effects to a mix.

# azimuth

Alignment co-ordinate of a tape head which references the head gap to the true vertical relative to the tape path.

# back-up

A safety copy of software or other digital data.

# bandpass filter (BPF)

Filter that removes or attenuates frequencies above and below the frequency at which it is set. Frequencies within the band are emphasised. Bandpass filters are often used as tone shaping elements in synthesisers.

# balance

This word has several meanings in recording. It may refer to the relative levels of the left and right channels of a stereo recording, or it may be used to describe the relative levels of the various instruments and voices within a mix.

# balanced wiring

Wiring system which uses two out-of-phase conductors and a common screen to reduce the effect of interference. In order for the process of balancing to be effective, both the sending and receiving device must have balanced output and input stages respectively.

# bandwidth

A means of specifying the range of frequencies passed by an electronic circuit, such as an amplifier, mixer or filter. The frequency range is usually measured at the points where the level drops by 3dB relative to the maximum.

# beta version

Software which is not fully tested and may include bugs.

# bias

High-frequency signal used in analogue recording to improve the accuracy of the recorded signal and to drive the erase head. Bias is generated by a bias oscillator.

# binary

Counting system based on only two states, represented by ones and zeros.

# bios

Part of a computer operating system held on ROM rather than on disk. This handles basic routines such as accessing the disk drive.

# bit

Abbreviation of binary digit, which may either be one or zero.

# bit depth

The number of bits used to represent a digital signal. See "Resolution".

# boost/cut control

Single control which allows a range of frequencies passing through a filter to be either amplified or attenuated. The centre position is usually the "flat" or "no effect" position.

# bouncing

The process of mixing two or more recorded tracks together and re-recording them onto another track. In the context of a computer audio system, this generally involves creating a new file of the mixed audio while leaving the originals intact.

# BPM

Beats Per Minute.

# breath controller

Device that converts breath pressure into MIDI controller data.

# buffer

Circuit designed to isolate the output of a source device from loading effects due to the input impedance of the destination device.

# buffer memory

Temporary RAM memory used in some computer operations, sometimes to prevent a break in the data stream when the computer is interrupted to perform another task. All audio software employs buffer memory to ensure a continuous stream of audio. The greater the buffer size, the less likely it is that glitches or other problems will occur. At the same time, however, a larger buffer size increases the system latency.

# bug

Slang term for a software fault or a problem with the design of equipment. Also sometimes used to describe a contact microphone or a similar type of pickup.

# buss

A common electrical signal path along which signals may travel. In a mixer, there are several busses carrying the stereo mix, the groups, the PFL signal, the aux sends and so on. Power supplies are also fed along busses. The spelling of buss may be buss or bus, depending on the source of the documentation.

# byte

A piece of digital data comprising eight bits.

# cardioid

Means literally "heart shaped". Describes the polar response of a unidirectional microphone.

# CD-R

A recordable type of compact disc that can only be recorded once. It cannot be erased and reused.

# CD-R burner

A device capable of recording data onto blank CD-Rs.

# CD-RW

A recordable type of Compact Disc that can be recorded many times. It may be erased and reused in a similar way to hard disks.

# CV

Control Voltage. Used to control the pitch of an oscillator or the frequency of a filter in an analogue synthesiser. Most analogue synths follow a one-volt-per-octave convention, although there are exceptions. To use a pre-MIDI analogue synthesiser under MIDI control, a MIDI-to-CV converter is required.

# capacitance

Property of an electrical component which enables it to store an electrostatic charge.

# capacitor

Electrical component exhibiting capacitance.

# capacitor microphone

Microphone that operates on the principle of measuring the change in electrical charge across a capacitor where one of the electrodes is a thin conductive membrane that flexes in response to sound pressure. Some older engineers may still refer to capacitor mics as condenser microphones. (Condenser was one of the original terms for capacitors.)

# channel

In the context of mixing, channel refers to a single strip of controls in a hardware or a virtual mixing console relating to either a single input or, alternatively, a pair of main/monitor inputs.

# channel

In the context of MIDI, channel refers to one of 16 possible data channels over which MIDI data may be sent. The organisation of data by channels means that up to 16 different MIDI instruments or parts may be addressed over a single cable.

# chase

Term describing the process whereby a slave device attempts to synchronise itself with a master device so that both play from the same part of the recording.

# chase

In the context of a MIDI sequence, this involves chasing events (ie looking back to earlier positions in the song to see if there are any program changes or other events that need to be acted upon).

# chip

Integrated circuit.

## chord

Two or more different musical notes played at the same time.

## chorus

Effect created by doubling a signal and adding delay and pitch modulation to one part.

## chromatic

A scale of pitches rising in steps of one semitone.

## click track

Metronome pulse which helps musicians to play in time.

## clipping

Severe form of distortion which occurs when a signal tries to exceed the maximum level boundary which a piece of equipment is equipped to handle. The sound of digital clipping tends to be much more unpleasant than that of analogue clipping, and so should be avoided.

## clone

Exact duplicate. The term often refers to digital copies of digital tapes or CD-Rs, where the numerical data contained in the original is passed on to the clone without being changed.

## common mode rejection

A measure of how well a balanced circuit rejects a signal that is common to both inputs. This is particularly important in the design of mic amps, as it dictates how effectively a balanced system will reject interference picked up on a mic cable.

## compander

Encode/decode device that compresses a signal while encoding it and then expands it while decoding it. This process is often used in systems that reduce noise in analogue tapes, but is largely irrelevant to digital audio systems.

## compressor

Device designed to reduce the dynamic range of audio signals by reducing the level of high signals or by increasing the level of low signals.

## computer

Device for storing and processing digital data.

## conductor

Material that provides a low resistance path for electrical current.

## console

Alternative term for mixer.

## contact enhancer

Compound designed to increase the electrical conductivity of electrical contacts, such as plugs, sockets and edge connectors.

## continuous controller

Type of MIDI message used to translate continuous change, such as from a pedal, wheel or breath-control device.

## copy protection

Method used by software manufacturers to prevent unauthorised copying.

## crash

Slang term relating to the malfunction of computer program.

## cut-and-paste editing

Editing by copying or moving sections of a recording to different locations.

## cut-off frequency

The frequency above or below which attenuation starts to occur in a filter circuit.

## cycle

One complete vibration of a sound source, or its electrical equivalent. One cycle per second is expressed as 1Hz (Hertz).

# CV

Control voltage used in analogue synths to control the frequency of oscillators or filters.

# damping

In the context of reverberation, damping refers to the rate at which the reverberant energy is absorbed by the various surfaces in the environment.

# daisy chain

Term used to describe the serial electrical connection between devices or modules.

# DAT

Digital Audio Tape. The commonly-used DAT machines are more correctly known as R-DAT machines because they use a rotating head similar to that of a VCR. Digital recorders using fixed or stationary heads (such as DCC) are known as S-DAT machines.

# data

Information stored and used by a computer.

# data compression

System used to reduce the amount of data that is necessary in order to accurately represent an audio signal, usually by discarding audio information that is being masked by more prominent sounds. Data-compression algorithms are based on psycho-acoustic principles designed to ensure that only components which cannot be heard are lost, although in practice heavy compression compromises subjective audio quality. Both MiniDisc audio and MP3 files use a type of data compression.

# daughterboard

Circuit board that fits into an expansion slot on a larger circuit board (motherboard), increasing its capabilities.

# dB

Decibel. Unit used to express the relative levels of two electrical voltages, powers or sounds.

# dBm

Variation on dB, referenced to 0dB = 1mW into 600 ohms.

## dBv

Variation on dB, referenced to 0dB = 0.775v.

## dBV

Variation on dB, referenced to 0dB = 1v.

## dB/octave

Means of measuring the slope of a filter. The more decibels per octave, the sharper the filter slope.

## DC

Direct Current.

## DCC

Stationary-head digital recorder format originally developed by Philips. DCC uses a data-compression system which reduces the amount of data that needs to be stored. DCC lost the marketing battle with MiniDisc, however, and is now rarely found in modern studios.

## DBX

Commercial analogue encode/decode tape noise reduction system that compresses the signal during recording and expands it by an identical amount on playback.

## DCO

Digitally-Controlled Oscillator.

## DDL

Digital Delay Line.

## de-esser

Device for reducing the effect of sibilance in vocal signals.

## de-oxidising compound

Substance which removes oxides from electrical contacts.

## decay

The progressive reduction in amplitude of a sound or electrical signal over time. In the context of ADSR envelope shapers, as used in synths and samplers, the Decay phase starts as soon as the Attack phase has reached its maximum level. In the Decay phase, the signal level drops (at a rate set by the Decay parameter) until it reaches the Sustain level, set by the user. The signal then stays at this level until the key is released, when the Release phase is entered.

## defragmentation

The process of rearranging the files on a hard disk so that all of the files are as contiguous as possible, and that the remaining free space is also contiguous. This is important for digital audio, as a fragmented drive delivers lower rates of data transfer.

## detent

Physical click stop in the centre of a control like a pan or EQ cut/boost knob.

## DI

Direct Injection, where a signal is plugged directly into an audio chain without the aid of a mic.

## DI box

Device for matching the signal level and impedance of a source to a tape machine or mixer input.

## digital

Electronic system which represents data and signals in the form of on/off states represented by ones and zeros.

## digital delay

Digital processor used for generating delay and echo effects.

## digital reverb

Digital processor used for simulating reverberation.

## DIN connector

Consumer multipin signal-connection format, also used for MIDI cabling. Various pin configurations are available.

## direct coupling

Means of connecting two electrical circuits so that both AC and DC signals may be passed between them.

## dither

System of adding low-level noise to a digitised audio signal in such a way that the low-level resolution is extended at the expense of a slight deterioration in noise performance. The effect of the added noise can be minimised by using noise-shaping techniques to move the noise high up in the audio spectrum, where the human ear is least sensitive.

## disc

Used to describe vinyl discs, CDs and MiniDiscs.

## disk

Abbreviation of diskette, now used to describe computer floppy, hard and removable disks.

## DMA

Direct Memory Access. Part of a computer's operating system which allows peripheral devices to communicate directly with the computer memory without going via the central processor or CPU.

## Dolby

Company responsible for Dolby analogue noise reduction and Dolby surround sound. Dolby analogue tape noise reduction is an encode/decode system that amplifies low-level, high-frequency signals during recording and then reverses this process during playback. There are several different Dolby systems in use, comprising types B, C and S for domestic and semi-professional machines and types A and SR for professional machines. Recordings made using one of these systems must also be replayed via the same system. Dolby Surround is a means of encoding a two-channel signal so that information can be extracted to drive rear speakers as well as stereo front speakers, and sometimes a front mid speaker. Many consumer TV systems now include the Dolby Pro Logic system.

## DOS

Disk Operating System. Part of the operating system of PC and IBM-compatible computers

## DSP

Digital Signal Processor. A powerful microchip used to process digital signals.

## driver

Piece of software that handles communications between the main program and a hardware peripheral, such as a soundcard, printer or scanner. Special drivers are needed for audio work in order to minimise the effect of latency. (See ASIO and EASI.)

## drum pad

Synthetic surface which produces electronic trigger signals in response to being hit with drum sticks.

## dry

Describes a signal that has had no effects added.

## dubbing

Adding further material to an existing recording. Also known as *overdubbing* or *tracking*.

## ducking

System used to control the level of one audio signal with another. For example, a segment of background music can be made to duck in level whenever there's a voice-over. There are some compressor plug-ins available which offer this facility.

## dump

To transfer digital data from one device to another. A sysex (system-exclusive) dump is a means of transmitting information about a particular instrument or module via MIDI, and may be used to store sound patches, parameter settings other criteria.

## dynamic microphone

Type of microphone that works on the electric generator principle, where a diaphragm moves a coil of wire within a magnetic field.

## dynamic range

Range in dB between the highest signal that can be handled by a piece of equipment and the level at which small signals are obscured by the noise floor.

# dynamics

Method of describing the relative levels within a piece of music.

# dynamics processing

Process such as compression, gating or limiting, which affect the dynamic range of a signal.

# EASI

Proprietary audio driver format developed by eMagic for use with compatible soundcards.

# early reflections

The first sound reflections from walls, floors and ceilings following a sound created in an acoustically-reflective environment.

# effect

Device for treating an audio signal in order to change it in some creative way. Effects often involve the use of delay circuits, and include such treatments as reverb and echo.

# effects loop

Connection system that allows an external signal processor to be connected into the audio chain. Virtual equivalents are available within software mixers for the use of effect plug-ins.

# effects return

Additional mixer input designed to accommodate the output from an effects unit.

# EIDE

Sometimes known as Ultra DMA, this is a type of hard-drive interface used within PCs and all recent Macintoshes. It's not as fast as SCSI but it's much cheaper.

# electret microphone

Type of capacitor mic, the operation of which is based on a permanently-charged capsule.

# encode/decode

System that requires a signal to be processed prior to recording, which is then reversed during playback.

## enhancer

Device designed to brighten audio material using techniques such as dynamic equalisation, phase shifting and harmonic generation.

## envelope

The way in which the level of a sound or signal varies over time.

## envelope generator

Circuit capable of generating a control signal which represents the envelope of the sound that you wish to recreate. This may then be used to control the level of an oscillator or some other sound source, although envelopes may also be used to control filter or modulation settings. The most common example is the ADSR generator. (See "ADSR".)

## E-PROM

Similar to ROM. The data on the chip can be erased and replaced using special equipment.

## equaliser

Device which selectively cuts or boosts selected parts of the audio spectrum.

## erase

To remove recorded material from an analogue tape, or digital data from any storage medium.

## event (MIDI)

In MIDI terms, an event is a single unit of MIDI data, such as a note being turned on or off, a piece of controller information, a program-change message etc.

## exciter

Enhancer that works by synthesising new high-frequency harmonics.

## expander

Device designed to decrease the level of low-level signals, thus increasing the dynamic range of the overall signal. Expanders are often used instead of gates to suppress low-level noise.

## expander module

Synthesiser with no keyboard, often being rack mountable or in some other compact format.

## fader

Sliding potentiometer control used in mixers and other processors.

## ferric

Magnetic tape coating made from iron oxide.

## FET

Field-Effect Transistor.

## figure of eight

Describes the polar response of a microphone that is equally sensitive at both the front and rear, and yet rejects sounds coming from the sides.

## file

Meaningful list of data stored in digital form. A standard MIDI File is a specific type of file designed to allow sequence information to be communicated between different types of sequencer.

## filter

Electronic circuit designed to emphasise or attenuate a specific range of frequencies.

## flanging

Modulated delay effect which uses feedback to create a dramatic, sweeping sound.

## flag

Digital data embedded in an audio data stream indicating its status (for example, SCMS copy code and track start IDs).

## floppy disk

Computer disk that stores digital information on a flexible magnetic medium encased in a protective plastic sleeve. The maximum information that can be stored on a standard high-density disk is 1.44Mb. Earlier double-density disks hold only around half of this.

## flutter echo

Resonant echo which occurs when sound reflects back and forth across two parallel, reflective surfaces.

## foldback

System for feeding one or more separate mixes to the performers for use while recording and overdubbing. Also known as a *cue mix*.

## formant

Frequency component or resonance of an instrument or voice which doesn't change with the pitch of the note being played or sung. For example, the body resonance of an acoustic guitar remains constant, regardless of the note being played.

## format

Procedure which is required to be performed in order prepare a computer disk or memory card for use. Formatting organises the disk's surface into a series of electronic pigeon holes", in which data can be stored. Different computers often use different formatting systems.

## fragmentation

Process by which the available space on a disk drive is split up into small sections as a result of the storing and erasing of files. See "Defragmentation".

## frequency

Indication of how many cycles of a repetitive waveform occur in one second. A waveform which has a repetition cycle of one cycle per second has a frequency of 1Hz (Hertz).

## frequency response

Measurement of the frequency range which can be handled by a specific piece of electrical equipment or loudspeaker. This is normally measured between the points at which the signal level drops by 3dB.

## FSK

Frequency Shift Keying. A method of recording a sync clock signal onto tape by representing it as two alternating tones.

# fundamental

Any sound comprises a fundamental (basic) frequency plus harmonics and partials at higher frequencies.

# FX

Short for "effects".

# gain

Amount by which a circuit amplifies a signal.

# gate (keyboard)

Electrical signal which is generated whenever a key is depressed on an electronic keyboard. This is used to trigger envelope generators and other events that need to be synchronised to key action.

# gate

Electronic device designed to mute low-level signals in order to improve noise performance during pauses in the wanted material. Sometimes know as a *noise gate*.

# General MIDI

An addition to the basic MIDI specification, designed to ensure a minimum level of compatibility when playing back GM format song files on different machines. The specification covers type and program number of sounds, drum sound mapping, minimum levels of polyphony and multitimbrality, response to controller information and so on.

# glitch

Describes an unwanted short-term corruption of a signal, or the unexplained short-term malfunction of a piece of equipment. An inexplicable click on a DAT tape is a glitch.

# GM reset

A universal sysex command which activates the General MIDI mode on a GM instrument. The same command also sets all controllers to their default values and switches off any notes that may be still playing by means of an All Notes Off message.

# graphic equaliser

Equaliser on which several narrow segments of the audio spectrum are controlled by individual cut/boost faders. The name derives from the fact that the fader positions provide a graphic representation of the EQ curve.

# ground

Electrical earth, or 0v. In mains wiring, the ground cable is physically connected to the ground via a long conductive metal spike.

# group

Collection of signals within a mixer that are submixed and then routed through a separate fader in order to allow overall control. The submix of signals produced is called a subgroup.

# ground loop

A condition caused by multiple ground paths between various pieces of equipment, leading to the circulation of mains-frequency currents in the ground wiring of an audio system. This results in hum that can be difficult to diagnose.

# GS

Roland's own extension to the General MIDI protocol.

# hard disk

High-capacity computer storage device, based on a rigid, rotating disk, coated with a magnetic surface onto which data may be recorded.

# harmonic

High-frequency component of a complex waveform related in frequency and phase to the original sound.

# harmonic distortion

Addition of harmonics that were not present in the original signal.

# head

Part of a tape machine or disk drive that reads and/or writes data to and from a storage medium.

# headroom

Safety margin between the highest peak signal being passed by a piece of equipment and the absolute maximum level which the equipment can handle. Measured in decibels

# high-pass filter (HPF)

Filter which attenuates those frequencies that fall below its cut-off frequency.

# hiss

Noise caused by random electrical fluctuations.

# hum

Signal contamination caused by low frequencies, usually related to mains power frequency.

# Hz

Hertz, the unit of frequency.

# IC

Integrated Circuit. (See chip.)

# impedance

Can be seen as the AC resistance of a circuit containing both resistive and reactive components.

# inductor

Reactive component that presents an increasing impedance with frequency.

# initialise

To automatically restore a piece of equipment to its factory default settings.

# insert point

Connector that allows an external processor to be patched into a signal path so that the signal flows through it. Virtual insert points are also provided within the mixer sections of most sequencers, allowing plug-ins (ie VST effects) to be inserted into an audio signal path.

# insulator

Material that does not conduct electricity.

## interface

Device that acts as an intermediary between two or more other devices. For example, a MIDI interface enables a computer to communicate with MIDI instruments and keyboards. An audio interface enables analogue signals to be converted into digital signals, or vice versa.

## intermittent

Something that appears occasionally and at unpredictable times. Usually used to describe a fault that only appears occasionally.

## intermodulation distortion

Form of distortion that introduces frequencies not present in the original signal. These are invariably based on the sum and difference products of the original frequencies.

## I/O

Part of a system that handles inputs and outputs, in both the digital and analogue domains.

## IPS

Inches Per Second. Used to describe tape speed.

## IRQ

Interrupt Request. Part of a computer's operating system that allows a connected device to request attention from the processor in order to transfer data to it or receive data from it.

## isopropyl alcohol

Alcohol commonly used for cleaning and de-greasing heads and guides of tape machines.

## jack

Commonly-used audio connector. May be mono or stereo.

## jargon

Specialised words associated with a specialist subject.

## k

Abbreviation for 1,000 (kilo). Used as a prefix to other values to indicate magnitude.

# kHz

1,000 Hertz.

# kohm

1,000 ohms

# LED

Light-Emitting Diode. A form of solid-state lamp constructed with semiconductor material.

# LCD

Liquid Crystal Display.

# LFO

See "Low-Frequency Oscillator".

# LSB

Least Significant Bit. If a piece of data has to be conveyed as two bits, one bit represents high-value numbers and the other represents low-value numbers, much in the same way as tens and units function in the decimal system. The high value, or most significant part of the message, is called the MSB (Most Significant Bit).

# limiter

Device which controls the gain of a signal in order to prevent it from ever exceeding a preset level. A limiter is essentially a fast-acting compressor with an infinite compression ratio.

# linear

Device from which the output is a direct multiple of the input.

# line level

Nominal signal level, around -10dBV for semi-pro and +4dBu for professional equipment.

# load

Electrical circuit which draws power from another circuit or power supply. Also describes the act of reading data into a computer.

# local on/off

Function which allows the keyboard and sound-generating section of a keyboard synthesiser to be used independently of each other.

# logic

Type of electronic circuitry used for processing binary signals.

# loop

Musical phrase or section that is arranged to be repeated continuously. The term may also be used to describe a situation in which the output of a circuit or system is connected back to its own input.

# low-frequency oscillator (LFO)

Oscillator used as a modulation source, usually below 20Hz. The most common LFO waveshape is the sine wave, although the user often has the option of choosing between sine, square, triangular and sawtooth waveforms.

# low-pass filter

Filter which attenuates frequencies above its cutoff frequency.

# mA

Milliamp (one thousandth of an amp).

# meg

Abbreviation for 1,000,000.

# MDM

Modular Digital Multitrack. A digital recorder that can be used in multiples in order to provide a greater number of synchronised tracks than a single machine. The first example of this was the Alesis ADAT digital tape machine, which provided eight mono tracks per machine.

# memory

RAM used to store programs and data. This data is lost when the computer is switched, off and so must be stored to disk or some other suitable medium.

# menu

List of choices presented by a computer program or a device with a display window.

# mic level

Low-level signal generated by a microphone. This must be amplified many times in order to increase it to line level.

# microprocessor

Specialised microchip at the heart of a computer. It is here that instructions are read and acted upon.

# MIDI

Musical Instrument Digital Interface.

# MIDI analyser

Device which provides a visual readout of MIDI activity when connected between two pieces of MIDI equipment.

# MTC

MIDI Time Code. A MIDI sync implementation based on SMPTE time code.

# MIDI bank change

Type of controller message which is used to select between alternate banks of MIDI programs where access to more than 128 programs is required.

# MIDI controller

Term used to describe the physical interface by means of which the musician plays the MIDI synthesiser or some other sound generating device. Examples of controllers include keyboards, drum pads, wind and keyboard synths.

# MIDI control change

Also known as *MIDI controllers* or *controller data*, these messages convey positional information relating to hardware performance controls, such as wheels, pedals, switches and other such devices. This information can then be used to control functions such as depth of vibrato, brightness, portamento, levels of effects and many other parameters.

# (standard) MIDI file

Standard file format for storing song data recorded on a MIDI sequencer in such as way as to allow it to be read by other makes and models of MIDI sequencer.

# MIDI implementation chart

Chart which provides information concerning which MIDI features are supported, usually found in MIDI product manuals. Supported features are marked with a "O" while unsupported feature are marked with a "X". Additional information may be provided, such as the exact form of the MIDI Bank Change message.

# MIDI merge

Hardware device or sequencer function that enables two or more streams of real-time MIDI data to be combined.

# MIDI module

Sound-generating device with no integral keyboard. Sometimes known as an *expander module*.

# multitimbral module

MIDI sound source capable of producing several different sounds at the same time and controlled on different MIDI channels.

# MIDI mode

MIDI information can be interpreted by the receiving MIDI instrument in a number of ways, the most common being polyphonically on a single MIDI channel (Poly/Omni Off mode). Omni mode enables a MIDI instrument to play all incoming data, regardless of the channel on which it is sent. (See the chapter "Introducing MIDI for a full description of the four most common MIDI modes.)

# MIDI note number

Every key on a MIDI keyboard has its own note number, ranging from 0 to 127, where the number 60 represents middle C. Some systems use C3 as middle C while others systems use C4.

# MIDI note on

MIDI message sent when a note is played (key depressed).

## MIDI note off

Message sent when a key is released.

## MIDI in

Socket used to receive information from a master controller or from the MIDI thru socket of a slave unit.

## MIDI out

Socket on a master controller or sequencer used to send MIDI information to the slave units.

## MIDI port

Physical MIDI connections of a MIDI-compatible device.

## MIDI program change

Type of MIDI message used to change sound patches on a remote module or the effects patch on a MIDI effects unit.

## MIDI splitter

Alternative term for MIDI thru box.

## MIDI sync

Description of the sync systems available to MIDI users (MIDI Clock and MIDI Time Code).

## MIDI thru

The socket on a slave unit used to feed the MIDI In socket of the next unit in line.

## MIDI thru box

Device which splits the MIDI out signal of a master instrument or sequencer in order to avoid the daisy chaining of connected devices. Powered circuitry is used to buffer the outputs in order to prevent problems when many pieces of equipment are driven from a single MIDI output.

## mixer

Device for combining two or more audio signals.

# monitor

Reference loudspeaker used for mixing.

# monitor

Action of listening to a mix or a specific audio signal.

# monitor

VDU display for a computer.

# monophonic

One note at a time.

# motherboard

Main circuit board within a computer or some other device, into which all of the other components plug or connect.

# MP3

Form of data compression used to minimise the size of audio files for transmission over the internet or for use in a portable MP3 player. Various levels of compression are available depending on how much quality can be sacrificed for the sake of small file size, but a typical MP3 file takes up around ten per cent of the size of the uncompressed 16-bit/44.1kHz file.

# MP3 player

Term used to describe either a hardware playback device for MP3 audio or a piece of software allowing MP3 audio to be replayed via the soundcard of a computer.

# multiport MIDI interface

Device with multiple MIDI output sockets, each capable of carrying data relating to a different set of 16 MIDI channels. Multiports are the only means of exceeding the limitations imposed by 16 MIDI channels when controlling external hardware synths.

# multisample

Creation of several samples, each covering a limited musical range, with a view to producing more natural sounds across the range of the instrument being sampled. For example, a piano may need to be sampled every two or three semitones in order to sound convincing.

# multitimbral

Synthesiser, sampler or module which can play several parts at the same time, each under the control of a different MIDI channel.

# multitrack

Recording device capable of recording several parallel parts or tracks , which may then be mixed or re-recorded independently.

# nearfield

Loudspeaker system designed to be used near the listener. The advantage is that the listener hears more of the direct sound from the speakers and less of the reflected sound from the room.

# noise reduction

System for reducing the amount of analogue tape noise or the level of hiss present in a digital or analogue recording.

# noise shaping

System for creating digital dither. Any added noise is shifted into those parts of the audio spectrum at which the human ear is least sensitive.

# non-registered parameter number (NRPN)

Addition to the basic MIDI specification that allows controllers to be used to control non-standard parameters relating to particular models of synthesiser. This is an alternative to using system-exclusive data to achieve the same ends, although NRPNs tend to be used mainly by Yamaha and Roland instruments.

# non-linear recording

Describes digital recording systems that allow any parts of the recording to be played back in any order with no gaps. This is associated with the random access capability of computer disks. Conventional tape is referred to as being *linear*, because the material can only play back in the order in which it was recorded.

# normalise

A socket is said to be normalised when it is wired in such a way that the original signal path is maintained unless a plug is inserted into the socket. The most common examples of normalised connectors are the insert points on a mixing console. The virtual insert points in a virtual mixer are also normalised, insofar as the signal flow is not interrupted if no plug-in is selected.

# normalise

In the context of digital audio, normalisation describes the process whereby the level of the audio within a file, or selected section of a file, is increased in level so that the loudest peak is at digital full scale. This makes the signal as large as possible without allowing any part of it to clip.

# Nyquist theorem

Rule which states that a digital sampling system must have a sample rate that is at least twice as high as that of the highest frequency being sampled, in order that aliasing may be avoided. Because anti-aliasing filters aren't perfect, the sampling frequency usually has to be made more than twice that of the maximum input frequency.

# octave

When a frequency or pitch is transposed up by one octave, its frequency is doubled.

# off-line

Process carried out while a recording is not playing. For example, some computer-based processes such as pitch-shifting have to be carried out off-line as the computer isn't fast enough to carry out the process in real time.

# ohm

Unit of electrical resistance.

# omni

Means literally "all". Refers to a microphone that is equally sensitive in all directions, or to the MIDI mode in which data on all channels is recognised.

# open circuit

Break in an electrical circuit that prevents current from flowing.

# open reel

Tape machine on which the tape is wound onto spools rather than sealed inside a cassette.

## operating system

Basic software that will enable a computer to load and run other programs.

## opto-electronic device

Device on which an electrical parameter changes in response to a variation in light intensity. Variable photoresistors are sometimes used as gain-control elements in compressors, where the side-chain signal modulates the light intensity.

## oscillator

Circuit designed to generate a periodic electrical waveform.

## overdub

To add another part to a multitrack recording or to replace one of the parts that already exist.

## overload

To exceed the operating capacity of an electronic or electrical circuit.

## pad

Resistive circuit for reducing signal level.

## pan pot

Control enabling the user of a mixer to move the signal to any point in the stereo soundstage by varying the relative levels fed to the left and right stereo outputs.

## parallel

Means of connecting two or more circuits together so that their inputs are connected together and their outputs are all connected together.

## parameter

Variable value which affects some aspect of a device's performance.

## parametric EQ

Equaliser with separate controls for frequency, bandwidth and cut/boost.

# passive

Describes a circuit with no active elements.

# patch

Alternative term for *program*. Refers to a programmed sound within a synth that can be called up using Program Change commands. MIDI effects units and samplers also have patches.

# patch bay

System of panel-mounted connectors used to bring inputs and outputs to a central point, from which they can be routed using patch cords.

# patch cord

Short cable used with patch bays.

# peak

The highest signal level in any section of programme material.

# PFL

Pre-Fade Listen. A system used within a mixing console in order to allow the operator to listen in on a selected signal, regardless of the position of the fader that controls that signal.

# phantom power

48v DC power supply for capacitor microphones, transmitted along the signal cores of a balanced mic cable.

# phase

Timing difference between two electrical waveforms expressed in degrees, where 360° corresponds to a delay of exactly one cycle.

# phaser

Effect which combines a signal with a phase-shifted version of itself in order to produce filtering effects, which may then be used creatively. Most phasers are controlled by means of an LFO.

# pitch

Hi-Fi connector developed by RCA and used extensively on semi-pro, unbalanced recording equipment. The same connector is also used for co-axial S/PDIF digital audio connections, although for this application they must be used in conjunction with 70-ohm digital cable.

# pitch

Musical interpretation of an audio frequency.

# pitch bend

Special control message specifically designed to produce a change in pitch in response to the movement of a wheel or lever. Pitch-bend data can be recorded and edited, just like any other MIDI controller data, even though it isn't part of the controller message group.

# pitch shifter

Device for changing the pitch of an audio signal without changing its duration.

# polyphony

An instrument's ability to play two or more notes simultaneously. If an instrument can only play one note at a time it is described as being monophonic.

# Poly mode

The most common MIDI mode, which allows an instrument to respond to multiple simultaneous notes transmitted on a single MIDI channel.

# port

Connection for the input or output of data.

# portamento

Gliding effect that allows a sound to change pitch at a gradual rate, rather than abruptly, when a new key is pressed or a new MIDI note is sent to it.

# post production

Work done to a stereo recording after mixing is complete.

# power supply

Unit designed to convert mains electricity to the voltages necessary to power an electronic circuit or device.

# post-fade

Aux signal taken after the channel fader so that the aux send level follows any channel fader changes. Normally used for feeding effects devices.

# PPM

Peak Programme Meter. A meter designed to register signal peaks rather than the average level.

# PPQN

Pulse Per Quarter Note. Used with sync signals derived from MIDI Clock.

# pre-emphasis

System for applying high-frequency boost to a sound before processing it in order to reduce the effect of noise. A corresponding de-emphasis process is required on playback in order to restore the original signal and attenuate any high-frequency noise contributed by the recording process. Early digital recordings used pre-emphasis, but the system is no longer in general use.

# pre-fade

Aux signal taken from before the channel fader so that the channel fader has no effect on the aux send level. Normally used for creating foldback and cue mixes.

# preset

Effects unit or synth patch that cannot be altered by the user.

# pressure

Alternative term for "aftertouch".

# print through

The undesirable process that causes some magnetic information from a recorded analogue tape to become imprinted onto an adjacent layer. This can produce low-level pre or post echoes. Digital tape does not suffer from this problem because any print through is ignored by any circuitry which recognises ones and zeros.

# processor

Device designed to treat an audio signal by changing its dynamics or frequency spectrum. Examples of processors are compressors, gates and equalisers.

# program change

MIDI message designed to change the patches of instrument or effects units.

# pulse wave

Similar to a square wave but not symmetrical. Pulse waves sound brighter and thinner than square waves, making them useful in the synthesis of reed instruments. The timbre changes according to the mark/space ratio of the waveform.

# pulse-width modulation

Means of modulating the duty cycle (mark/space ratio) of a pulse wave. This changes the timbre of the basic tone. LFO modulation of pulse width can be used to produce a pseudo chorus effect.

# punch in

Action of putting an already recorded track into Record at the correct time during playback so that the existing material may be extended or replaced.

# punch out

Action of switching a recording device out of Record after executing a punch in. With most multitrack recording systems, both punching in and punching out can be accomplished without stopping playback.

# PQ coding

Process for adding pause, cue and other subcode information to a digital master tape or CD-R in preparation for CD manufacture.

# PZM

Pressure Zone Microphone. A type of boundary microphone, designed to reject out-of-phase sounds reflected from the surface to which the microphone is fixed.

# Q

Measure of the resonant properties of a filter. The higher the Q, the more resonant the filter and the narrower the range of frequencies that are allowed to pass through it.

## quantise

Means of moving notes recorded in a MIDI sequencer so that they line up with user-definable subdivisions of a bar (16ths, for example). May be used to correct timing errors.

## RAM

Random Access Memory. This is a type of memory used by computers for the temporary storage of programs and data, and all data stored in this way is lost when the power is turned off. For this reason, work needs to be saved to disk if it is not to be lost.

## RBUS

Roland proprietary audio data format for interconnecting RBUS-compatible equipment. The interface supports only eight audio channels, although it may be used in multiples.

## RAM

Describes a hard disk or RAM-based storage system, where the data may be accessed in any desired order.

## R-DAT

Digital tape machine that uses a rotating head system.

## real time

Audio process that can be carried out as the signal is being recorded or played back. The opposite is off-line, where the signal is processed in non-real time.

## release

The time taken for a level or gain to return to normal. Often used to describe the rate at which a synthesised sound decays in level after a key has been released. The term is also used in the context of the parameters of gates and compressors.

## resistance

Opposition to the flow of electrical current. Measured in ohms.

# resolution

Accuracy with which an analogue signal is represented by a digitising system. The more bits that are used, the more accurately the amplitude of each sample can be measured. However, there are other elements of the design of a converter that also affect accuracy. High conversion accuracy is known as high resolution.

# resonance

See "Q".

# reverb

Acoustic ambience created by multiple reflections in a confined space.

# ReWire

Audio routing software protocol developed by Steinberg which allows multiple channels of audio to be routed between programs in real time.

# RF interference

Radio-frequency interference, significantly above the range of human hearing, sometimes due to radio transmissions.

# ribbon microphone

Microphone in which the sound-capturing element is a thin metal ribbon suspended in a magnetic filed. When sound causes the ribbon to vibrate, a small electrical current is generated within the ribbon.

# roll-off

Rate at which a filter attenuates a signal once it has passed the cut-off point.

# ROM

Read Only Memory. This is a permanent or non-volatile type of memory, which contains data that can't be changed. Operating systems are often stored on ROM because the memory will then remain intact when the power is removed.

# ring modulator

Device that accepts and processes two input signals in a particular way. The output signal does not contain any of the original input signal but instead comprises new frequencies based on the sum and difference of the input signal's frequency components. The best-known application of ring modulation is the creation of robot voices, but it may also be used to create dramatic instrumental textures. Depending on the relationships between the input signals, the results may either be musical or extremely dissonant – for example, ring modulation can be used to create bell-like tones. (The term *ring* is used because the original circuit which produced the effect used a ring of diodes.)

# RMS

Root Mean Square. Used in a method of calculating the mean level of an alternating audio signal.

# safety copy

Copy or clone of an original tape to be used if the original is lost or becomes damaged.

# sample

Digitised sound used as a musical sound source in a sampler or additive synthesiser.

# sample rate

The number of times that an A/D converter samples an incoming waveform per second.

# sample and hold

Circuit that stores an instantaneous value. Used in A/D converters to hold sample values until the next sample is taken

# sampling

Process carried out by an A/D converter, where the instantaneous amplitude of a signal is measured many times per second (44.1kHz on CDs).

# sawtooth wave

So called because it resembles the teeth of a saw. Contains both odd and even harmonics.

# SDII

This was originally a Digidesign software editor called Sound Designer II, although it's no longer in production. The SDII file format is still supported by a number of Mac-based software packages, and has become an industry standard.

# SCMS

Serial Copycode Management System, a system of data flags carried by the S/PDIF digital audio interface which indicates whether the source material may be copied for one generation, unlimited generations, or not at all. The SCMS code is generated by some consumer DAT machines as an anti-piracy measure. However, if the material if transferred to any system via an AES/EBU interface the SCMS flags will be ignored. SCMS is also not transferred via analogue connections.

# SCMS stripper

Hardware or software device for resetting the SCMS flags in order to allow unlimited copying of a program. The stripper is connected between the source and destination devices when transferring the data to be stripped.

# SCSI

(Pronounced "skuzzi".) Small Computer System Interface, an interfacing system for using hard drives, scanners, CD-ROM drives and similar peripherals with a computer. Each SCSI device has its own ID number, and no two SCSI devices in the same chain can be set to the same number. The last SCSI device in the chain should be terminated, either via an internal terminator, if one is provided, or via a plug-in terminator fitted to a free SCSI socket.

# session tape

Original tape made during a recording session.

# sequencer

Device for recording and replaying MIDI data, usually in a multitrack format, allowing complex compositions to be built up one part at a time. Most modern sequencers allow the user to record and edit audio

# short circuit

Low resistance path that allows electrical current to flow. The term is usually used to describe a current path that exists through a fault condition.

# sibilance

High-frequency whistling or lisping sound that affects vocal recordings because of either poor mic technique or excessive equalisation.

## side chain

Part of the circuit that splits off a proportion of the main signal so that it can then be processed in some way in order to derive a control signal.

## signal

Electrical representation of an input, such as sound.

## signal chain

Route taken by a signal from a system input to its output.

## signal-to-noise ratio

Ratio of maximum signal level to residual noise, expressed in decibels.

## sine wave

The waveform of a pure tone with no harmonics.

## single-ended noise reduction

Device for removing or attenuating the noise component of a signal but which doesn't require previous encoding, as with Dolby or dbx.

## slave

Device under the control of a master device.

## SMPTE

Time code that was originally developed for use in the film industry but now extensively used in music and recording. SMPTE is a real-time code and it's measurements are related to hours, minutes, seconds and film or video frames rather than to musical tempo.

## S/PDIF

Stereo digital audio interconnection format developed jointly by Philips and Sony to facilitate the interconnection of digital audio equipment. The connections may be either co-axial (via phono connectors) or optical in nature. The data stream has flags embedded in it which indicate the copy code status (SCMS) and track start IDs of the material.

## SPL

Sound Pressure Level, measured in decibels.

## SPP

MIDI Song Position Pointer.

## standard MIDI file

Standard file format that allows MIDI files to be transferred between different sequencers and MIDI file players.

## step time

System for programming a sequencer in non-real time.

## stereo

Two-channel system feeding left and right loudspeakers.

## sticky shed syndrome

Problem affecting some brands of analogue tape after a long time in storage. A breakdown of the binder causes the oxide to shed, and the tape adheres to the tape heads and guides when played. A short-term cure can be effected by baking the tape for several hours at 50° C.

## stripe

To record time code onto one track of a multitrack tape machine.

## square wave

Symmetrical rectangular waveform. Square waves contain a series of odd harmonics.

## sub-bass

Frequencies below the range of typical monitor loudspeakers. Sub-bass is often defined as frequencies that can be felt rather than heard.

## subwoofer

Loudspeaker that handles only very low frequencies.

## subcode

Hidden data within the CD and DAT format that includes such information as the absolute time location, the number of tracks and the total running time.

## subtractive synthesis

Process of creating a new sound by filtering and shaping a raw, harmonically-complex waveform.

## surge

Sudden increase in mains voltage.

## sustain

Part of the ADSR envelope (Attack, Decay, Sustain and Release) which determines the level to which the sound will settle if a key is held down. Once the key is released, the sound decays at a rate set by the Release parameter. The term also refers to a guitar's ability to hold notes which decay very slowly.

## sweet spot

Optimum position for a listener relative to monitor loudspeakers.

## switching power supply

Type of power supply that uses a high-frequency oscillator before the transformer so that a smaller, lighter transformer may be used. These power supplies are commonly used in computers and some synthesiser modules.

## sync

System for making two or more pieces of equipment run in synchronism with each other.

## synthesiser

Electronic musical instrument designed to create a wide range of sounds, both imitative and abstract.

## tape head

Part of a tape machine that transfers magnetic energy to the tape during recording or reads it during playback.

# TDIF

Audio interfacing standard developed by Tascam, on which up to eight channels can be handled per connection. Connection is via a multipin connector.

# toslink

Standard optical interface used by the S/PDIF and ADAT interfaces.

# tempo

The rate of the "beat" of a piece of music, measured in beats per minute. (See "BPM".)

# test tone

Steady, fixed-level tone recorded onto a multitrack or stereo recording to act as a reference during the matching of levels.

# THD

Total Harmonic Distortion.

# thru

MIDI connector which passes on the signal received at the MIDI in socket.

# timbre

The tonal colour of a sound.

# track

This term dates back to the days when multitrack tape was more commonly used, on which the tracks are physical stripes of recorded material located side by side along the tape.

# tracking

System whereby one device follows another. Tracking is often discussed in the context of MIDI guitar synthesisers or controllers on which the MIDI output attempts to track the pitch of the guitar strings.

# transparency

Subjective term often used to describe the quality of a section of audio material in which the high-frequency detail is clear and in which the individual sounds are easy to identify and separate.

# tremolo

Modulation of the amplitude of a sound with an LFO.

# transducer

Device which converts one form of energy into another. A microphone is a good example of a transducer. In its operation it converts mechanical energy to electrical energy.

# transpose

To shift a musical signal by a fixed number of semitones.

# triangle wave

Symmetrical triangular shaped wave containing only odd harmonics, but with a lower harmonic content than the square wave.

# TRS jack

Stereo jack with tip, ring and sleeve connections.

# unbalanced

Two-wire electrical signal connection on which the inner or hot (positive) conductor is usually surrounded by the cold (negative) conductor, which forms a screen against interference.

# unison

To play the same melody using two or more different instruments or voices.

# valve

Vacuum tube amplification component, also known as a tube.

# velocity

Rate at which a key is depressed. This may be used to control loudness (in order to simulate the response of instruments such as pianos) or other parameters.

## vocoder

Signal processor that imposes a changing spectral filter on a sound based on the frequency characteristics of a second sound. By taking the spectral content of a human voice and imposing it on a musical instrument, talking instrument effects can be created.

## voice

Indicates the capacity of a synthesiser to play a single musical note. An instrument capable of playing 16 simultaneous notes is said to be a 16-voice instrument.

## vibrato

Pitch modulation achieved by using an LFO to modulate a VCO.

## virtual instrument

Synth or sampler generated within a computer using specialised software.

## VST

Virtual Studio System. An industry standard developed by Steinberg designed to be used as a plug-in with their Cubase VST software. It is now supported by other leading sequencers, including eMagic's Logic Audio.

## VU meter

Meter designed to interpret signal levels in roughly the same way as the human ear, responding more closely to the average levels of sounds rather than to the peak levels.

## watt

Unit of electrical power.

## warmth

Subjective term used to describe sound in which the bass and low-mid frequencies have depth and the high frequencies sound smooth rather than aggressive or fatiguing. Warm-sounding tube equipment may also exhibit some of the aspects of compression.

## .WAV

Type of audio file format first used for PC audio programs but now also supported by Macs.

# waveform

Graphic representation of the way in which a sound wave or electrical wave varies over time.

# white noise

Random signal with an energy distribution that produces an equal amount of noise power per Hertz.

# write

To save data on a digital storage medium, such as a hard drive.

# XG

Yamaha's alternative to Roland's GS system, enhancing the General MIDI protocol by providing additional banks of patches.

# XLR

Type of three-pin connector commonly used to carry balanced audio signals, including the feeds from microphones.

# Y-lead

Lead split so that one source can feed two destinations. Y-leads may also be used in console insert points, in which case a stereo jack plug at one end of the lead is split into two monos at the other.

# Z

Electrical term for impedance.

# zero-crossing point

Point at which a signal waveform crosses over from being positive to negative, or vice versa.

# zipper noise

Audible steps that occur when a parameter is being altered in a digital audio processor.